BIBA'S ITALY

BIBA'S ITALY

BIBA CAGGIANO

FAVORITE RECIPES FROM THE
SPLENDID CITIES

ARTISAN | NEW YORK

Published by Artisan
A Division of Workman Publishing, Inc.
225 Varick Street
New York, NY 10014
www.artisanbooks.com

Library of Congress Cataloging-in-Publication Data
Caggiano, Biba.
Biba's Italy : favorite recipes from the splendid cities / Biba Caggiano.
p. cm.
ISBN-13: 978-1-57965-317-0
ISBN-10: 1-58965-317-0
1. Cookery, Italian. I. Title.
TX723.C244 2006
641.5945—dc22   2006045951

10 9 8 7 6 5 4 3 2 1
Printed in the United States of America

Book design by Jan Derevjanik

TO MY FAMILY

Andrew, Alex, Aidan, and William, my splendid
grandchildren, who have enriched my life to the fullest.

Carla and Paola, my daughters, my pride, my joy, my heart.

Brian and Tim, the best sons-in-law anyone could hope for.

Vincent, my husband, whose support and confidence
allowed me to achieve goals I never thought I could.
Ti amerò sempre!

CONTENTS

Introduction

There are so many beautiful countries in Europe, all with major breathtaking cities. France has Paris, England has London. Austria has Vienna, Greece has Athens. And Italy? Italy has Rome, Florence, Pisa, Siena, Venice, Verona, Bologna, Parma, Naples, Palermo, Milan, Turin, Genoa . . . and so many more. Travelers flock to these cities like bees swarm to honey. They might be drawn because of the city's history, its art, its architecture, its culture, its landscapes, its fashionable streets, its outdoor caffès, its warm sun, its blue oceans, its majestic mountains and great lakes, and for its ludicrously palpable *gioia di vivere.* Or they might go there simply to pursue the pleasures of the Italian table.

What is it that makes a country that is only 750 miles long so jam-packed with delectable food? And why is it that in spite of the many culinary changes that Italy has gone through during the last few decades, the popularity of the Italian table has never been greater? (Surveys show that Italian is the most popular food in the United States and indeed around the world.) Perhaps it is Italy's enormous variety of regional dishes and its equally enormous number of superlative regional ingredients. Or because this is a food that is approachable, honest, and straightforward, whose flavors, textures, and character belong to and are dictated by its local, unique history, traditions, climate, and geography. Or again, maybe it is because Americans are beginning to discover all the permutations of what is broadly called *Italian cuisine.*

When in 1960 I moved to New York from Bologna to follow my American-born husband, most people I met had no idea where Bologna, the capital of the Emilia-Romagna region, was. At that time Italian food was defined as *Northern Italian* and *Southern Italian,* and Italian cooking generally meant red-check tablecloths and pasta covered with thick, garlicky tomato sauces or with heavy cream. During the first months I lived in New York City I was so homesick for the food of my city that I hunted Manhattan for a Bolognese restaurant. When I finally found one, I realized that the very nice American-born owners had lost touch with the real food of Bologna.

What a difference forty-five years have made. Today many Americans have a much broader understanding of the food of Italy, thanks to scores of food magazines, cookbooks, and television shows. They easily hop on a plane and visit what until a decade ago were unknown regions, thus discovering a wealth of regional cuisines. They eat *risi e bisi* in Venice, *carciofi alla giudea* in Rome, *ossobuco* in Milan, and *parmigiana de melanzane* in Naples. They know that the food of Bologna has almost nothing in common with the food of Florence, even though the two cities are only seventy miles apart; and that the food of Palermo, with its Baroque sweet-and-sour dishes bestowed on them by the Arabs, has no relation whatsoever to the food of Turin, whose refined cuisine was influenced by the French.

And yet despite Italy's great food traditions, it is obvious that the country is going through culinary and social transitions. Today, whether we like it or not, we are all globally connected. Television, the Internet, airplanes, and superhighways allow us to communicate with one another faster, and to get to our destination quicker. Supermarkets are sprouting up all over Italy, in many cases replacing the little specialty-food store. International chains are everywhere. Young Italians love eating hamburgers and french fries, while small-scale food artisans are struggling to stay alive. Yet despite a modernization that has created a somewhat more homogeneous landscape, Italy maintains a big heart, charming people, a prodigal table, and tightly knit family life.

The idea for this book came to me because of the large number of people who routinely ask for the names of places to eat while in Italy. The country is blessed with many cities, towns, and hamlets with a rich history of food. A handful of Italy's world-class cities are perennial favorites: Rome, Milan, Venice, Bologna, and Florence were constantly mentioned. Thus a book on the food of these cities began to formulate in my mind—a good book that would not only offer sinfully delicious recipes, easily doable in an American kitchen, but also would suggest where to go to have a good meal. Which food market was not to be missed. Which of the many wine bars also served food. Where to find the best gelato. And so on.

When in the spring of 2000 I began researching this book, my daughter Paola joined me for the first of several Italian trips. Our journey began in Rome, a city I dearly love. I told my daughter that while I had nothing against art and historic sights, the purpose of our visit was to totally immerse ourselves in the Italian culture of food. And so we did. From the moment we arrived and dropped our bags at the hotel, we jumped in a taxi and headed straight to a well-known trattoria. We ate, we drank, we laughed, and we reconnected with a bang to the outspoken flavors of Italian food.

Each day, from morning until night, we walked the cities in search of my favorite food markets, bakeries, specialty food stores, grand old caffès, and ice cream parlors. We ate pizza by the slice on the go. We sipped frothy cappuccino while munching on those to-die-for Italian brioches. We ate sandwiches at the *paninoteche*, Italy's glorious sandwich shops. We visited old, venerable trattorie that served time-honored dishes. While eating lunch, we made plans for dinner. Along the way, we rekindled old friendships while making new ones. It was a magic time, a time when we pursued, savored, and shared the pleasures of the Italian table just as the Italians do: leisurely, one bite at a time.

This book draws from several years of eating experiences in five of Italy's grand cities. Some of the establishments in each chapter are expensive and offer fine dining; others are unassuming *trattorie, osterie,* and *enoteche* that serve mostly the traditional food of the area. All have one thing in common: good food.

OPPOSITE: *The Spanish Steps, Rome*

Eating in Italy

So, you are finally in Italy, tired but hungry. You took a walk in the center of town looking for a place to eat, and you found more than you bargained for. You probably know what a *ristorante* and a *trattoria* are, but what is an *osteria,* a *tavola calda,* a *paninoteca,* or an *enoteca?* Although these are all eating establishments, they often differ in the type of food they serve and in the style in which they serve it. The following list sorts out some of Italy's most common eating establishments.

Ristorante: Italian restaurants are as diverse as the Italian landscape. Some elegant, expensive restaurants are the domains of celebrity chefs who specialize in creative cooking. Others are simpler establishments that serve the traditional food of the area. Restaurants will provide the customer with a printed menu and a wine list (see "A Typical Restaurant Menu" on page xv).

Trattoria: A small, unassuming restaurant, generally family owned, that serves traditional homestyle food at reasonable prices. A trattoria is often a home away from home for many; students, young families, and people on a budget are ardent patrons. A trattoria usually serves a limited number of dishes. The service might be less polished than restaurant service. However, the bonus is that eating in a trattoria is like eating with an Italian family, whose basic, simple, and honest food tells the story of a people and a place. Often, trattorie do not have menus. Instead, the owner or the waiter will recite the menu of the day and suggest dishes and wines. Stay away from trattorie that offer a *a menù turistico,* which is a set meal for tourists that offers very standard, often uninspired food.

Osteria or Hostaria: Generally a tavern or a wine shop that serves wine by the glass and offers a limited number of homey dishes. Soups, cheeses, cold cuts, savory breads, and pickled vegetables are some of the offerings, generally listed on a blackboard. It is a great place to relax over a glass of wine and some snacks, and to connect with your fellow man seated next to you.

Enoteca: An urban, more gentrified wine bar than the humble osteria. Enoteche serve wine by the bottle and by the glass, and many have added more ambitious dishes to their menus. These are great spots to visit.

Tavola Calda (hot table): An informal eatery that serves a selection of hot dishes to eat informally, standing up or to take out.

Rosticceria: A shop that sells food to go, primarily roasted and spit-roasted meats, roasted potatoes, and sautéed vegetables at reasonable prices. The *rosticceria* is where Italians shop when pressed for time. A great place to visit and to pick up something for a picnic.

Pizzeria: Pizzerias are divided into two categories: shops that make pizza and sell it by the slice or by square pieces (Italian teenagers seem to be eating pizza to go constantly), and regular pizzerias where you can sit at a table and choose from the many toppings. For Italians, the best pizzas are thin-crusted and crisp, and topped with only a few outstanding ingredients. Today these informal establishments often serve a small selection of pasta, salads, calzone, and savory pies as well as pizza.

Paninoteca: A sandwich shop. But, boy, what great sandwiches. *Panini* (thus *paninoteca*) stuffed with seafood, ham, vegetables, and cheeses, alone or in appetizing combinations, can be bought there. These places are very popular in the larger cities, where most workers have only a one-hour break at lunch.

Gelateria: An ice cream parlor. Italians rarely make gelato at home, nor do they regularly order it in restaurants or trattorie, for they prefer to walk to any gelateria or caffè and choose from a large number of flavors. Sitting at an outdoor caffè with a large glass of voluptuous gelato is a great Italian experience.

Pasticceria: A pastry shop where pastries can be purchased to eat there or take away. Often a *pasticceria* also has a bar area that serves espresso, cappuccino, tea, and so on.

Bars and Caffès: A *bar* is a place to stop for a quick espresso, cappuccino, tea, pastry, or an aperitivo, which are generally consumed standing at the counter. (An Italian bar has nothing in common with an American bar.) A *caffè* is a bar that has the addition of inside and possibly outside tables, and has waiter service. For Italians a bar also becomes an extension of home, a warm, comforting, hospitable place where you can, for a while, escape the pressure of daily life. The bar is also an important social institution that allows its citizens an active participation in simple everyday rituals where people of every walk of life mingle and pause, waiting at the shining counter for their beloved espresso.

ESPRESSO GLOSSARY

Ask any Italian what they order when they drop in at a bar, and their answer will probably be *espresso.* Espresso is, without any doubt, the national drink. The best espresso comes from the bars' and caffès' professional machines, which supply the required pressurization and hot temperature to make a good espresso. Most Italians prefer their espresso straight and strong.

Espresso: Often called simply *caffè,* it is drunk throughout the day, from early morning to late at night. A good espresso should be drunk really hot, should fill a demitasse cup a little less than halfway, and should be topped by the thin, brown layer of foam that Italians call *crema.*

Decaffeinato: A decaffeinated espresso.

Corretto: An espresso that has the addition of a shot of grappa or brandy.

Macchiato: An espresso that has a touch of warm milk.

Ristretto: Concentrated and strong.

Lungo: An espresso that is less concentrated and generally fills the demitasse almost to the top.

Doppio: A double espresso.

Cappuccino: An espresso served in a large cup, topped by thick, foamy, hot milk. Cappuccino is consumed mostly in the morning and very seldom after a meal.

Caffè Latte: Half espresso, half hot milk. Just as cappuccino, it is consumed in the morning.

If you are a first-time traveler to Italy reading through a restaurant menu, its sequence of courses might be a bit intimidating and somewhat confusing. Don't worry. Keep in mind the following:

- Menus are generally à la carte, meaning you pay for each dish you order. Soup and salad are seldom offered with the entrée. And if they are, you are probably in a restaurant that offers a *menù turistico*, a menu for tourists.

- To familiarize yourself with the food and wine culture of the area, eat and drink regionally. Ask the waiter to suggest local dishes and local wines. Many restaurants and trattorie will be happy to serve you wine by the glass, or their house wine.

- Food portions are smaller than in the United States. This is because an Italian meal generally includes three or four courses.

- The salad is generally served *after* the entrée, not before, since the pungency of the vinegar in the dressing would interfere with the wine drunk with the meal. The salad is also meant to cleanse the palate and prepare it for the next course.

- On most menus, the vegetables, *contorni*, are listed and priced separately and don't come automatically with the entrée.

- Most restaurants, with the exception of tourist-oriented places, don't open for dinner until 8:00 P.M.

- Butter is generally not served in restaurants and trattorie. Ditto for the oil–balsamic vinegar dip (a California concotion).

- At the bottom of most menus you will read *Coperto Lire* . . . That is a cover charge for the bread, linen, and silverware.

- In many restaurants the taxes and the service charges are already included on the bill. Check with the server. If it is not included, a tip of 15 percent is expected.

- Make reservations well in advance.

A TYPICAL RESTAURANT MENU

- *Antipasti:* Literally "before the meal," appetizers. The role of antipasti is to stimulate the appetite and tease the palate, preparing it for the courses to come.

- *Primi Piatti* (or *Primi*): First courses, usually pasta, risotto, gnocchi, or soups. These are the dishes that have captured the world's attention. (Italians never have pasta and soup at the same time.)

- *Secondi Piatti* (or *Secondi*): Second courses (entrées) that include meat, game, and seafood. Often the meat and seafood are listed separately. The *secondi* are generally served alone on the plate without the addition of vegetables, so you must choose a vegetable listed under *contorni*.

- *Contorni:* Vegetable side dishes that are priced separately. Salads can be found in this category.

- *Formaggi:* Cheeses. Given a choice, at the end of a meal Italians would prefer to eat cheese, often paired with walnuts or a fruit condiment.

- *Dolci e Frutta:* Desserts and fruit to end the meal.

The following are additional listings that might appear on restaurant menus:

- *Piatti del Giorno:* Specials of the day

- *Piatti Espressi:* Express dishes

- *Bolliti:* Boiled dishes

- *Pesce Fresco:* Fresh fish

- *Nostre Specialità:* House specials

- *Alla Brace:* Grilled dishes

Buon appetito.

ROME

APPETIZERS

Bruschetta with Roasted Caramelized Cherry Tomatoes {*Bruschetta con Pomodorini Canditi*}

Fava Bean Purée with Bitter Greens {*Incapriata*}

Stuffed Artichokes Roman-Style {*Carciofi alla Romana*}

Stuffed Zucchini Blossoms {*Fiori di Zucchine Ripieni*}

PASTA

Fettuccine with Roman Ragù {*Fettuccine con Ragù alla Romana*}

Spaghetti with Fresh Tomatoes, Olives, and Capers {*Spaghetti alla Checca*}

Spaghetti with Guanciale, Eggs, and Parmigiano {*Spaghetti alla Carbonara*}

Bucatini with Pancetta, Pecorino, and Black Pepper {*Bucatini all Gricia*}

Green Tea Tonnarelli with Shrimp and Candied Cherry Tomatoes
{*Tonnarelli al Tè Verde con Gamberi e Pomodorini Canditi*}

Potato Gnocchi in Spicy Tomato Sauce {*Gnocchi all'Amatriciana*}

Baked Semolina Gnocchi Roman-Style {*Gnocchi di Semolino alla Romana*}

Pasta and Chickpea Soup {*Minestra di Pasta e Ceci*}

ENTRÉES

Roman Oxtail Stew {*Coda alla Vaccinara*}

Veal Scaloppine with Prosciutto, Sage, and Wine {*Saltimbocca alla Romana*}

Lamb Hunter-Style {*Agnello alla Cacciatora*}

Spicy Baby Chicken "Devil-Style" {*Pollo alla Diavola*}

Chicken with Peppers alla Romana {*Pollo con Peperoni*}

The Rack of Lamb of Ristorante Troiani {*L'Agnello del Ristorante Troiani*}

Pan-Fried Sausage with Spicy Broccoli Rabe
{*Salsicce e Broccoli Rape con Aglio, Olio, e Peperoncino*}

Salt Cod with Tomatoes, Raisins, and Pine Nuts {*Baccalà in Guazzetto*}

VEGETABLES

Escarole with Garlic, Anchovies, and Red Pepper Flakes
{*Cicoria Saltata in Padella con Acciughe e Peperoncino*}

Stew of Fava Beans, Peas, and Artichokes {*La Vignarola*}

Pan-Fried Zucchini with Vinegar and Chili Pepper {*Zucchine in Padella con Aceto e Peperoncino*}

DESSERTS

Tart Cherry Crostata {*Crostata di Visciole*}

Roman Sweet Buns with Raisins and Pine Nuts {*I Maritozzi Romani*}

There is an old Italian saying, *Tutte le strade conducono a Roma*—

every street will take you to Rome. For many, the capital, with its three million inhabitants, is the most beautiful city in the world. A city of great art, architecture, and history. Ancient roads, monuments, statues, fountains, majestic squares, churches, and old buildings dot the Roman landscape stretching the twenty-seven centuries of history to modern times. For others, Rome is synonymous with *la dolce vita,* the "sweet life" of elegantly clad city dwellers and visitors alike lingering at the outdoor caffès of Via Veneto or shopping at the exclusive boutiques of Via Condotti, oblivious to the chaotic traffic and the roaring noises of the Vespas and cars that zip past them. Then, for many more, Rome is synonymous with extraordinarily tempting good food.

The first time I tasted Roman food at its source was when I turned fifteen and my mother's oldest sister, *zia* Maria, invited me to spend a week with her family. My aunt had a lovely apartment on the second floor of an old building. The two large terraces were an extension of their living room, and in the morning, we would sip our espresso or *caffè latte* on the terrace while listening to the almost synchronized sounds of the church bells. My fondest memories of that week are still with me: the daily excursions to the most important sights of Rome. Saint Peter's Square and the Sistine Chapel. Castel Sant'Angelo, the Colosseum, the

Fontana di Trevi, the Pantheon, and the Spanish Steps gleaming with multicolored azaleas . . . magical sights that evoked the wisdom of a highly advanced, ancient civilization.

After our daily adventure my aunt and I would often stop at her neighborhood food market to select the ingredients for the evening meal. Everything was luscious and fresh. The plump Roman artichokes would be trimmed and stuffed with a mixture of mint, parsley, and garlic and then cooked with wine and oil. The bitter chicory would be sautéed in fragrant oil with specks of chili pepper. And the porcini mushrooms, always so abundant in the fall, would become the topping of homemade fettuccine. One time we visited Campo de' Fiori, which, at that time, was considered by many the best open food market of the city. Stall after stall displayed perfectly arranged baskets of colorful vegetables, fruit, and fresh herbs, and mounds of dried spices. Partially enclosed stalls featured meat and poultry, often showcasing a just-slaughtered suckling pig or baby lamb. Others displayed fresh fish still alive in small tanks of water. And others again had a variety of tempting cheeses, hams, and sausages. But what made all of this a lively theater was the interaction of customers and merchants, often talking in high-pitched voices in Roman dialect, gesturing, posturing, and disputing with one another.

Then there were unforgettable meals at humble neighborhood trattorie, where I ventured into uncharted territory and tasted true Roman food. I remember the first time I had *rigatoni con la pagliata*, which my aunt had described as one of the oldest, most succulent pasta dishes of Rome. I ate the pasta and cleaned the plate in no time at all. I loved it. Only later did I learn that the wonderful sauce I had scooped up with bread was made by using what in Rome is called *quinto quarto*, or "fifth quarter," the butcher's inexpensive leftovers of the slaughtered animal, including liver, sweetbreads, heart, tripe, and lungs. That information prevented me from ordering that dish again for several years.

Any reference to the culture, customs, and cooking of Latium points directly to Rome. No other city in Italy, with the exception perhaps of Florence, dominates its region gastronomically as does the capital of Italy and of world Christianity. Rome, with its history of domination, greatness, and lavish banquets, has probably the most plebeian food of Italy.

As I learned throughout the years and during my many trips, the traditional Roman *cucina* has been largely influenced not by the refined dishes and banquets of Imperial Rome, but by three distinct communities: the ancient Roman-Jewish population, with their marinated fish, savory cakes, and flavorful deep-fried vegetables; the *vaccinari*, as the Roman slaughterhouse workers were once called, who developed a flavorful but humble *cucina* obtained from lowly cuts of meats and innards cooked slowly in order to tenderize them and extract the maximum amount of flavor; and the shepherds' lamb and chicken dishes, flavorful cheeses, and simple yet irresistible pasta dishes.

Thankfully, many of these dishes have stood the test of time and can be found in many of the *trattorie* and *osterie* of the city, especially the ones located in the Jewish quarter and in Trastevere. In these two of Rome's most colorful areas you can eat extravagantly well but somewhat inexpensively, choosing from a variety of dishes such as *carciofi alla giudea*, a typical Roman-Jewish dish that fries the long-stemmed artichokes twice until crisp; or *bucatini all'amatriciana*, a hollow, tubular pasta with a sauce of *guanciale* (cured pork jowl) or pancetta, tomatoes, and red chili pepper; *fettuccine con ragù alla Romana*, fresh egg pasta tossed in a luscious, dense beef ragù; and *coda di bue alla vaccinara*, oxtail beef stew, simmered at length with vegetables, wine, and tomatoes. Other dishes especially popular with the Romans are *abbacchio* and *capretto*, very young milk-fed baby lamb and baby goat that have not yet tasted grass. These dishes are generally prepared roasted (always accompanied by sinfully delicious roasted potatoes) or *alla cacciatora*, hunter-style, with white wine, vinegar, and herbs, and are a reminder of the city's pastoral tradition. These are the dishes that the *Romani de' Roma* (true Romans) go back to time after time, because they are hearty, direct, colorful, and faithful to its traditions, and as comforting and nurturing as mother's milk.

Although the traditional Roman *cucina* is still alive and well, changes are everywhere, especially in more expensive restaurants, where young, ambitious chefs tackle the city's traditional dishes, lightening and refining them, to the delight of many and to the distress of others. This lighter approach banishes lard in favor of olive oil, limits the number of deep-fried dishes, and stresses the freshness of vegetables and seafood. I still remember the incomparable shellfish risotto I had at La Rosetta, a popular, hip seafood restaurant that caters to Roman and visitor alike. And the glorious lamb medallions of Il Convivio Troiani, hinting of fragrant rosemary and mint. Beautiful food, lightly prepared, that tasted great.

Romans, like most other Italians, prefer to take their sweets at the *pasticceria* or nearby caffè during the day, but not at the end of a meal. Unless of course it is a special occasion. While the desserts of upscale restaurants are creative and luxuriously decadent, the simpler, homey fare of the trattorie rely on time-honored recipes. Delicious Roman ricotta is used in cakes, tarts, puddings, and fritters. *Biscotti* and baked fruit, sweet polenta cake, *zuppa Inglese alla Romana*, sour cherry tart, and gelato are other standard trattoria fare. A popular way to end a Roman meal is with a wedge of local Pecorino cheese and some fresh fruit.

I fell in love with Rome when I first visited it so many years ago, and today that Rome is more beautiful than ever, thanks to the grand renovation that occurred during the Catholic Church Jubilee of 2000. Churches have been restored, monuments and fountains have been polished. Museums have been reopened and palaces have been renovated. The city as a whole is sparkling and aglow with pride.

Rome is a city that needs to be walked to be understood, to have its true heart revealed. After you have visited the prerequisite historical sights, walk for pleasure. Go to the open food market of Campo de' Fiori, or the lesser known Testaccio market, to gaze at the vegetables, fruit, herbs, and spices. Check out the Museo Nazionale delle Paste Alimentari (the National Pasta Museum), located near the Fontana di Trevi. It is dedicated to the history and craft of pasta production through the centuries. On a Sunday morning go to Porta Portese's flea market in a colorful quarter of Trastevere. Go to Piazza Navona and have one of the street artists sketch you. Take time to pause and observe what is around you: the fresco painted on the side of the building; the fountains that gurgle on the squares; the geraniums on the windows; the hip Roman teenagers lingering on their motor scooters; the shopkeeper who is sweeping the front of his store; the chestnut seller who entices you with the tempting, smoky aroma of just-roasted chestnuts. And when you are tired, find a little trattoria that serves typical Roman comfort food. Or just sit at an outdoor caffè, sip a cappuccino, and linger, just as the Romans do, appreciating the moment and observing the theater of daily Roman life.

Bruschetta with Roasted Caramelized Cherry Tomatoes

Bruschetta con Pomodorini Canditi

Years ago, bruschetta was simply a slice of grilled Italian bread, rubbed with garlic and drizzled with flavorful olive oil. This delicious humble country dish, once a mainstay of farmers and peasants, has now been gentrified and embellished, and in Rome is prepared with a variety of ingredients. Bruschetta with roasted cherry tomatoes seems to be the up-to-the-minute favorite Roman variation. The addition of sugar during the last half hour of the tomatoes' slow cooking caramelizes the tomatoes to a delicious crispness. ♦ *serves 8*

2 pounds large cherry tomatoes (2 baskets), washed, dried, and halved

Salt to taste

1 tablespoon sugar

8 to 10 fresh basil leaves, julienned

Freshly ground black pepper to taste

1/3 cup extra-virgin olive oil

8 slices crusty Italian bread, cut 1/2-inch thick

2 large garlic cloves, peeled and halved

Preheat the oven to 250°F.

Place half of the tomatoes, cut side up, on a small baking pan that can accommodate them snuggly in one layer. Season lightly with salt. Place on the middle rack of the oven and roast for about 2 1/2 hours, checking them every half hour or so, making sure they don't burn. (If that happens, lower the temperature to 200°F.) Sprinkle the tomatoes with the sugar during the last half hour of cooking. When done the tomatoes will be dried and will have a crinkled appearance and an intense aroma. Allow to cool to room temperature.

In a medium bowl, combine the cool tomatoes with the uncooked tomatoes, add the basil, season lightly with salt and pepper, and toss with the olive oil. Set aside at room temperature until ready to use.

Preheat the oven to 400°F. Brush the bread on both sides with the olive oil that has pooled in the bowl, place the bread on a baking sheet, and bake until lightly golden on both sides, about 5 minutes. Rub one side of the bread with the cut sides of garlic. Spoon the tomato mixture over each slice, place on a large platter, and serve.

Fava Bean Purée with Bitter Greens

Incapriata

Enoteca Ferrara, one of the best and best-known wine bars of Rome, came to us highly recommended. We were told that this upscale place had, besides an incredible wine list, deliciously ambitious food. And so we went. As we walked into the restaurant at eight-thirty, the place was already packed, quite unusual in a city where people don't go out to dinner before nine. Two enormous books were brought to the table, and the pleasant waitress said with a twinkle in her eye, "One for the white wines and one for the reds." My husband, who loves wine, grinned from ear to ear. Our meal, at a leisurely pace, lasted for over three hours. My favorite dishes were the traditional ones of *la cucina povera*, the hearty but inventive cooking of the poor. Maria Paolillo, who with her sister cooks and runs the restaurant and who is extremely choosy about the ingredients she uses and the quality of the food she serves, suggested as a starter this purée of fresh fava beans and bitter chicory, a typical dish of Puglia. We liked this place so much that the next evening at eight-thirty sharp we went back for more. ◆ *serves 4 to 6*

2 pounds fresh, unshelled fava beans

1 medium Idaho or russet potato, peeled and cut into small chunks

Salt to taste

$^1/_2$ cup extra-virgin olive oil, plus more for brushing the bread

1 pound broccoli rabe, escarole, or any other bitter green

Red pepper flakes to taste

4 slices crusty Italian bread, cut $^1/_2$-inch thick

1 large garlic clove, peeled and halved

PREPARE THE FAVA BEAN PURÉE

Shell the beans and discard the pods. Bring a medium pot of water to a boil over high heat and prepare an ice-water bath in a medium bowl. Add the fava beans to the pot and cook for 1 to 2 minutes, depending on size. Drain the beans and place in the ice bath. Drain again. Pinch the skin of each bean, breaking it at one end, and squeeze the bean out of its skin.

(continued on next page)

Put the shelled beans and the potato chunks into another pot with just enough water to cover. Season with salt and bring the water to a gentle boil. Cook, uncovered, over medium heat until the water is completely evaporated and the potato and beans are very tender and begin to fall apart, 12 to 15 minutes. If the water evaporates too quickly and the beans and potatoes are not yet soft, stir in a little more water.

Purée the fava beans and the potatoes through a food mill (or food processor) directly into a large bowl. Add about half of the olive oil a few tablespoonfuls at a time, and mix thoroughly with a wooden spoon. Taste and adjust the seasoning.

PREPARE THE BITTER GREENS AND ASSEMBLE

While the beans and potato are cooking, trim and discard any large woody stalks and wilted leaves from the broccoli rabe. Wash the bitter greens under cold running water, then place in a pot with 2 cups of water and a few pinches of salt. Bring to a boil, then reduce the heat to medium and cook until very tender (7 to 8 minutes for broccoli rabe; 2 to 3 minutes for escarole). Drain and dry well with paper towels. Place the greens in a bowl, season with the red pepper flakes and salt to taste, and dress with the remaining oil.

Preheat the oven to 400°F. Brush the bread on both sides with a bit of oil, place the slices on a baking sheet, and bake until lightly golden on both sides, about 5 minutes. Remove from the oven and rub one side of the bread with the cut side of garlic.

Spoon the bean purée into individual serving bowls, forming a small mound. Place some of the bitter greens over or around the purée, and serve warm or at room temperature with the toasted bread.

VARIATION

Fava Bean Purée with Dried Fava Beans ◆ Soak the peeled or unpeeled fava beans overnight. If using unpeeled beans, plunge them in a pot of boiling water for a few minutes. Drain and remove the skin as instructed above. Put the beans and the potato into a pot with enough water to cover by 1 inch. Bring to a gentle boil over medium heat. As soon as the beans begin to release their foam (fresh beans will not do that), skim it off with a large spoon. Lower the heat, season with salt, and cook until the beans and potatoes are very tender, about 1 hour. (Dry beans require a longer cooking time than fresh ones.) If the water in the pot evaporates too quickly and the beans are not quite tender, add small amounts of water as needed. Drain, then purée the beans and potato and add the oil as instructed above.

OLD WAYS

There are still many cooks in Puglia who prepare this dish the old-fashioned way. As the beans cook on the stove, the cook stirs occasionally with a long wooden spoon. During the last 10 to 15 minutes of cooking, when the water is almost all evaporated and the beans and potatoes are falling apart, the stirring needs to be vigorous in order to mash everything. Then the oil is beaten in with the wooden spoon until everything turns into a smooth purée.

Stuffed Artichokes Roman-Style

Carciofi alla Romana

Artichokes are one of Rome's most prominent vegetables. In spring, eating establishments all over the city display cooked and uncooked artichokes as a badge of honor. Of the many types of artichokes that Italy produces, perhaps the most succulent is the round, plump *carciofo romanesco cimarolo*, harvested in the countryside of Rome and picked from the top of the bush. These meaty artichokes become utterly irresistible when stuffed with mint, parsley, and garlic and cooked stem side up in wine and olive oil until soft and tender. Paris, a very popular restaurant in the heart of Trastevere, serves mouthwatering *carciofi alla Romana*. If you are ever in Rome in spring, order this dish and ask them to serve it with a few wedges of local Pecorino cheese. A combination made in heaven. ◆ *serves 4*

1 lemon, halved	Salt and freshly ground black pepper to taste
4 long-stemmed medium artichokes	
1/2 cup chopped fresh flat-leaf parsley	3/4 cup extra-virgin olive oil
1/4 cup chopped fresh mint leaves	3 cups dry white wine
3 garlic cloves, finely minced	

Fill a large bowl with cold water and add the juice of 1/2 lemon. Pull off and discard the tough outer leaves of the artichokes, until you get to the tender, lightly colored leaves. With a sharp paring knife, peel the green, tougher part of the stems and the green parts of the artichoke bases. Slice off about 1 inch from the tops of the artichokes. Gently spread open the leaves and remove the fuzzy inner chokes with a spoon or a melon scooper. Rub half of the lemon all over the artichokes to prevent discoloration, then plunge the artichokes in the bowl of lemon water.

In a medium bowl, combine the parsley, mint, garlic, salt and pepper, and 2 to 3 tablespoons of the olive oil. One at a time, hold the artichokes over the bowl and press some of the herb mixture between the leaves and in the center of each artichoke. With your hands, push the leaves closer together, then place the artichokes, stem side up, in a deep, heavy pot that holds them snugly in one layer. Pour in the rest of the oil and the wine. Bring the liquid to a boil over high heat. Reduce the heat to medium low, cover, and cook until a thin knife can be inserted easily at the base of the artichokes, 30 to 40 minutes.

With a large spatula, transfer the cooked artichokes to a platter. If the liquid in the pot is watery, cook it over high heat until it is reduced enough to coat the back of a spoon. Spoon the juices over the artichokes, cool completely, and serve at room temperature, drizzled with some of the reduced juices. (The artichokes can be stored in the refrigerator for several days. Bring them back to room temperature before serving.)

The Colosseum

Stuffed Zucchini Blossoms

Fiori di Zucchine Ripieni

After eating *bucatini all'amatriciana, coda alla vaccinara,* and other traditional Roman dishes in fun-filled boisterous trattorie, you may long for a quiet, elegant, romantic, expensive dinner. I have a place for you: Il Convivio, near Piazza Navona. The staff at this excellent restaurant greet you with a flute of champagne, then navigate you through their menu and large wine list while offering helpful suggestions. One of their dishes I've enjoyed most is the zucchini blossoms stuffed with superlative Roman ricotta and plump minced anchovies, dipped in a light beer batter and fried. (Because Roman ricotta is not available here, the recipe below adds some goat cheese to the ricotta mixture to heighten the flavor of the filling.) This is a dish that needs to be fried at the last moment and quickly served. However, if you prepare the filling several hours ahead and stuff the blossoms one hour or so before you begin the frying, it will be a snap to complete the dish. ◆ *serves 4 to 6*

FOR THE BATTER

2 eggs, separated

1¼ cups beer

1 cup all-purpose flour

Small pinch of salt

FOR THE STUFFING AND ZUCCHINI

6 ounces ricotta cheese

2 ounces goat cheese

4 to 5 anchovy fillets, finely chopped

Pinch of salt

20 large zucchini blossoms
(about 5 ounces)

Vegetable oil for frying

PREPARE THE BATTER

In a medium bowl, whip the egg whites until soft peaks form. In another medium bowl, lightly beat the yolks, then whisk in the beer. Gradually add the flour, whisking well after each addition. Season with salt, then fold in the egg whites. Set aside for about 30 minutes.

PREPARE THE STUFFING AND ZUCCHINI

In a medium bowl, combine the ricotta, goat cheese, and anchovies. Season lightly with salt, and mix well with a spatula to blend. Test and adjust the seasoning. Put the filling in a small pastry bag and refrigerate until ready to use.

If the stems of the zucchini blossoms are very long, cut them down to about 2 inches in length. Open the flowers gently and remove the pistils. Pipe a small amount of the ricotta mixture into the blossom cavities. Twist the blossom leaves *very lightly* (just like the ends of a loosely wrapped candy) so that the filling will not escape during the frying. Repeat with the remaining blossoms.

Heat 1 inch of oil in a medium saucepan over high heat. When the oil is hot but not smoking, working with one blossom at a time, hold a blossom with your fingers, dip it into the batter, and slip it into the oil. Do not fry more than four blossoms at a time or the temperature of the oil will decrease. When they are golden on one side, turn them over and brown the other side, about 2 minutes. With a slotted spoon, transfer them to paper towels to drain. When all the blossoms have been fried, place them on a large serving platter, sprinkle lightly with salt, and serve at once.

VARIATION

The blossoms are also heavenly delicious when they are deep-fried without a stuffing. Remove and discard the stems and pistils. Dip the blossoms in the batter and fry a few at a time; their golden, crisp leaves will spread out like the petals of flowers. Sprinkle with salt before serving.

Fettuccine with Roman Ragù

Fettuccine con Ragù alla Romana

Just imagine sitting in a little trattoria overlooking a beautiful Roman square, sipping wine and eating a delightful plate of *fettuccine col ragù* while watching the world go by. Some dishes need to be eaten in their own setting to be really appreciated. The trattoria where I enjoyed this and other memorable dishes is Fortunato al Pantheon, a bastion of authentic Roman cooking. This basic and somewhat pristine meat ragù becomes utterly tantalizing when paired with the homemade egg fettuccine of the city.

◆ *serves 4 to 6*

FOR THE RAGÙ

- 1/3 cup extra-virgin olive oil
- 1/2 small onion, minced (about 1/2 cup)
- 1 small carrot, minced (about 1/2 cup)
- 1 medium celery stalk, minced (about 1/2 cup)
- 1 pound ground beef chuck
- 1/4 pound sliced prosciutto, finely minced
  Salt and freshly ground black pepper to taste
- 1/2 cup medium-bodied red wine
- 3 cups canned imported Italian plum tomatoes, with their juices, finely chopped
- 1 cup Meat Broth (page 298) or low-sodium canned beef broth

FOR THE FETTUCCINE AND TO SERVE

- 1 tablespoon coarse salt
- 1 recipe Basic Pasta Dough, rolled out and cut into fettuccine (page 301), or 1 pound imported dried fettuccine
- 1 tablespoon unsalted butter
- 1/2 cup freshly grated Parmigiano-Reggiano

PREPARE THE RAGÙ

Heat the oil in a heavy, wide-bottomed saucepan over medium heat. Add the onion, carrot, and celery and cook, stirring with a wooden spoon, until the vegetables are soft and lightly golden, about 8 minutes. Add the beef and prosciutto and season with salt and just a little pepper. Cook over high heat, breaking the meat up with the wooden spoon, until the meat has a rich golden color, 8 to 10 minutes.

Add the wine and cook, scraping the bottom of the pan, until the wine is almost all evaporated. Add the chopped tomatoes with all their juices and the broth. As soon as the tomatoes begin to bubble, reduce the heat to the barest simmer, partially cover the pan, and cook, stirring every half hour or so, for 1½ hours. At the end of cooking the sauce should have a rich, reddish color and a medium-thick consistency. Taste, adjust the seasoning, and turn off the heat. (The ragù can be prepared several hours or a few days ahead. Refrigerate tightly covered.)

PREPARE THE FETTUCCINE

Bring a large pot of water to a boil over high heat. Add the 1 tablespoon coarse salt and the fettuccine and cook until the pasta is tender but still firm to the bite. Drain the pasta and place in a large bowl. Add about half of the ragù, the butter, and a nice handful of the Parmigiano. Toss quickly until the pasta and sauce are well combined. Stir in a little more sauce if needed. Serve at once with the remaining Parmigiano on the side.

HOW TO REFRIGERATE RAGÙ

If you are planning to use the ragù a few days after you have made it, place the sauce in a large baking dish or wide casserole and refrigerate uncovered. Stir the ragù every 20 minutes or so until it is cooled all the way through. Transfer the chilled ragù to a large bowl, cover tightly with plastic wrap, and refrigerate for up to a few days, or freeze it.

THE WINES OF ROME

The region of Lazio, of which Rome is the capital, produces mainly white wines, although lately some notable reds have made an impression on the international scene. Some of my favorites are:

WHITE WINES

Est! Est!! Est!!! di Montefiascone, a white wine from the village of Montefiascone near Lake Bolsena. Produced from trebbiano, malvasia bianca, and the local rossetto, it is a pleasant, fragrant white, with an enviable legendary history: It is called Est! Est!! Est!!! because legend has it that the servant of a German bishop, sent ahead of his master to check the quality of the wines in the villages along the road leading to Rome, was to write *Est,* "it is (good)," on the walls of the inns where he found good wine. In Montefiascone he could not contain himself and wrote, *Est, Est, Est.* The wine may be still, slightly bubbly, or spumante style, or even slightly sweet (*amabile.*) Bigi is an excellent producer whose wines are available in the United States. Poggio dei Gelsi, a late-harvest Est! Est!! Est!!!, is a wonderful dessert wine produced by Falesco.

Frascati, a blend mainly of trebbiano and malvasia grapes, is perhaps the most widely recognized white wine of Lazio. Often a simple, nondescript wine, it can also be lively, fresh, and flowery, with hints of tropical fruit and a lingering finish. It is excellent with seafood, fettuccine alla romana, and some lighter meat dishes. Castel de Paolis is the producer of note, and the single-vineyard Vigna Adriana is superb. Another excellent producer is Fontana Candida, and the single-vineyard Santa Teresa is not to be missed.

RED WINES

Reds produced in Lazio are generally a blend of cesanese, merlot, montepulciano d'Abruzzo, and sangiovese, but many variations exist. Here are two producers whose reds I always enjoy:

In the Alban hills south of Rome, Paola di Mauro produces fine red wines under the Colle Picchioni label. The Vigna del Vassello, a blend of merlot, cabernet sauvignon, and cabernet franc, is a full-bodied, rich red wine. The Colle Picchioni Rosso is a bit softer, a blend of merlot, cabernet sauvignon, sangiovese, and montepulciano. Both can accompany most red-meat dishes.

Falesco, owned by the Cotarella brothers, produces a hundred-percent merlot called Montiano that rivals many Bordeaux and California reds. It has become an international favorite.

Spaghetti with Fresh Tomatoes, Olives, and Capers

Spaghetti alla Checca

This is perhaps one of the most "modern" of all the traditional pasta dishes of Rome, for it seems it was invented in the early 1970s by a family-run establishment, Osteria dell'Antiquario. Perhaps it was the sultry summer heat that prompted the chef to forgo the cooking of the tomatoes, or perhaps it was merely a burst of creativity. The fact is that on a hot summer day, very few dishes taste as good. ◆ *serves 4 to 6*

1 garlic clove, minced

4 plump anchovy fillets packed in salt, rinsed and chopped

1/3 cup extra-virgin olive oil

3 tablespoons capers, rinsed and dried

1 cup pitted green and black olives, halved

1/4 cup chopped fresh flat-leaf parsley

8 to 10 basil leaves, shredded

1 1/2 pounds ripe plum tomatoes, washed, seeded, and diced

Salt and freshly ground black pepper to taste

1 tablespoon coarse salt

1 pound imported dried spaghetti

Put the garlic, anchovies, and olive oil in a large serving bowl and mix well. Add the capers, olives, parsley, basil, and diced tomatoes. Season with salt and pepper. Let the mixture stand for about 15 minutes.

Meanwhile, bring a large pot of water to a boil over high heat. Add the coarse salt and the pasta, and cook until the pasta is tender but still firm to the bite.

Drain the pasta and place in the bowl with the tomatoes. Toss quickly until the pasta and sauce are well combined. Add a little more olive oil if needed. Taste, adjust the seasoning, and serve.

Spaghetti with Guanciale, Eggs, and Parmigiano

Spaghetti alla Carbonara

Lately in Italy, as well as in the United States, the classic carbonara sauce has been "enriched" with a variety of other ingredients: mushrooms, peas, fava beans, prosciutto, broccoli, and cream (ouch!) have been added to the basic preparation, to the distress of many. The following carbonara is traditional to the core. It uses *guanciale* (cured pork jowl) or pancetta, the freshest eggs possible, a mixture of Parmigiano and Pecorino cheeses, and lots of black pepper. This is the exact same dish that the famous trattoria La Carbonara in Rome serves day in and day out. This is a dish that does not wait for anyone. So when you are ready to serve, make sure to have everyone seated. ◆ *serves 4*

2 whole large eggs

2 large egg yolks

1/4 cup freshly grated Parmigiano-Reggiano

1/4 cup freshly grated Pecorino Romano

1/2 teaspoon salt plus more to taste

1/2 teaspoon freshly ground black pepper plus more to taste

1 tablespoon coarse salt

1/2 pound dried spaghetti

1/3 cup extra-virgin olive oil

1/4 pound thickly sliced *guanciale* (see note) or pancetta, diced

In a large serving dish that can later accommodate the pasta, beat the eggs and the egg yolks with 2 tablespoons each of the Parmigiano and Pecorino Romano. Season with 1/2 teaspoon salt and 1/2 teaspoon black pepper and set aside.

Bring a large pot of water to a boil. Add the 1 tablespoon of coarse salt and the spaghetti. Cook, uncovered, over high heat until the spaghetti is tender but still a bit firm to the bite.

While the pasta is cooking, heat the oil in a large skillet over medium heat until hot. Add the *guanciale* or the pancetta and cook until it is lightly golden, 1 to 2 minutes.

Drain the spaghetti and add to the skillet. Season lightly with salt and mix over low heat until the pasta is well coated with the oil. Add the pasta to the dish with the eggs. Sprinkle with a little more Parmigiano and Pecorino, and toss quickly to coat. Taste, adjust the seasoning, and serve at once with more cheese if desired.

GUANCIALE

Guanciale is a salt-cured pork jowl that Romans like to use in a variety of recipes. It's not always available in the United States, but can be found in some gourmet stores, especially those focusing on Italian foodstuffs. If you can't find it, pancetta, which is somewhat leaner, is a good substitute.

Bucatini with Pancetta, Pecorino, and Black Pepper

Bucatini alla Gricia

One of Rome's most loved pasta dishes is *bucatini all'amatriciana,* in which thick, hollow spaghetti are tossed with a sauce of *guanciale* (cured pork jowl) or pancetta, tomatoes, and red pepper flakes. However, sixty miles from Rome in the tiny town of Amatrice, in the Abruzzo region, you can still find a humbler ancestor of this dish, called *bucatini alla gricia.* The ancient shepherds of Amatrice would prepare this simple dish during the long stretches they spent with their flocks in the region's lush pastures. At the time bucatini alla gricia was made only with guanciale and seasoned with aged Pecorino cheese, made from sheep's milk. The guanciale, with its large amount of savory fat, coated the pasta, while the cheese added pungency. While pasta all'amatriciana with tomatoes can be found on most Roman menus and on the menus of Italian restaurants all over the world, the tomato-less version seems to be available only in some of the most traditional trattorie of Rome. ◆ *serves 4 to 6*

I tablespoon coarse salt, plus more to taste

I pound dried bucatini or spaghetti

1/2 cup extra-virgin olive oil

6 ounces thickly sliced *guanciale* (see note, page 21) or pancetta, diced

Freshly ground black pepper to taste

I tablespoon chopped fresh flat-leaf parsley

I cup freshly grated Pecorino Romano

Bring a large pot of water to a boil over high heat. Add the I tablespoon coarse salt and the pasta and cook until the pasta is tender but still firm to the bite.

While the pasta is cooking, heat the oil in a large skillet over medium heat. Add the *guanciale* or pancetta and cook, stirring, until the pancetta is lightly golden, 2 to 3 minutes.

Scoop out 1/2 cup of the pasta cooking water and reserve. (Pasta's cooking water, enriched by the starch of the pasta, is often used in Italian kitchens to thicken and give more body to sauces.) Drain the pasta and add to the skillet. Season with salt and generously with pepper. Add the parsley, $1/3$ cup of the Pecorino, and the pasta water. Mix over medium heat until the pasta is well coated with the sauce. Taste and adjust the seasoning. Serve hot with a bit more cheese, if desired.

THE SECRET IS IN THE INGREDIENTS

It is hard to imagine that a pasta made with only five basic ingredients can be as irresistible as this one. Look for imported bucatini (thick, hollow spaghetti), a Roman favorite. Buy the best extra-virgin olive oil you can afford, and don't be stingy in using it. Select a nice piece of imported Pecorino Romano cheese and, if you can't find guanciale, select pancetta that has the same amount of fat and lean meat (flavor is in the fat). Then get in the kitchen and cook as the Romans do, with abandon, joy, and anticipation.

Green Tea Tonnarelli with Shrimp and Candied Cherry Tomatoes

Tonnarelli al Tè Verde con Gamberi e Pomodorini Canditi

The trip from San Francisco to Paris to Rome was long but uneventful. Once in Rome we waited for our luggage, and waited and waited, only to finally find out that the bags were still in Paris. By the time we arrived at our hotel, my husband and I were exhausted and hungry. So we opted to have a bite at the hotel. We were escorted to a large, beautiful garden, half full with smartly dressed people. A piano was playing softly in one end of the garden. A minute after we were seated, a waiter came with a flute of champagne and took our order. "I strongly recommend the green tea tonnarelli with shrimp and candied tomatoes," he said. "Our chef is one of the best of Rome." When the pasta arrived, preceded by the intense aroma of the candied tomatoes, our spirits were lifted immediately. The pasta was fantastic, the creation of the talented chef Paolo Londero of the Hotel Hassler in Rome, who after having spent several years in Japan was inspired to create a pasta flavored with one of Japan's most loved ingredients, tea, and pair it with a flavorful Italian sauce. Of course this splendid sauce can also be paired with pappardelle, penne, spaghetti, and linguine. ◆ *serves 6*

FOR THE TONNARELLI

5 large eggs

8 teabags (about 4 tablespoons) Japanese powdered green tea

2 cups all-purpose unbleached flour combined with 1 cup finely milled semolina flour

FOR THE CANDIED TOMATOES

1 pound large cherry tomatoes, about 2 baskets, washed and halved

FOR THE SAUCE

$1/3$ cup extra-virgin olive oil

1 pound medium shrimp, shelled, deveined, and cut into $1/2$-inch pieces

1 garlic clove, minced

Red pepper flakes to taste

Salt to taste

$1/2$ cup dry white wine

1 to 2 tablespoons unsalted butter

2 tablespoons chopped fresh flat-leaf parsley

1 tablespoon coarse salt

PREPARE THE TONNARELLI

Beat the eggs in a medium bowl. Add the green tea powder and mix thoroughly with a fork or small whisk. Proceed to make the Basic Pasta Dough using the Hand Method or the Machine Method on pages 301–2. Roll out the pasta and cut it into tonnarelli as instructed on page 303.

PREPARE THE CANDIED TOMATOES

Preheat the oven to 250°F. Place the tomatoes cut side up on a large baking sheet and roast on the middle rack of the oven for 2½ to 3 hours. Check occasionally, making sure the tomatoes don't burn. If that happens, lower the temperature to 200°F. When done, the tomatoes will have a crinkled appearance and an intense aroma. They should not be too dry. They can be used immediately, or allowed to cool to room temperature. When cool, place them in a bowl, cover with extra-virgin olive oil, and refrigerate tightly covered until ready to use. They will keep well for about 1 week.

PREPARE THE SAUCE AND ASSEMBLE

Heat the oil in a large skillet over medium-high heat. When the oil just begins to smoke, add the shrimp and cook until they just begin to color, 1 to 2 minutes. Add the garlic, red pepper flakes, and the reserved candied tomatoes. Season with salt and stir for about 1 minute. Add the wine and butter and stir until the sauce has thickened, 2 to 3 minutes. Stir in the parsley and turn off the heat.

Meanwhile, bring a large pot of water to a boil over high heat. Add the 1 tablespoon coarse salt and the tonnarelli and cook until the pasta is tender but still firm to the bite. Scoop up about ½ cup of the pasta cooking water and reserve. Drain the pasta, add it to the skillet, and toss quickly over medium heat until the pasta and sauce are well combined. Stir in some of the reserved pasta water if the pasta looks too dry. Taste, adjust the seasoning, and serve.

Potato Gnocchi in Spicy Tomato Sauce

Gnocchi all'Amatriciana

Sora Margherita, a small trattoria in Piazza delle Cinque Scole, is one of those establishments that are the heart and soul of Rome. The food relies on time-honored dishes, made with first-quality ingredients. The owner or a waiter will recite the dishes of the day. And so on Monday you might order the potato gnocchi. On Tuesday, oxtail stew. On Wednesday, the fettuccine with ragù. The day I was there, I ordered the potato gnocchi with a most divine *amatriciana* sauce. The gnocchi were plump and soft. The sauce was spicy and savory with a lingering, satisfying flavor. And the red wine was the uncomplicated, straightforward one of the Castelli Romani that paired so well with this type of food. Pasta with amatriciana sauce is one of the many dishes that Rome "borrowed" from neighboring regions and through the centuries made its own. This sauce is also traditionally paired with *bucatini,* which is thick, hollow spaghetti. ◆ *serves 4 to 6*

4 to 5 tablespoons extra-virgin olive oil

4 ounces thickly sliced *guanciale* (see note, page 21) or pancetta, diced

Red pepper flakes to taste

$^1/_2$ cup dry white wine

6 large fresh tomatoes, peeled, seeded, and finely diced (see note) or 4 cups finely diced canned Italian plum tomatoes with their juices

Salt to taste

1 tablespoon coarse salt

1 recipe Basic Potato Gnocchi (page 304, refrigerated, uncovered)

$^1/_2$ cup freshly grated Pecorino Romano or Parmigiano-Reggiano

Heat the oil in a large skillet over medium-high heat. Add the *guanciale* or the pancetta and a nice pinch of pepper flakes and stir until the guanciale is lightly colored but not crisp, 1 to 2 minutes. Add the wine and cook briskly until it is all evaporated. Stir in the tomatoes, season with salt to taste, and cook, stirring occasionally, until the tomatoes are very soft and their juices have thickened, about 10 minutes.

Meanwhile, bring a large pot of water to a boil over high heat. Add the 1 tablespoon coarse salt and the gnocchi. Cook until the gnocchi rise to the surface of the water, about 2 minutes. Remove the gnocchi a few at a time with a slotted spoon and add to the sauce. Add a small handful of cheese and stir with a wooden spoon over medium heat until the gnocchi and sauce are well combined. Taste, adjust the seasoning, and serve with the remaining cheese.

HOW TO PEEL AND SEED TOMATOES

Cut an X at the bottom of each tomato and drop them into a pot of boiling water. Boil until the skin begins to split, about 1 minute. Transfer to a bowl of ice water. As soon as you can handle them, peel off the skin, place the tomatoes on a cutting board, and halve. Squeeze out the seeds or pull them out with your fingers. Dice, mince, or chop the flesh as desired.

Baked Semolina Gnocchi Roman-Style

Gnocchi di Semolino alla Romana

While potato gnocchi are made in many parts of Italy, semolina-flour gnocchi is a uniquely Roman dish. Just walk into a typical Roman trattoria during the fall or winter and you will probably find written on the blackboard "today *gnocchi alla Romana.*" The last time I had this dish was at Corsi, a small, authentic trattoria where the local folks meet to drink and play cards. The baked gnocchi came to the table basted in sweet butter and topped generously with Parmigiano, which melted and laced the gnocchi voluptuously. It was pure, simple food at its best. ◆ *serves 4 to 6*

4 cups whole milk

2 teaspoons salt

$^{1}/_{2}$ pound semolina flour (about $1^{1}/_{2}$ cups)

5 tablespoons unsalted butter, melted, plus softened butter to grease the baking pan

1 cup freshly grated Parmigiano-Reggiano

2 large eggs, lightly beaten in a small bowl

Oil to grease the sheet pan

In a medium-size heavy pot over medium heat, bring the milk to a gentle boil. Add the salt and reduce the heat to medium low. As soon as the milk begins to simmer, start pouring in the semolina flour by the handful in a thin stream, very slowly, stirring constantly with a long wooden spoon to prevent lumps from forming. When all the flour has been incorporated, keep cooking and stirring with the wooden spoon, reaching all the way to the bottom of the pan, for about 10 minutes. The semolina is cooked when it sticks heavily to the spoon and comes away clean from the sides of the pan.

Remove the pan from the heat and stir in half of the melted butter, half of the Parmigiano, and both eggs. Mix for a couple of minutes, until everything is well incorporated.

Lightly oil a rimmed baking sheet. With a spatula, spread the semolina mixture $^{1}/_{2}$ inch thick on the sheet. Dip the spatula in cold water and smooth the top with it. Place in the refrigerator and chill, uncovered, for a couple of hours, or until firm.

Preheat the oven to 400°F. Butter a deep 10 by 12-inch baking dish.

With a 2-inch round cookie cutter (or a small glass), cut the cooled semolina into rounds. Arrange the rounds in the buttered baking dish, slightly overlapping one another. Brush the rounds with the remaining $2^1/2$ tablespoons butter and sprinkle with the remaining $^1/2$ cup Parmigiano. (The dish can be prepared up to this point a few days ahead. Cover and refrigerate.)

Bake on the middle rack of the oven until the gnocchi have a golden color, 10 to 15 minutes. Let stand 5 minutes before serving.

NOTE

After you cut the chilled semolina into rounds, you will have a nice amount of semolina scraps. Cut the scraps into fairly equal pieces and toss them in a skillet with butter, Parmigiano, and sage. The look of this improvisation will be very homey, but its taste will be delicious and satisfying.

Pasta and Chickpea Soup

Minestra di Pasta e Ceci

This is a heartwarming dish of *la cucina povera Romana*—simple, unsophisticated, but savory food, popular in Roman households and traditional trattorie. As always, there are several versions of *pasta e ceci*. The most traditional, which was generally made on Fridays, the "meatless" day of the week, omits the pancetta in favor of minced anchovies. Others omit the pasta in favor of grilled or toasted bread. And some dribble the soup with fruity olive oil instead of Pecorino. At Nino Trattoria, located near Piazza di Spagna, this soup was so thick that it could have been eaten with a fork. When I asked for a sprinkling of Pecorino Romano, the waiter said, "Signora, absolutely not," then proceeded to lace my soup with gorgeously green olive oil.

◆ *serves 8*

I pound (about 2 cups) dried chickpeas, picked over and soaked overnight in cold water to cover generously

1/3 cup extra-virgin olive oil, plus more for drizzling

1/4 pound thickly sliced pancetta, finely minced

2 garlic cloves, minced

2 tablespoons finely minced fresh rosemary, or I tablespoon crumbled dried rosemary

3 cups canned Italian plum tomatoes with their juices, put through a food mill to remove the seeds

Salt and freshly ground black pepper to taste

1/2 pound dried thin spaghetti, broken into 2- to 3-inch pieces

Discard any chickpeas that rise to the surface of the water. Drain and rinse the chickpeas well under cold running water and put in a large pot. Add 2 1/2 quarts (12 cups) cold water and bring to a gentle boil over medium heat. Partially cover the pot, reduce the heat to low, and cook, stirring from time to time, until the chickpeas are tender, 2 to 2 1/2 hours.

Meanwhile, heat the oil in a medium saucepan over medium heat. Add the pancetta and cook, stirring, until lightly golden, about 2 minutes. Add the garlic and rosemary and cook, stirring, for about I minute. Add the tomatoes, season with salt and pepper, and bring to a gentle simmer. Cook, stirring occasionally, until the sauce has a medium-thick consistency, 10 to 15 minutes.

Add the tomato mixture to the pot with the chickpeas and bring to a gentle boil. Taste, adjust the seasoning, then add the pasta. Cook uncovered over medium heat until the pasta is tender but still firm to the bite. Turn off the heat and let the soup rest for a few minutes. Serve with a few drops of the best extra-virgin olive oil you have in your house.

THE UBIQUITOUS LEGUMES

Some of the most delicious dishes of Italy are made with legumes. Beans, lentils, fava beans, and chickpeas, either fresh or dried, are used in soups, stews, salads, and braised dishes. While pasta and bean soup is a much loved combination all over Italy, in Rome pasta and chickpea soup is the undisputed favorite. While the chickpea (also called *garbanzo bean* and *ceci*) is a basic, unassuming ingredient, it takes a little knowledge to cook it properly. This is what I have learned:

• The older the dried chickpeas are, the longer they need to soak. To be safe, soak your chickpeas in cold water to cover, not less than 24 hours.

• Chickpeas should be cooked over *very low heat*. Fast cooking will toughen the beans.

• The cooking time changes depending on how old the beans are. Simmer the beans not less than 2 hours, then taste them. If still too firm, cook longer, in which case you might need to add a little more water.

• Keep in mind that a chickpea soup, just like a bean soup, will thicken as it sits, especially if it includes pasta.

WHEN IN ROME
Restaurants, Trattorie, and Wine Bars

From the U.S., dial 011, followed by the country code of 39. The area code for all numbers below is 06.

Al Bric
Via del Pellegrino 51/52
Campo de' Fiori
Tel. 687 9533
As you enter this cozy wine bar, you will notice an enormous book placed on a large stand. That is the wine list. So if you are not serious about wine, you had better leave. The food is a mixture of traditional and creative; the ones I enjoyed most were the traditional.

Checchino dal 1887
Via di Monte Testaccio 30
Testaccio
Tel. 574 3816
Since 1887 this restaurant has served outstanding Roman food. Make sure to order *abbacchio* (milk-fed baby lamb), either roasted or *alla cacciatora*.

Enoteca Corsi
Via del Gesù 87/88
Tel. 679 0821
I never get tired of Corsi. Why? Because its food is simple but delicious, and the price is right. This unassuming little eatery has now added a wine bar to its well-established trattoria. The wine choices are many, and the dishes of the day are recited quickly by the owner. Great pastas and soups. But if the *polpettine con purè* (meatballs with mashed potatoes) are offered that day, grab them.

Enoteca Ferrara
Via del Moro 1/a
Tel. 583 33 920
If you have time to visit only one place in Rome, go to Enoteca Ferrara. The wine lists (one for whites and one for reds) is tremendous, and the food, which is influenced by several Southern Italian regions, is simply outstanding.

Fortunato al Pantheon
Via del Pantheon 55
Tel. 679 2788
Fortunato al Pantheon has been one of my favorites for years. Nothing has changed, not even the waiters, who now seem to be moving slower than usual. The food is basic but delicious. The pastas are not to be missed, especially the Carbonara and the Bucatini alla Gricia.

The Palm Court Garden of the Hotel Hassler
Piazza Trinità dei Monti 6
Tel. 69 9340
This beautiful hotel has two outstanding restaurants. The garden is more informal; the rooftop more elegant. The Honey-Flavored Young Smoked Turkey Hen with Baby Salad and Aged Balsamic Vinegar is outstanding. Bonus: the view from the rooftop restaurant is spectacular.

Hostaria Romanesca
Piazza Campo de' Fiori 40
Tel. 686 4024
This simple eatery is located in the picturesque
Campo de' Fiori square. The food is unpretentious
and basic, but the homemade fettuccine with the
Roman ragù makes you want to go back for more.
Ask for an outside table and watch the world go by.

Il Convivio Troiani
Vicolo dei Soldati 31
Tel./Fax 686 9432
Three brothers, Massimo, Giuseppe, and Angelo,
run this elegant restaurant that serves creative and
traditional dishes. Try the "light as feathers" Potato
Gnocchi with Small Calamari and Peas.

L'Angolo Divino
Via Balestrari 12
Tel. 686 4413
A rustic wine bar where you can taste a large
number of wines by the glass. The food is simple
and often consists only of soups, pasta, pizza,
salads, and cured meats.

La Rosetta
Via della Rosetta, 8/9
Pantheon
Tel. 686 1002
Expensive and noisy, but boy do they know how
to cook seafood! This place is, without any doubt,
one of the best seafood restaurants in the city. The
splendid risotto with shellfish is my favorite.

Lo Sgobbone
Via dei Podesti 8/10
Tel. 323 2994
Lo Sgobbone, a place where you feel instantly at
ease, is located in the outskirts of Rome and is
patronized mostly by Romans. Try the bruschette,
the stuffed zucchini, and the *polpette*, delicious
meatballs in a tomato sauce.

Nino
Via Borgognona 11
Tel. 678 6752
The food at this popular spot is very tasty and
served in generous portions. The service is informal
yet reassuring, and you know right away you are in
good hands. Try any of the pasta dishes or, if on
the menu, the classic Pasta and Chickpea Soup and
the Bistecca all'Arrabbiata, a large steak cooked
with a peppery tomato sauce.

Paris
Piazza San Calisto 7/a
Trastevere
Tel. 581 5378
Traditional food prepared with a sure hand.

Sabatini
Piazza Santa Maria in Trastevere 13
Tel. 581 2026
A busy, bustling trattoria with outdoor tables that
face the beautiful Piazza Santa Maria in Trastevere.
Try the Chicken with Peppers alla Romana or the
roasted Abbacchio (baby lamb).

Sora Lella
Via di Ponte Quattro Capi 16
Isola Tiberina
Tel. 686 1601
Sora Lella is one of the most popular trattorie
of Rome. The food is traditional, straightforward,
delicious, and reasonable. If available, try the
Vignarola, a stew of fava beans, fresh peas, and
artichoke hearts.

Sora Margherita
Piazza delle Cinque Scole 30
Tel. 686 4002
A typical Roman trattoria that serves the classic
dishes at reasonable prices. Try the Potato Gnocchi
all'Amatriciana, a sure winner.

Roman Oxtail Stew

Coda alla Vaccinara

A few years back, when the idea for this book was just beginning to take shape, my daughter Paola and I spent a week in Rome. I told her that because I was researching the food for a book, we needed to eat in as many places as we could, and we needed to take good notes and talk to the chefs, cooks, and owners of the establishments we enjoyed most. And so we did. The first night we arrived in Rome, in spite of the long, exhausting trip from San Francisco, we unloaded the luggage at the hotel and hopped in a taxi. Ten minutes later we were at Perilli, a well-known trattoria that serves traditional Roman food in the colorful Testaccio area. This small, boisterous, crowded place was still jumping at ten o'clock at night. We sat at a small table by the entrance. The waiter brought us "just something to perk you up": two slices of charred bruschetta, rubbed with garlic and drizzled with fragrant green olive oil. We ordered a bottle of local Frascati wine, fettuccine with Roman ragù, oxtail stew, and several other dishes that we knew we could never finish. Back at our hotel, we fell soundly asleep, and I dreamed about the glorious days that awaited us in Rome, and all the splendid food we would eat.... ◆ *serves 4 to 6*

3 pounds thick, meaty oxtail, trimmed of excess fat and cut into 2¹/₂- to 3-inch pieces

¹/₃ cup extra-virgin olive oil

1 small white onion, finely chopped

2 ounces pancetta, finely minced

2 garlic cloves, chopped

¹/₄ cup finely chopped fresh flat-leaf parsley

1 teaspoon salt plus more to taste

¹/₂ teaspoon freshly ground black pepper plus more to taste

1 cup dry red wine

2 (28-ounce) cans Italian plum tomatoes, preferably San Marzano (see note), with their juices, put through a food mill to remove the seeds

3 celery stalks, cut into 1-inch pieces

3 medium carrots, cut into 1-inch pieces

Preheat the oven to 350°F.

Rinse the oxtail under cold running water and pat dry on paper towels.

Heat the oil in a large, heavy ovenproof casserole over medium heat. Add the onion, pancetta, garlic, and parsley and cook, stirring, until the mixture is lightly golden, 4 to 5 minutes. Add the oxtail, season with the salt and pepper, and cook, turning the pieces in the savory base until the oxtail is browned on all sides, 5 to 6 minutes. Raise the heat to high and add the wine. Cook, stirring and scraping the bottom of the pan with a wooden spoon, until the wine has reduced approximately by half, 2 to 3 minutes.

Add the tomatoes and bring to a boil. Cover the pot partially and place on the middle rack of the oven. Cook for 1½ hours, stirring a few times.

Stir the celery and carrots into the sauce and cook gently until the meat is so tender that it begins to fall away from the bone, 1½ hours longer. Check the sauce from time to time and, if too thick, add some warm water. At the end of cooking the sauce should have a medium-thick consistency.

Transfer the meat to individual serving plates, taste the sauce and adjust the seasoning, and spoon over the meat. Serve hot.

ABOUT SAN MARZANO TOMATOES

San Marzano tomatoes, or *pomodori di San Marzano*, are a type of plum tomato that is cultivated all over the Campania region and that Neapolitans consider the best in the world. Canned San Marzano tomatoes are available in the United States and can be found in Italian markets and specialty food shops. For authentic canned San Marzano tomatoes, look for the official DOP seal of the consortium of Italian growers.

ABOUT OXTAIL

Oxtail is the skinned tail of an adult, castrated male of the bovine family. This very humble but very tasty meat became one of the city's most popular dishes at a time when the *vaccinari*, as the Roman slaughterhouse workers were once called, received oxtails and other lowly cuts of meat as a part of their pay. In turn the vaccinari would take the oxtail to the local *osteria* (wine pub) to be cooked. With time this dish became a much loved savory staple of popular Roman *cucina*.

As always there are many variations to a dish. Some cooks drop the oxtail pieces in boiling water for a few minutes to eliminate part of the fat. Others blanch the vegetables before adding them to the pot. And still others add pine nuts, raisins, and chocolate to the sauce during the last few minutes of cooking. Everyone agrees, however, that oxtail should be cooked covered on gentle heat for no less than 3 hours.

Veal Scaloppine with Prosciutto, Sage, and Wine

Saltimbocca alla Romana

Saltimbocca means, literally, "jump in the mouth," because of its instant gratifying flavor. It is one of the most loved Roman dishes and can be found in modest trattorie as well as in refined restaurants. The Romans take thin slices of white veal, top them with slices of rosy prosciutto and fresh sage, and brown them quickly in oil or butter. The sauce consists simply of the pan juices and reduced wine. This tantalizing, savory dish can be prepared in less than 10 minutes. I like to serve saltimbocca with creamy mashed potatoes or stuffed tomatoes. ◆ *serves 4*

8 slices thinly cut prosciutto di Parma (about 5 ounces)

8 large slices veal scaloppini (about 1 1/2 pounds), pounded thin

8 large fresh sage leaves

1/3 cup extra-virgin olive oil

1 cup dry white wine

2 tablespoons unsalted butter

Salt to taste

Place 1 slice of prosciutto over each veal slice, top the prosciutto with 1 sage leaf, and secure the layers with a wooden toothpick.

Heat the oil in a large nonstick skillet over medium-high heat. When the oil is nice and hot but not smoking, add the veal prosciutto side down and cook, without crowding, until the prosciutto is lightly golden, about 2 minutes. Turn and brown the other side, 1 to 2 minutes. Transfer the veal to a platter and keep warm in a low oven while you are making the sauce.

Discard the fat from the skillet and put the skillet back on high heat. Add the wine and stir with a wooden spoon to pick up the flavorful bits attached to the bottom of the skillet. When the wine is reduced almost by half, 2 to 3 minutes, swirl in the butter and season lightly with salt. Cook, stirring, until the sauce has a medium-thick consistency, about 2 minutes. Taste and adjust the seasoning.

Arrange the veal, prosciutto side up, on individual serving dishes. Remove the toothpicks and spoon the sauce over the veal. Serve at once.

Lamb Hunter-Style

Agnello alla Cacciatora

Checchino dal 1887 is a temple of Roman gastronomy whose fairy-tale story spans five generations. In 1887, Lorenzo and Clorinda, a young married couple who had an *osteria* (wine shop) in the Testaccio area, decided to serve food as well as wine. The food was unpretentious, with many dishes relying on second cuts of meats obtained from the nearby slaughterhouse. After five generations, the food of Checchino has evolved and been refined, while maintaining the basic heartiness and honesty of its predecessors. In the fall of 2000, after a morning of sightseeing, I took my daughter Paola to Checchino. We were greeted by Elio Mariani, one of the two managers and sons of Ninetta, the restaurant owner, and began tasting one dish after another. My absolute favorite was the *abbacchio alla cacciatore*, made with milk-fed baby lamb cooked in a sauce of anchovies, garlic, vinegar, chili pepper, and extra-virgin olive oil. This is an adaptation of the original dish, using the older lamb available in the United States.

◆ *serves 4 to 6*

1/3 cup extra-virgin olive oil

3 pounds boneless lamb shoulder, trimmed of fat and cut into 2-inch pieces

Salt to taste

4 anchovy fillets packed in salt, rinsed and minced

2 garlic cloves, finely minced

2 to 3 tablespoons finely chopped fresh rosemary or 1 teaspoon dried rosemary

1/2 teaspoon finely minced fresh red chili pepper, or crushed red pepper flakes to taste

1 1/2 cups dry white wine

1/4 cup good-quality red-wine vinegar

Preheat the oven to 325°F.

Heat the oil in a large, heavy ovenproof pot or casserole over medium-high heat. When the oil is nice and hot, add the lamb without crowding (brown the lamb in two batches if necessary) and season lightly with salt. Cook, stirring and turning the meat, until the lamb is lightly golden, 5 to 6 minutes. With a slotted spoon, transfer the lamb to a large plate.

Discard some of the fat in the pan. Add the anchovies, garlic, rosemary, and chili pepper and cook over medium heat, stirring with a wooden spoon, for 1 to 2 minutes. Return the lamb to the pan and stir the pieces around briefly to coat them with the savory base. Add the wine and vinegar and bring to a simmer. Cover the pot and place on the middle rack of the oven. Bake for $1^{1}/_{2}$ to 2 hours, or until the meat is tender enough to be cut with a fork. At the end of cooking there should be just enough sauce to coat the meat. If too much sauce is left in the pan, transfer the meat to a large, warm platter and reduce the sauce over high heat. Pour the sauce over the lamb, taste for seasoning, and serve.

ABBACCHIO

Abbacchio, baby lamb, is the sheep's offspring, fed on milk, that has not yet eaten grass. It is without any doubt one of Rome's utmost delicacies. Since abbacchio was once available only in spring, it became the much-sought-after meat to cook at Easter. Today the supply of abbacchio is much larger, so this flavorful treat can be had year-round. Ideally abbacchio should not be older than 60 days, and should weigh no more than 20 pounds. In the United States, sometimes milk-fed lamb is available to top restaurants willing to buy the whole animal. In buying lamb, look for the youngest possible lamb. Keep in mind that one-year-old lamb has a strong flavor and is technically considered mutton.

Spicy Baby Chicken "Devil-Style"

Pollo alla Diavola

In Rome they butterfly a baby chicken, marinate it in oil and lemon juice, season it with salt and *plenty* of hot red pepper flakes, then grill it until its skin is crisp and its flesh is meltingly tender. This is country food at its best! In many Roman trattorie, *Pollo alla diavola*, "devilishly" hot from the coals and from the large amount of pepper, generally comes to the table surrounded by golden crisp roasted potatoes. ◆ *serves 4*

4 baby chickens or Cornish hens (I to I½ pounds each), washed and patted dry

½ cup extra-virgin olive oil

3 lemons, I juiced and 2 halved

I teaspoon salt

I teaspoon red pepper flakes plus more to taste

Remove the chickens' backbones by using kitchen shears or a sharp knife (or ask your butcher to do it for you). Place the butterflied baby chickens on a work surface skin side up, cover with plastic wrap, and flatten them by pressing down with your hands or with a rolling pin. Transfer the chickens to a deep dish.

In a medium bowl, whisk together the olive oil and lemon juice. Brush both sides of the chickens generously with the oil-lemon mixture. Season liberally with the salt and red pepper flakes. Set aside for about 30 minutes.

Preheat the grill. When nice and hot, add the chickens skin side down and cook until they are golden brown and crisp, about 15 minutes. (Lower the heat and turn the chickens if the skin is browning too fast.) Turn the chickens and brown the other side, 10 to 15 minutes longer. Brush with a bit of additional oil if needed. The chickens are done when the thigh juices run clear when pricked with a thin knife.

Place the chickens on individual serving plates and serve with the halved lemons and additional pepper flakes, if desired.

VARIATION

Spicy Baby Chicken "Under a Brick" ◆ This dish is also very popular in Tuscany, where it may be called *pollo al mattone,* or "chicken under a brick." In that preparation the chicken is put either on a hot grill or in a cast-iron pan and pressed down with a brick or another heavy pan, which ensures that the chicken remains nice and flat. There, black pepper is generally used instead of red pepper flakes.

FOR EASY GRILLING

Before you put the chickens on the grill, pat them with paper towels to remove excess oil. Too much oil will result in flare-ups and splattering. If possible, grill the birds covered, which will reduce the cooking time and will generate a more even cooking. If the birds brown too fast, reduce the heat and turn them a few times as they cook.

Chicken with Peppers alla Romana

Pollo con Peperoni

Chicken with peppers is one of the many straightforward but tasty preparations of Roman cooking. Sabatini, a rustic trattoria that opened in 1954 in the heart of Trastevere, serves a particularly hearty version. When I asked our waiter, Francesco, for the "secret" of such moist chicken, he said, "Signora, these are farm-raised chickens. We brown them on high heat and finish cooking them on low heat with sweet peppers. As simple as that." Thank you, Francesco! ♦ *serves 4*

1/2 cup extra-virgin olive oil

I large plump chicken (4 to 5 pounds), cut into 8 serving pieces, thoroughly washed and patted dry with paper towels

I teaspoon salt plus more to taste

1/4 teaspoon freshly ground black pepper plus more to taste

I garlic clove, minced

2 to 3 ounces thickly sliced prosciutto, diced

I cup dry white wine

I (28-ounce) can Italian plum tomatoes, preferably San Marzano (see note, page 35), coarsely chopped, with their juices

4 large green, red, or yellow bell peppers (preferably a mixture of all colors), washed, seeded, and cut into 1-inch strips

Heat half of the oil in a large skillet over medium-high heat. Add the chicken and cook, turning the pieces to brown on all sides, about 8 minutes. Season with salt and pepper.

Add the garlic and the prosciutto, and stir for about 1 minute. Add the wine and cook, stirring and moving the chicken pieces around, until the wine is almost all evaporated, 5 to 6 minutes. Add the chopped tomatoes and their juices and bring to a boil. Reduce the heat to low, partially cover the pan, and simmer very gently, stirring and basting the chicken from time to time, for about 30 minutes.

Meanwhile, heat the remaining oil in another large skillet over medium-high heat. Add the peppers and cook, stirring, until they begin to soften and their skin is somewhat charred, 8 to 10 minutes.

Scoop up the peppers with a large slotted spoon or tongs and add to the chicken. Simmer gently, stirring occasionally, until the meat is tender and the sauce has a rich brown color and a medium-thick consistency, 8 to 10 minutes. Taste, adjust the seasoning, and serve. (The whole dish can be prepared a few hours ahead. Reheat gently before serving.)

A CHICKEN ON EVERY TABLE

There was a time when chickens were raised primarily for their eggs. My aunt Rina had a small farm just outside Bologna, and she harvested her flock's eggs while still warm from the nests. These chickens were called *ruspante*, barnyard birds raised outdoors, and they were the ancestors of today's naturally raised free-range chickens. The birds would find their way into the pot only on special occasions.

During the Second World War, Italy's chickens and eggs became a prime commodity for black-market entrepreneurs, who sold them at outrageously high prices. After the war, as Italy slowly began its recovery, the chicken became the symbol of affluence, and took its place of honor on the Italian table.

The Rack of Lamb of Ristorante Troiani

L'Agnello del Ristorante Troiani

When in Rome . . . one must eat lamb. Roman lamb usually means *abbacchio*, very young milk-fed baby lamb that simply dissolves in the mouth. I had such a dish at Il Convivio Troiani, one of Rome's best high-end restaurants, which serves a mix of beautifully presented traditional and creative dishes. The small rack of lamb came to the table basted with a very unusual ginger-flavored sauce, served with velvety mashed potatoes and the crisp fried leaves of small zucchini blossoms (see variation of fried stuffed zucchini blossoms on page 15). This is the recipe, which I have slightly adapted to the ingredients available in the United States. ◆ *serves 4 to 6*

FOR THE LAMB

1/3 cup extra-virgin olive oil

2 racks of lamb (about 1 1/2 pounds, 8 chops, each), chine bone removed (see note)

1/2 teaspoon salt

1/4 teaspoon freshly ground black pepper

1 garlic clove, peeled

1 small sprig of fresh rosemary

FOR THE SAUCE

2 small shallots, finely minced

2 teaspoons finely minced peeled fresh ginger

2 garlic cloves, finely minced

1 tablespoon chopped fresh rosemary

1 1/2 cups Meat Broth (page 298) or low-sodium canned beef broth

Salt and freshly ground black pepper to taste

2 tablespoons unsalted butter

PREPARE THE LAMB

Preheat the oven to 400°F.

Heat the oil in a large, heavy, ovenproof pan over medium-high heat. Season the lamb with the salt and pepper and place in the pan, meaty side down. Add the whole clove of garlic and the sprig of rosemary, and cook until the meat is lightly golden, 3 to 4 minutes. Turn the racks over and cook 1 to 2 minutes longer. Discard the garlic and the rosemary. Turn the racks again, meaty side down, and place the pan on the middle rack of the oven. Roast until the meat is done to your liking: 10 to 12 minutes for medium rare, 15 to 16 minutes for medium.

Remove the pan from the oven and transfer the racks to a carving board. Cover the racks loosely with foil and let them rest for about 5 minutes. (Keep in mind that the meat will cook a little more as it rests.)

PREPARE THE SAUCE

Meanwhile, discard about half of the fat in the pan. Add the shallot, ginger, minced garlic, and chopped rosemary, and place the pan over medium heat. Stir quickly for about 1 minute. Add the broth, season with salt and pepper, and cook until the sauce is reduced approximately by half, 3 to 4 minutes.

Strain the sauce through a fine-mesh sieve and pour it back into the pan over medium-high heat. Stir in the butter. Cook for a minute or two, until the sauce is medium thick and velvety. Taste and adjust the seasoning.

Slice the racks into chops and place on warm serving dishes. Spoon some of the sauce over each chop, and serve.

NOTE

When buying a rack of lamb, make sure to have your butcher remove the chine bone and scrape the rack bones of all the fatty meat attached to them.

Pan-Fried Sausage with Spicy Broccoli Rabe

Salsiccie e Broccoli Rape con Aglio, Olio, e Peperoncino

This is a typical dish of many Roman trattorie that pairs the assertive taste of Roman sausage with the tanginess of broccoli rabe. The sausage is cooked in the typical Italian way, in a large skillet with about 1/2 inch of water. As the water slowly evaporates, a bit of oil is added to the skillet, so the sausage finishes browning partially in its own fat. A variation of this dish grills the sausage, then pairs it with the broccoli. ◆ *serves 4 to 6*

2 pounds broccoli rabe

Salt

2 pounds mildly spicy Italian sausage

1/3 cup extra-virgin olive oil

2 garlic cloves, minced

Chopped fresh red chili pepper or hot red pepper flakes to taste

1/2 cup dry white wine

Trim and discard any large woody stalks and wilted leaves from the broccoli rabe, and wash well under cold running water.

Bring a pot of water to a boil and prepare an ice-water bath in a large bowl. Add a large pinch of salt and the broccoli rabe to the boiling water. Cook, uncovered, over high heat, until the broccoli is tender but still a little al dente, about 2 minutes. Drain and place the broccoli in the ice-water bath to stop the cooking. When cool, drain again and set aside.

Preheat the oven to 250°F.

Prick the sausages in a few places with a fork and place in a large skillet. Add enough cold water to come a little less than halfway up the sides of the sausage. Place the skillet on high heat. When the water begins to boil, reduce the heat to medium and cook, turning the links a few times, until all the water in the pan has evaporated and only the fat of the sausage is left in the skillet, 10 to 15 minutes. Add 2 to 3 tablespoons of the oil to the skillet and keep cooking the sausage over medium heat until it is golden brown on all sides, 2 to 4 minutes. Transfer to a platter and keep warm in the oven.

Add the garlic, chili pepper, and, if needed, a little more oil to the skillet, and stir for less than 1 minute. Add the wine and stir over medium heat until the wine is almost all evaporated, 3 to 4 minutes. Add the reserved broccoli rabe, season lightly with salt, and cook until the broccoli is thoroughly heated through, 3 to 4 minutes. Taste and adjust the seasoning.

Place the broccoli rabe on serving dishes, top with the sausage, and serve hot.

The Forum

Salt Cod with Tomatoes, Raisins, and Pine Nuts

Baccalà in Guazzetto

Nino is an unassuming establishment not too far from Piazza di Spagna that serves good, honest food and has a large selection of wines at reasonable prices. I discovered this place about fifteen years ago, and I visit every time I am in Rome. One of the dishes I order is *baccalà in guazzetto,* salt cod slowly simmered with wine, tomatoes, pine nuts, and raisins, a very old, traditional dish that seems to have roots in Roman-Jewish cooking. There was a time when *baccalà* was considered poor man's food because it was abundant and inexpensive. Even though baccalà is now considerably more expensive, some of Rome's most traditional eating places, following the old church rule of not eating meat on Fridays, still routinely prepare baccalà on that day. ♦ *serves 4*

1 1/2 pounds *baccalà,* soaked (see note, opposite)

1/3 cup extra-virgin olive oil

1/2 small onion, minced (about 1/2 cup)

1 garlic clove, finely minced

1/2 cup dry white wine

1 (28-ounce) can plum tomatoes, preferably San Marzano (see note, page 35), coarsely chopped, with their juices

1/3 cup pine nuts

1/3 cup raisins, soaked in lukewarm water for 20 minutes and drained

Freshly ground black pepper to taste

1 to 2 tablespoons chopped fresh flat-leaf parsley

Rinse the soaked cod under cold running water, pat dry with paper towels, then cut it into 2-inch pieces. Heat the oil in a large skillet over medium heat. Add the onion and cook, stirring, until soft, 4 to 5 minutes. Add the garlic, stir for 20 to 30 seconds, then add the wine. Cook until the wine is almost all evaporated. Add the tomatoes, pine nuts, and raisins, season with just a bit of pepper, and bring the sauce to a gentle simmer. Place the cod in the pan, cover, and simmer over very low heat until the cod is tender and flakes easily when pierced with a fork, 40 minutes to 1 hour.

With a flat spatula, transfer the cod to warm serving dishes. Return the sauce to medium-high heat and add the parsley. Stir until the sauce has a medium-thick consistency, 2 to 4 minutes. Taste and adjust the seasoning. Spoon the sauce over the cod and serve.

ABOUT *BACCALÀ*

Baccalà is salt-preserved cod that has a rich, unique, complex character and texture, which in the United States can often be found in Italian, Spanish, Portuguese, and French specialty food stores. However, the majority of salt cod in the U.S. probably comes from Canada, and is generally available in high-end supermarkets. Because salt cod has a wide range of provenance, its texture and cooking time differ considerably. Select a piece that has a light, creamy color with no dark parts, and that is meaty with a minimal amount of bones. Before using the cod, make sure to soak it for 2 to 3 days in plenty of cold water to cover, changing the water 3 times a day. The soaking will soften the cod and remove most of its salt. Then cook the cod over very low heat; fast cooking will toughen it.

WHEN IN ROME
Food Markets, Specialty Food Stores, Bakeries, and Cooking Schools

Antico Forno Campo de' Fiori
Piazza Campo de' Fiori 22
Tel. 688 06662
Great breads and focaccia, a *pizza bianca* to die for, sweet rolls, cookies, and pastries.

Associazione Enogastronomica Pepe Verde
Via Santa Caterina da Siena 46
Tel. 679 0528
A well-respected cooking school. For information, write or call.

A Tavola con lo Chef
Via dei Gracchi 60
Tel. Fax 320 3402
English-taught classes for groups of twelve. Contact Fiorella d'Agnano for information.

Campo de' Fiori Open-Air Food Market
Campo de' Fiori
This central, historic food market is still enticing, but in the last few years it has lost some of its luster, since several of its stands have been replaced by others offering knickknacks. Nevertheless, it is still worth a visit. Of particular interest are the brightly colored stands selling fruit, vegetables, and herbs.

Gastronomia E. Volpetti
Via Marmorata 47 Testaccio
Tel. 574 2352
A terrific food store with large selections of cheeses, hams, sausages, breads, and more.

Giovanni Riposati
Via delle Muratte 8
Tel. 679 2866
This bakery opened in 1700, and is the oldest in Rome. In addition to terrific breads, sweet rolls, cookies, pastries, and *crostate*, you can find pizza and *panini imbottiti*, Italian sandwiches that are stuffed with all kinds of mouthwatering concoctions.

Museo Nazionale delle Paste Alimentari
Piazza Scanderberg 117
Tel. 699 1120
A museum devoted entirely to pasta through the centuries.

Testaccio Food Market
Piazza Testaccio
The Testaccio market was, and still is, one of the most popular of the city, and it is the place where many restaurateurs find top-quality ingredients.

Escarole with Garlic, Anchovies, and Red Pepper Flakes

Cicoria Saltata in Padella con Acciughe e Peperoncino

Romans are very fond of the bitter vegetables of the chicory family, especially the green, leafy ones such as escarole and broccoli rabe. And they are absolutely wild about the wild chicory that can still be gathered in summer in the lush fields and meadows outside Rome, or bought at any of the food markets of the city. The Roman way of cooking these vegetables is quite simple: they are first boiled, then quickly pan-fried with olive oil, garlic, anchovies, and red pepper flakes. Or they are turned into a salad and tossed simply with olive oil and lemon juice. These dishes are staples in traditional Roman trattorie. ◆ *serves 4*

Salt, plus more to taste

2 pounds escarole or broccoli rabe, trimmed, cored, and washed

$1/4$ to $1/3$ cup extra-virgin olive oil

2 garlic cloves, peeled and lightly crushed

Red pepper flakes to taste

4 plump anchovy fillets packed in salt, rinsed and chopped

Bring a large pot of water to a boil over high heat and prepare an ice-water bath in a large bowl. Add 2 large pinches of salt and the escarole to the boiling water, and cook until soft but not completely wilted, 2 to 3 minutes. Drain and cool in the ice water. Drain again and pat dry with paper towels. Set aside until ready to use.

Heat the oil in a large skillet over medium heat. Add the garlic and cook until golden on all sides, 1 to 2 minutes, then discard the garlic. Add the pepper flakes and the anchovies, and stir until the anchovies are soft and almost melted, 1 to 2 minutes. Add the escarole and cook, stirring for 2 to 3 minutes, or until the escarole is heated through. Taste, adjust the seasoning, and serve.

VARIATION

Escarole Salad ◆ Omit the anchovies and the garlic. Clean and boil the chicory as instructed above, dry it well, and place in a salad bowl. Dress the chicory with extra-virgin olive oil and lemon juice, and season with salt and freshly ground black pepper. I love to pair this salad with a slice of delicious Pecorino Romano.

Stew of Fava Beans, Peas, and Artichokes

La Vignarola

In spring, when fava beans, peas, and artichokes are at their peak, a dish called *la vignarola* can be found in Rome. This dish glorifies all that is seasonally fresh, and is cooked with the addition of *guanciale* (cured pork jowl) or pancetta, onion, celery, and flavorful extra-virgin olive oil. It can be served as an appetizer, main course, or side dish. It can also be turned into a very thick soup by simply adding a few cups of meat broth. A terrific vignarola can be found at Sora Lella, one of the best and best-known Roman trattorie, located on the Isola Tiberina, a small island in the Tiber. ◆ *serves 6 to 8*

2 pounds unshelled fresh fava beans

1 1/2 pounds unshelled fresh peas, or a 10-ounce package frozen peas, thawed

Salt

1/3 cup extra-virgin olive oil, plus more for drizzling

1/2 small onion, minced (about 1/2 cup)

1/2 small celery stalk, minced (about 1/3 cup)

4 ounces *guanciale* (see note, page 21) or thickly sliced pancetta, minced

1 1/2 pounds baby artichokes, cleaned and cooked (see note, opposite)

Freshly ground black pepper to taste

Bring a medium pot of water to a boil over high heat and prepare an ice-water bath in a large bowl. Shell the fava beans and discard the pods. Add the fava beans to the pot and cook for 2 to 3 minutes. Drain the beans (do not empty the water) and place in the ice bath to cool. Drain again. Pinch the skin of each bean, breaking it at one end, and squeeze the bean out of its skin. Set aside.

If you are using fresh peas, shell them and plunge them in the boiling water with some salt. Cook until tender, 1 to 3 minutes depending on size. Drain and place in the ice bath to cool. Drain again and set aside. (The cooking of the vegetables can be done several hours or a day ahead.)

Heat the oil in a large skillet over medium heat. Add the onion, celery, and *guanciale* or pancetta. Cook, stirring, until the mixture is soft and lightly brown, 4 to 5 minutes. Add the artichokes, stir for a couple of minutes, then add the reserved fava beans and peas. Season with salt and several grindings of pepper. Cook and stir until the vegetables are well coated with the savory base and are heated all the way through. Serve hot with a few drops of good extra-virgin olive oil.

CLEANING AND COOKING THE ARTICHOKES

Fill a large bowl halfway with cold water. Squeeze in the juice of 2 halved lemons and drop in the squeezed halves. Remove the outer green leaves of each artichoke by snapping them off at the base. Stop when you get to the pale yellow central cone. Slice off the tip of the cone. Cut the stems off at the base and with a small knife, trim off the remaining green part at the base. Drop the artichokes in the lemon water.

Bring a medium pot of salted water to a boil over medium heat and prepare an ice-water bath in a large bowl. Drain the artichokes and add to the boiling water. Cook gently until the artichokes are tender when pricked with a thin knife, 6 to 8 minutes depending on size. Drain and place in the ice water to cool. Drain again, cut them into wedges, and set aside.

Pan-Fried Zucchini
with Vinegar and Chili Pepper

Zucchine in Padella con Aceto e Peperoncino

Fried zucchini are popular all over Italy, and change little from area to area. In Rome this appetizing dish is given extra flavor by the addition of *peperoncino* (small, red chili pepper) and crushed garlic that browns in the oil and infuses it with its aroma before being discarded. The last-minute splash of vinegar rounds up all the flavors. It can be served as an appetizer, or it makes an especially good side dish with grilled meat or fish. ◆ *serves 4*

$^1/_4$ cup extra-virgin olive oil

2 large garlic cloves, peeled and lightly crushed

$1^1/_2$ pounds zucchini, the smallest you can find, washed, dried, ends trimmed, and cut into $^1/_4$-inch-thick rounds

Salt to taste

1 small red *peperoncino*, finely shredded, or crushed red pepper flakes to taste

2 to 3 tablespoons red-wine vinegar

1 tablespoon chopped fresh flat-leaf parsley

Heat the oil in a large frying pan or skillet over medium-high heat. When the oil is hot but not yet smoking, add the garlic and cook until golden brown on both sides, 2 to 3 minutes. Discard the garlic. Add the zucchini without crowding (fry in 2 batches if needed) and cook, stirring and turning the zucchini until golden brown on both sides, about 2 minutes.

Season with salt and the *peperoncino* or pepper flakes. Add the vinegar and stir until almost all evaporated, 1 to 2 minutes. Stir in the parsley, taste, and adjust the seasoning. Serve warm or at room temperature.

WHEN IN ROME
Caffès, Pastry Shops, and Gelaterie

Antico Caffè Greco
Via Condotti 86
Tel. 679 1700
Antico Caffè Greco, which opened in 1760, is perhaps the oldest caffè of Rome. Located in the fashionable Via Condotti, this establishment caters to locals and tourists alike.

Gelateria Alberto Picca
Via della Seggiola 12
Tel. 686 8405
Located only a few blocks from Campo de' Fiori food market, this gelateria offers as many as 40 varieties of terrific gelatos, some with exotic flavors.

Giolitti
Via Uffici del Vicario 40
Giolitti, one of the best known gelaterie in the city, often offers as many as 50 types. One of their specialties is the *coppa*, a large glass layered with several varieties of creamy gelato.

Gran Caffè La Caffettiera
Piazza di Pietra 65
Tel. 679 8147
One of the most beautiful, historic caffès in the heart of the city, it draws a fashionable crowd. The selection of sweet pastries, paired with delectable espresso and cappuccino and courteous service, makes this a destination.

Il Gelato di San Crispino
Via Acaia 56/56 a
Tel. 7045 0412
This gelateria is an institution and the place to go for an exceptional gelato made with the best of natural ingredients.

Rosati
Piazza del Popolo 5
Tel. 322 5859
Another legendary old caffè that has drawn a crowd since 1923.

Tart Cherry Crostata

Crostata di Visciole

This Italian crostata is as dear to Italians as apple pie is to Americans. It is made with a buttery dough and filled with *visciole* or *amarene* (mild, tart Italian cherries) or other fresh or dried fruit and homemade preserves in a simple but absolutely delicious tart that evokes memories of mothers and grandmothers canning fresh fruit. Today, when most Italian women work outside the home and have considerably less time on their hands, they often buy the *crostata* at their local bakery, or make it at home using one of the many outstanding prepared preserves available in specialty food stores. Several of the traditional Roman eating establishments, including Sora Margherita, a small but comfortable trattoria in the historic Jewish quarter, serve a version of this delicious crostata. ◆ *serves 8*

I recipe Basic Pie Dough (page 308)
Butter for greasing the pan
I (15- to 16-ounce) jar sour cherry preserves

Grated zest of $^1/_2$ lemon
Grated zest of I orange
I large egg, lightly beaten

Prepare the pie dough and shape into a disk. Wrap in plastic wrap and refrigerate for a few hours.

Preheat the oven to 350°F. and butter a 9-inch fluted tart pan with a removable bottom.

In a medium bowl, combine the preserves with the grated lemon and orange zests.

Cut the chilled dough into 2 pieces, one a little larger than the other. On a lightly floured surface, roll out the larger piece of dough into a 12-inch circle. Place the dough in the tart pan and press it gently and evenly into the bottom and sides of the pan. Remove any overhanging dough by rolling the rolling pin over the top of the pan. Spoon the preserves mixture into the tart shell, and smooth the top with a spatula.

Roll out the smaller piece of dough into a 10-inch circle. With a scalloped pastry wheel, cut it into $^1/_2$-inch-wide strips. Arrange the strips on top of the filling to make a lattice pattern. Brush the dough with the beaten egg.

Put the tart on a sheet pan or cookie sheet, and place on the middle rack of the oven. Bake for about 30 minutes, or until the crust is golden brown. Cool the tart for 10 to 15 minutes, then gently remove from its ring. Cool for several hours or overnight before serving.

Roman Sweet Buns
with Raisins and Pine Nuts

I Maritozzi Romani

The Roman *maritozzi* are part of a category of homey desserts that Italians call *dolci di credenza* and that includes biscotti, tarts, and sweet breads. These sweets were once baked regularly at home because they were simple to prepare and one could always have a nice supply at hand, often displayed on the family credenza for unexpected guests, since they would keep well for several days. I first tasted them at a Roman hotel, where they were stacked on a large platter, golden and bursting at the seams with sweet raisins and pine nuts. Maritozzi are great when eaten while still warm next to a nice cappuccino and are equally wonderful when dunked into a glass of dessert wine. They are also terrific when sliced and stuffed with thick, lemon-scented, whipped cream. ◆ *makes 18 to 20 buns*

FOR THE SPONGE

- 4 teaspoons active dry yeast
- Pinch of sugar
- $^1/_2$ cup lukewarm water
- $^3/_4$ cup unbleached all-purpose flour

FOR THE DOUGH

- 3 cups unbleached all-purpose flour
- 5 ounces unsalted butter at room temperature, cut into small pieces
- $^3/_4$ cup granulated sugar
- Pinch of salt
- Grated zest of 1 lemon
- 4 large eggs, lightly beaten
- 3 tablespoons extra-virgin olive oil
- 1 cup golden raisins, soaked in dried Marsala wine for 30 minutes, then drained and dried on paper towels
- $^1/_2$ cup pine nuts
- 1 to 2 tablespoons all-purpose flour
- Butter for greasing the baking sheet
- 1 egg, lightly beaten in a small bowl

MAKE THE SPONGE

In a medium bowl, combine the yeast, pinch of sugar, and lukewarm water, and mix well to dissolve the yeast. Let stand until small bubbles appear on the surface of the water, about 10 minutes. Stir the flour into the dissolved yeast, then work the mixture briefly into a soft, sticky ball. Flour a clean bowl lightly and add the dough. Cover with plastic wrap and let rise at room temperature until it is doubled in size and its surface is full of tiny bubbles, 25 to 30 minutes.

MAKE THE DOUGH

Put the flour, butter, sugar, salt, and grated lemon zest in the bowl of an electric mixer. Mix by hand, rubbing the flour and butter between your palms, until the butter has a fine, crumbly consistency. Add the eggs, 2 tablespoons of the oil, and the risen sponge and beat with the dough hook at medium speed until the dough is soft, shiny, and pliable, 4 to 5 minutes. (If you are making the dough by hand, knead on a lightly floured surface for about 10 minutes.)

Brush a large bowl lightly with the remaining oil and add the dough. Cover with plastic wrap and let rise in a draft-free place until doubled in bulk, 1½ to 2 hours.

Place the risen dough on a lightly floured surface. Flatten it out into a large circle with your hands or a rolling pin. Sprinkle the raisins and pine nuts all over the dough surface, then roll up the dough loosely. Knead lightly until the mixture is well incorporated. If some raisins or pine nuts fall out, simply knead them back into the dough. Dust the dough with a bit of additional flour if somewhat sticky.

Preheat the oven to 400°F. and butter a baking sheet lightly.

Cut the dough into pieces about the size of a large egg, then roll each piece into a small ball. Line the rolls a few inches apart on the baking sheet, brush them with the beaten egg, and place them on the middle rack of the oven. Bake until they have almost doubled in size and have a rich golden color, 15 to 20 minutes. Remove from the oven and cool on wire racks before serving. Store *maritozzi* in an airtight container at room temperature for up to 1 week.

THE ROMAN TABLE

APPETIZERS

Bruschetta: Sliced grilled bread rubbed with garlic and drizzled with oil, or topped with tomatoes, capers, and garlic.

Carciofi alla Giudea: Whole, very fresh, deep-fried young artichokes, a specialty of the many Roman-Jewish trattorie.

Fave e Pecorino: Shelled, raw fava beans dipped in salt, with Pecorino cheese.

Mozzarella Fritta: Deep-fried mozzarella. Thick slices of mozzarella are dipped into beaten eggs, coated with bread crumbs, and fried until crisp. Delicious.

Supplì al Telefono: Deep-fried, crisp rice croquettes stuffed with ham and mozzarella. The name comes from the strings of mozzarella, which look like telephone wires.

FIRST COURSES

Bucatini all'Amatriciana: Thick, hollow spaghetti with chili-pancetta-tomato sauce and Pecorino Romano.

Fettuccine Alfredo: Homemade egg fettuccine with a lot of butter and Parmigiano-Reggiano.

Fettuccine alla Romana: Homemade fettuccine generally tossed with the typical ragù of beef and chicken livers of Rome.

Penne all' Arrabbiata: A sauce made with tomatoes and plenty of chili pepper.

Spaghetti alla Carbonara: Spaghetti tossed with a luscious sauce of eggs, guanciale, cheese, and black pepper.

Spaghetti Cacio e Pepe: Spaghetti with Pecorino Romano and black pepper.

ENTRÉES

Abbacchio al Forno: Whole roasted suckling baby lamb accompanied by roasted potatoes, a typical spring Roman dish.

Abbacchio alla Cacciatora: Baby lamb that is slowly simmered in a sauce of tomatoes, pancetta, vegetables, and herbs. Another version of *cacciatore* cooks the lamb without the tomatoes in a sauce of wine, vinegar, and herbs.

Agnello in Bianco alla Cacciatora: A lamb stew that omits the tomatoes in favor of wine, vinegar, chili pepper, herbs, and vegetables.

Baccalà in Agrodolce: Sweet-and-sour salt cod, slowly stewed with raisins, sugar, and vinegar. A dish that was typically prepared on Fridays, the lean day of the week.

Coda alla Vaccinara: Oxtail stew. Oxtail is simmered at length with a variety of vegetables, pancetta, wine, and tomatoes until the meat falls away from the bone. Any Roman trattoria worth its salt will have oxtail on its menu.

Porchetta allo Spiedo: A whole pig cooked on a spit. A dish that is still prepared at country fairs; occasionally, it can also be found in country trattorie.

Saltimbocca: Sautéed veal slices topped with prosciutto and sage. Another variation of *saltimbocca* rolls up the veal.

VEGETABLES

Bieta all'agro: Bitter chicory with garlic, oil, and lemon.

Piselli al Prosciutto: Sautéed peas with prosciutto.

Puntarelle: Bitter Roman chicory salad with anchovy dressing.

Spinaci alla Romana: Sautéed spinach with raisins.

DESSERTS

Bignè di San Giuseppe: Deep-fried sweet pastry balls.

Le Frappe: Sweet pastry fritters.

Pizza di Polenta e Ricotta: Sweet polenta cake.

Torta di Ricotta: Ricotta cake.

SOME BASIC INGREDIENTS

Acciughe: Anchovies, fresh or packed in oil or salt.

Aglio: Garlic.

Ceci: Chickpeas, which have been a staple of the Roman table since Roman times, and are used in soups, salads, and stews.

Fiore di Latte: Fresh cow's-milk mozzarella.

Guanciale: Salt-cured pork jowl.

Lardo: Lard. Because of its flavor, lard has, until recently, been the favorite Roman fat. It is often solid enough to be sliced.

Mozzarella di Bufala: Fresh-water buffalo mozzarella.

Olio d'Oliva: Olive oil. Roman extra-virgin olive oils range from fruity and fragrant to delicate.

Pancetta: Unsmoked, cured pork belly.

Pasta Secca: Dry pasta such as bucatini, spaghetti, penne, and rigatoni.

Pecorino Romano: Hard, pasteurized sheep's-milk cheese for grating.

Peperoncino: Fresh or dried chili pepper.

Pomodori: Tomatoes, fresh or canned.

Ricotta Romana Fresca: Fresh, creamy sheep's-milk ricotta.

Ricotta Salata: Salted sheep's-milk ricotta for grating.

Scamorza: A pear-shaped semisoft cheese made from cow's milk or from a combination of cow's and sheep's milk. It is often grilled.

FLORENCE

APPETIZERS

Fettunta with Kale {*Fettunta con Cavolo Nero*}

Baked Scamorza and Pear Skewers {*Spiedini di Scamorza e Pere*}

Deep-Fried Salt Cod {*Baccalà Fritto*}

Allegra's Vegetable Tart {*Il Tortino di Verdure di Allegra*}

Tomato, Bread, and Cucumber Salad {*Panzanella*}

FIRST COURSES

Twice-Cooked Florentine Vegetable Soup {*Ribollita*}

Tuscan Farro Soup {*Zuppa di Farro*}

Ganino's Ricotta-Parmigiano-Spinach Dumplings {*Gli Strozzapreti di Ganino*}

Rigatoni Dragged with Florentine Meat Ragù {*Rigatoni Strascicati col Ragù*}

Penne with Porcini {*Penne con Porcini Trifolati*}

Risotto with Spinach {*Risotto alla Fiorentina*}

ENTRÉES

Roasted Pork with Rosemary, Sage, and Garlic {*Arista alla Fiorentina*}

T-Bone alla Fiorentina {*Bistecca alla Fiorentina*}

The Braised Beef of Florence {*Stracotto di Manzo alla Fiorentina*}

Rabbit Braised with Wine, Olives, and Sage {*Coniglio con Olive e Salvia*}

Roasted Quail Wrapped in Pancetta {*Quaglie Arrosto con la Pancetta*}

Grilled Spareribs {*Rosticciana*}

Grilled Trout with First-Pressed Olive Oil {*Trota alla Griglia con Olio Novello*}

Braised Squid with Tomatoes, Chili, and Swiss Chard {*Calamari in Inzimino*}

VEGETABLES

Deep-Fried Baby Artichokes {*Carciofini Fritti*}

Green Beans with Garlic and Tomatoes {*Fagiolini al Pomodoro*}

Mushroom Salad with Celery and Pecorino {*Insalata di Funghi, Sedano, e Pecorino*}

DESSERTS

Drunken Pears {*Pere Ubriache*}

Chocolate-Coated Zuccotto {*Zuccotto alla Cioccolata*}

Tuscan Pastry Fritters {*Cenci*}

Ponte alla Carraia

In the Italian landscape, Tuscany stands out like a brilliant jewel.

Its cities, towns, and hamlets bestow the region with a profusion of art, a simple yet refined cuisine, and superlative wines. This was the home of extraordinary people: Michelangelo, Leonardo da Vinci, Dante, Galileo, Machiavelli, Botticelli, Puccini, and so many others. The region as a whole, and Florence in particular, were also the cradle of the Italian Renaissance, where from the fourteenth through the seventeenth centuries, under the tutelage of the Medici, Tuscany's greatest patrician family, the arts flourished as at no other time in history. The pleasures of the table flourished too, thanks to the courts' lavish banquets—an interminable succession of spectacular dishes that kept guests at the tables for food marathons. When in 1533 Caterina de' Medici married the future king of France, Henry II, and moved to Paris, she took along typical Tuscan ingredients such as olive oil, white beans, and Pecorino cheese, so that her chefs could reproduce her favorite dishes. She also introduced to her new court the Florentine custom of eating with a fork.

The breathtaking beauty of Tuscany—soft rolling hills studded with farmhouses, vineyards, olive groves, imposing cypresses, and noble small towns—has been documented in films, books, magazines, and newspapers the world over. Florence, Tuscany's capital and its center of art and architecture, is a shining masterpiece. The city was founded around 1000 B.C. by the Etruscans, a highly erudite people who called the land they inhabited *Etruria*. Through the centuries Etruria was colonized by waves of invaders—Romans, Lombards, and Franks—who left their marks.

Unlike several other large Italian cities, Florence is a walker's paradise. Its tightly compact city center, jam-packed with art and architecture, can easily be explored by foot. What should one see in Florence? Basically everything:

- The gorgeous Piazza della Signoria, which is dominated by the Palazzo Vecchio with its soaring turret and copy of Michelangelo's *David*. (The original *David* is now at the Accademia delle Belle Arti.)
- The Duomo, flanked by Giotto's Campanile.
- The famed Ponte Vecchio, Florence's oldest bridge, which dates back to the mid-1300s and is clustered with some of the most splendid jewelry and art stores of Florence.
- The Piazzale Michelangelo with its magnificent sweeping view of the city below.
- Santa Maria Novella, a gorgeous church that displays dazzling frescoes.
- Via Tornabuoni, the most elegant street of Florence, for its great shops and superb restaurants that offer comforting authentic cuisine.

Walk through the narrow, medieval streets and you will discover tiny, dark shops that house some of the city's outstanding craftsmen. Discover small squares, hidden gardens, caffès, and food markets. Browse through the many antique stores. And when you are tired, find a quiet corner or sit at an outdoor caffè. While sipping an espresso or savoring a creamy gelato, you will fall hopelessly in love with this magnificent city.

For many, Florence is a food lover's paradise. The city's food draws from its many pasts: from the sophisticated cuisine of the courts with its sweet-and-sour-spiked dishes that a handful of restaurants still try to keep alive to the food of *la cucina povera*, poor and peasant cooking, which is based on the products of the land, the season, and frugality. Bread, olive oil, vegetables, grains, beans, wild mushrooms, fresh herbs, and wild game are the star elements of cucina povera; treated with reverence, they produce a cuisine that is fresh, uncomplicated, and maddeningly tasty. The unsalted bread of the region appears in almost every course: turned into thick slices of *fettunta* (country bread) and toasted over the fire, rubbed with garlic, and dribbled with luscious green olive oil; crostini, small canapés, are topped with a variety of savory ingredients; a few days' old bread gives identity and thickness to hearty country soups such as *pappa al pomodoro, ribollita,* and *acquacotta;* stale bread is turned into panzanella, one of the region's most popular salads. Bread is skewered between meat or fowl, vegetables, and herbs, and grilled as *spiedini.* Bread crumbs become part of a vegetable filling and give a crisp coating to little *polpette.* And rolled-out bread dough studded with grapes and dusted with sugar becomes *schiacciata,* a sweet yet wholesome treat to be enjoyed at the end of a meal or any time of the day.

Tuscans, like most other Italians, love pasta, but for first courses they prefer the thick country soups of beans, vegetables, and bread. This preference probably stems from the fact that pasta is a relative newcomer to the Tuscan table, since it became part of the local diet only around two hundred years ago.

Many of the traditional *secondi* are justifiably famous. First and foremost is *Bistecca alla Fiorentina,* a mainstay of Florentine trattorie and upscale restaurants. This charcoal-grilled two-inch-thick T-bone comes from the finest grass-fed Chianina cattle, a Tuscan breed that goes back to Roman times, and is the pride of the city; tradition dictates that a real bistecca alla Fiorentina must be grilled over a fire and served *al sangue,* rare. Other favorites are *Arista di maiale,* a delectable pork loin roast that is rubbed with a mixture of fresh herbs and garlic; *Rosticciana,* grilled pork ribs that are often marinated in lemon, extra-virgin olive oil, and garlic; and *Pollo fritto,* a crisp, deep-fried small chicken. Typically, these dishes are generously seasoned.

Because Tuscan food is defined by its straightforward clarity, the vegetables play a very important role. Fresh, ripe, seasonal *primizie,* the first vegetables of the season, are what the people of Florence look for when they go to the market. Fresh cannellini beans for a salad with tuna and onion. Delicate zucchini blossoms ready to be stuffed and deep-fried. Tender peas to be cooked simply with prosciutto, onion, and olive oil. Small string beans to be sautéed with very ripe tomatoes. And heavenly meaty porcini mushrooms that need only to be grilled and brushed with good olive oil and garlic. At Mercato di Sant'Ambrogio, one can marvel at the large variety of seasonal vegetables and fruit as well as homemade breads, cheeses, cured meats, and much more. Buy some bread, cured Tuscan prosciutto or *salame,* and Pecorino; find a quiet spot; sit back; and start thinking about where you will have dinner.

Florence is a diner's paradise, with the many charming, unpretentious trattorie and equally appealing restaurants housed in centuries-old buildings. Florence is also one of the world's most visited cities, and at the peak of summer it seems to transform into an eerily crowded fairground. For me the best time to visit is late winter, early spring, and late fall, when there is a crispness in the air and the city belongs again to the Florentines. This is the Florence for a passionate food and wine lover, where one can still experience not only truly Florentine dishes that have been made in the same ways for centuries, but also the great, natural conviviality and genuineness of the people. And I am absolutely elated when I realize that in spite of the mass tourism that engulfs this great city, Florence's warm soul, magnificent art treasures, and delectable cuisine still have so much to offer.

Reproduction of Michelangelo's David, *Palazzo Vecchio*

Fettunta with Kale

Fettunta con Cavolo Nero

Fettunta is a simple country dish that takes thick slices of unsalted Tuscan country bread, grills them until crisp and a bit charred, rubs them with a garlic clove, and drizzles them with dense, flavorful extra-virgin olive oil. This was, and still is, the typical soul food of Tuscan farmers, greatly enjoyed throughout the year but especially in late fall, after the harvest and pressing of the new oil. This very pristine dish can also be enriched by a variety of toppings.

At Cantinetta Antinori, one of Florence's best and most sophisticated restaurants, I enjoyed a fettunta that was topped by an intensely flavored *cavolo nero* (Tuscan black kale) the dark, curly leaves of which had been boiled, then tossed simply with the Cantinetta extra-virgin olive oil. The simple purity of this type of dish is what makes the food of Florence and Tuscany so very outstanding.

Fettunta can be served alone or next to slices of Tuscan *salame*, prosciutto, Pecorino, and marinated pickled vegetables, as a casual appetizer or an easy-to-prepare luncheon. ◆ *serves 4*

I bunch of *cavolo nero* (black kale), about 1/2 pound

Salt

1/3 cup plus 2 tablespoons extra-virgin olive oil

4 slices coarse, crusty Italian bread

2 garlic cloves, peeled and halved

Freshly ground black pepper

Remove the kale leaves from the stalks and wash them well under cold running water.

Put 3 to 4 inches of water in a large pot and bring to a boil; in a large bowl, prepare an ice-water bath. Add a large pinch of salt and the leaves to the boiling water, and cook until tender, about 10 minutes. Drain and plunge the leaves in the ice bath. When cool, drain again. Squeeze the leaves with your hands to remove as much water as possible. Set aside.

Preheat the oven to 375°F.

Brush a baking sheet with 1 to 2 tablespoons of the olive oil. Add the bread and toast until the slices are lightly golden on both sides, 3 to 5 minutes. Rub the garlic on one side of the toasted bread and set aside.

Heat the remaining ⅓ cup oil in a large skillet over medium-high heat. Add the kale and season with salt and pepper to taste. Stir for 2 to 3 minutes, or until the kale is heated through and is well coated with the oil. Pile the kale on the toasted bread and serve warm.

VARIATION

Add a handful of cooked cannellini beans to the skillet with the kale, season, and stir for a few minutes, then pile on the bread.

Baked Scamorza and Pear Skewers

Spiedini di Scamorza e Pere

Just mention Benedetta Vitali's name in Florence food circles and everyone will agree that her food is terrific. Her new restaurant, Zibibbo, named after a Sicilian grape, serves a mixture of hard-to-find trattoria food as well as creative and personal interpretations of dishes from other parts of Italy. The night my husband and I were there we wanted to try everything on the menu. As we were waiting for our first appetizers to arrive, the server brought us a flute of delicious *prosecco* and these skewers of smoked, baked scamorza and pears. What a way to start a meal! ◆ *serves 4*

2 lightly firm Anjou pears

$^1/_2$ pound smoked scamorza cheese

Extra-virgin olive oil

Freshly ground black pepper

1 to 2 tablespoons dried oregano

Preheat the oven to 500°F.

Core, seed, and quarter the pears, then cut them into 1-inch pieces.

Cut the scamorza into 1-inch cubes. Alternate 4 pieces of pear and 4 pieces of cheese on 4 wooden or metal skewers. (If using wooden ones, sok them in water first.)

Place the skewers on a lightly oiled baking sheet. Sprinkle the skewers with pepper and dried oregano, and drizzle with olive oil. Place the pan on the middle rack of the oven and bake until the cheese begins to melt, but before it turns runny or burns, 3 to 5 minutes. Serve at once.

ABOUT SCAMORZA

Scamorza is a typical cow's-milk cheese of Southern Italy that can be eaten fresh or may be aged for a short time; it can also be smoked. This cheese typically has a flask shape; a fine outer rind, and a dense, solid body. It can be used for grating as a table cheese, or as an ingredient in many typical Southern Italian dishes. Scamorza can now be found in many Italian specialty food stores.

Deep-Fried Salt Cod

Baccalà Fritto

Baccalà, dried salt cod, used to be a staple of several Northern Italian regions, and every family had a treasure chest of baccalà recipes that were handed down from mothers to daughters. Today baccalà can still be found in many trattorie and wine bars, especially in Florence and Venice, where many consider its assertive taste pure heaven. ◆ *serves 4 to 6*

I^1/$_2$ pounds salt cod, soaked as directed on page 49

4 cups whole milk

2 large eggs

I^1/$_2$ cups all-purpose flour

Olive oil or vegetable oil for deep-frying

Salt to taste

I lemon, cut into 6 wedges

Drain the cod and place in a large saucepan. Add the milk and enough water to cover the cod. Bring the liquid to a simmer and cook for about 5 minutes. Drain the cod and pat dry with paper towels. Pick out and discard any bones and pieces of skin. Cool the cod to room temperature, then cut into I^1/$_2$- to 2-inch pieces.

Prepare the batter: Beat the eggs in a medium bowl. Stir in I^1/$_2$ cups water. Gradually add the flour, beating well with a wire whisk until the batter is smooth. (Do not add salt to the batter.) Let the batter sit and thicken for about I hour.

Pour 2 to 2^1/$_2$ inches of oil in a heavy, medium saucepan and place over medium-high heat. When the oil is very hot and registers 370° to 375°F. on a thermometer, dip 3 or 4 pieces of cod at a time into the batter and, using a slotted spoon, lower them into the hot oil. Fry until golden brown on all sides, 3 to 4 minutes. Remove from the oil with the slotted spoon and drain on paper towels.

When all the pieces have been fried, arrange them on a warm platter, season lightly with salt, and serve hot with lemon wedges.

Allegra's Vegetable Tart

Il Tortino di Verdure di Allegra

One of the most charming wine-bar-restaurants of Florence is Cantinetta Antinori, where you can enjoy not only delicious traditional Tuscan dishes, but also a large gamut of the Antinoris' wine served by the glass or the bottle. This is one of the Cantinetta's savory appetizers. Allegra Antinori, one of Marchese Antinori's daughters, graciously shared the recipe with me. ◆ *serves 6*

FOR THE DOUGH

1 cup unbleached all-purpose flour

3 ounces unsalted butter, at room temperature for hand mixing, or cold and in small pieces for the food processor

Salt

1 large egg

3 to 4 tablespoons chilled white wine or water

Butter for greasing the tart pan

2 cups uncooked beans or rice to weight down the pastry

FOR THE FILLING

$1/3$ cup extra-virgin olive oil

1 small onion, diced (about 1 cup)

1 small carrot, diced ($1/2$ to $3/4$ cup)

1 small red bell pepper, cored, seeded, and diced (about 1 cup)

1 small yellow bell pepper, cored, seeded, and diced (about 1 cup)

1 small zucchini, diced ($3/4$ to 1 cup)

4 canned plum tomatoes, minced, without their juices (about 1 cup)

1 tablespoon chopped fresh flat-leaf parsley

8 to 10 fresh basil leaves, finely shredded

Freshly ground black pepper to taste

2 large eggs, lightly beaten

$1/3$ cup freshly grated Parmigiano-Reggiano

PREPARE THE DOUGH

In a medium bowl or in a food processor fitted with the metal blade, mix the flour and butter until crumbly. Add a pinch of salt, the egg, and the wine or water, and mix into a soft dough. (If you use a food processor, remove the dough when it is loosely gathered around the blade.) Shape the dough into a dish, wrap in plastic, and refrigerate for a few hours, or until ready to use.

Preheat the oven to 375°F. Butter a 10-inch straight-sided tart pan with a removable bottom. Unwrap the refrigerated dough and place on a lightly floured work surface. Roll out the dough to a 12-inch circle. Place the dough into the tart pan and trim the excess dough. Refrigerate the shell for about 30 minutes. Line the shell with foil and fill the bottom with uncooked beans or rice.

Bake on the middle rack of the oven for 15 minutes, then remove the foil and the beans or rice, and bake until the dough is barely colored, 5 to 6 minutes longer. Remove from the oven and cool the shell in its pan. (The shell can be prepared several hours or a day ahead.)

PREPARE THE FILLING

Heat the oil in a large skillet over medium-high heat. Add the onion, carrot, and red and yellow peppers, and cook until the vegetables begin to soften, 8 to 10 minutes. Add the zucchini and cook until tender but still a bit firm to the bite, 3 to 4 minutes. Stir in the tomatoes, parsley, and basil, and cook until the tomatoes begin to soften, 3 to 4 minutes. Season with salt and pepper, transfer to a bowl, and cool. Stir in the eggs and Parmigiano.

Fill the pastry shell with the vegetable mixture and bake on the middle rack of the oven until the top is lightly golden and firm and the crust is golden brown, 15 to 20 minutes.

Cool the tart in its pan, then transfer to a serving dish. Serve at room temperature.

From the U.S., dial 011, followed by the country code of 39. The area code for all numbers below is 055.

Cammillo
Borgo San Jacopo 57/r
Tel. 212 427

One of the top trattorie of Florence, it has been in the same family for three generations. Today, Francesco, the grandson of the original owner, runs this place. The food at Cammillo is a mixture of traditional Tuscan dishes and classics from other parts of Italy. The soups at Cammillo are thick and filling. Their homemade taglierini, which are generally paired with porcini mushrooms, fresh peas, or white truffle, are outstanding.

Cantinetta Antinori
Piazza Antinori 3
Tel. 292 234

A soothing, classic restaurant-wine bar that belongs to the Antinoris, a patrician wine-making family that has been making wines for over six hundred years. A great place to indulge in wine tasting, and to enjoy classic Tuscan cuisine prepared with a light but sure hand.

Cantinetta dei Verrazzano
Via dei Tavolini 18/r
Tel. 268 590

A charming spot for a casual lunch that serves freshly baked bread; sandwiches; crostini topped by mouthwatering ingredients such as marinated vegetables and figs; country-cured meats; a large assortment of cheeses; and a wide selection of wines by the glass.

Enoteca Le Volpi e l'Uva
Piazza dei Rossi 1
Tel. 239 8132

A nice place to taste some interesting wines and to snack on some typical cheeses, cured meats, and delicious sandwiches.

Frescobaldi Wine Bar
Via dei Magazzini 2-4/r
Tel. 284 724

A brand-new, sleek wine bar owned and operated by the Frescobaldis, another great Tuscan wine family. There one can taste Tuscan and other Italian wines as well as wines from other countries. Delicious traditional dishes, cold and warm, are often chosen to match the Frescobaldis' wines.

Il Cibrèo
Via dei Macci 118/r
Tel. 234 1100

A much-celebrated restaurant that serves wonderful, refined Tuscan food but not pasta! It has become a destination for foodies from all over the world.

La Baraonda
Via Ghibellina 67/r
Tel. 234 1171

A rustic trattoria run by two passionate owners, Elena and Duccio, who try to keep alive the dishes so dear to Tuscan grandmothers. Try the Tagliatelle with Ragù alla Fiorentina and the Farinata, an old-fashioned, thick soup of black cabbage and cornmeal; the *risolata* (risotto with romaine lettuce); and the veal meat loaf with salsa verde.

Osteria Caffè Italiano
Via Isola delle Stinche 11/13/r
Tel. 289 368
Fun, boisterous place that serves very good food, and an incredible Bistecca alla Fiorentina.

Osteria del Cinghiale Bianco
Via Borgo San Jacopo 43/4
Tel./Fax 215 706
A terrific trattoria nestled on the ground floor of a thirteenth-century tower in Borgo San Jacopo, one of the most historical streets of Florence, that serves superlative traditional Tuscan cuisine. Try the scrumptious Pappardelle with Wild Boar Ragù or, if on the menu, Salt Cod Livorno-Style.

Procacci
Via Tornabuoni 64/r
Tel. 211 656
Procacci is one of those establishments that are hard to classify. Part caffè, part wine bar, part specialty foods store, Procacci attracts its customers for all of the above. Located in the most fashionable street of Florence, this wonderful old-fashioned store is one of the most charming places to stop for a quick bite. Choose one of the freshly baked small rolls, stuffed with all sorts of delicate ingredients (my favorite was the truffle sandwiches), and sip a glass of prosecco or any other wine of the Marchese Antinori's family, which now owns the place.

Ristorante Zibibbo
Via di Terzollina 3/r
Tel. 433 383
This fairly new, attractive restaurant belongs to Benedetta Vitali, chef and former co-owner of the famous Cibrèo restaurant. Benedetta is a master at preparing traditional, hard-to-find Florentine dishes. Try the fantastic, large tortelli stuffed with pears and Pecorino cheese.

Sostanza
Via del Porcellana 25/r
Tel. 212 691
A simple, always jammed trattoria that serves excellent traditional Tuscan dishes. Here, the soups seem to be thicker and more flavorful than anywhere else in the city.

Trattoria Garga
Via del Moro 48
Tel. 211 396
A colorful, ebullient establishment that serves, besides classic Tuscan fare, also some creative dishes. Giuliano Garga and his wife, Sharon Oddson, a Canadian, run the kitchen with joyous vitality.

Tomato, Bread, and Cucumber Salad

Panzanella

Panzanella, one of the most typical Tuscan dishes, began as the humble staple of peasants and farm workers, who would dress slices of stale bread with a water-vinegar mixture and top it with sliced onion. While the panzanella of today has many faces, most of Florence's trattorie still serve this most traditional version. As always, the right ingredients play the most important role in any dish. Select the best olive oil. Seek out garden-ripe tomatoes and the freshest basil. And, if at all possible, look for the unsalted, coarse-textured *pane toscano* (often available in larger cities) or other coarse-textured country bread. I love this type of spontaneous food that takes advantage of great seasonal ingredients. ♦ *serves 4*

$^1/_2$ pound coarse-textured bread,
2 to 3 days old

3 large, ripe tomatoes, diced
(about 2 cups)

I small cucumber, sliced into thin
rounds (about $1^1/_2$ cups)

I small red onion, thinly sliced
(about $1^1/_2$ cups)

10 to 15 fresh basil leaves, shredded

Salt and freshly ground black pepper
to taste

$^1/_3$ cup extra-virgin olive oil

2 tablespoons red-wine vinegar

Break the bread into pieces. Place in a bowl and add cold water to barely cover. Soak for about 10 minutes.

Drain the bread. With your hands, squeeze out as much water as possible. Crumble the bread into a large salad bowl. Add the tomatoes, cucumber, onion, and basil. Season with salt and several grinds of pepper. Add the oil and vinegar, and mix well to combine. Taste and adjust the seasoning. Chill the salad for about I hour before serving.

VARIATIONS

Panzanella with Scampi ◆ Sauté or grill 8 ounces of medium shrimp, cut them into 1-inch pieces, and toss with the salad.

Panzanella with Tuna and Olives ◆ Drain the oil from one 7-ounce can of imported white Italian tuna, and flake it into the salad. Stir in 8 to 10 pitted black olives, quartered.

Panzanella with Grilled Bread ◆ Grill several medium-thick slices of Italian bread. When cool, cut them into small cubes. Toss the grilled bread (instead of soaked bread) with the other ingredients.

Twice-Cooked Florentine Vegetable Soup

Ribollita

Buca in Italian means "hole," and indeed Buca dell'Orafo Trattoria seems to be housed in an underground hole. The small, barely visible entrance leads a few steps down to a grotto-like room with small tables so close together that once you are seated you are basically touching elbows with the people at the next table. As I was beginning to be put off by the crowded surroundings, a white-haired waiter slid between the tables and began pouring us some red wine while singing softly, almost to himself, "Firenze stanotte sei bella . . . ," a beautiful old Florentine song. As he put the wine on the table, he looked at my daughter Paola and said, "Signorina, Firenze is beautiful, but you are even more beautiful." He then proceeded to bring us two large bowls of the classic *ribollita* soup, and drizzled it with a few drops of golden extra-virgin olive oil. The ribollita was incredibly flavorful, loaded with vegetables, beans, black cabbage, and bread, and was so thick that it could have been eaten with a fork. The food that came to our table afterward was equally good. The service was charming and attentive. The crowded surroundings did not matter anymore. ◆ *serves 10 to 12*

1/2 pound dried cannellini beans (about 1 cup), picked over and soaked overnight in cold water to cover generously, drained, and rinsed

1/2 cup plus 2 tablespoons extra-virgin olive oil

1 small onion, finely minced (about 1 cup)

2 garlic cloves, finely minced

1/4 cup finely chopped fresh flat-leaf parsley

1 bunch of *cavolo nero* (black kale), tough center stalks removed, coarsely shredded (about 7 cups)

3 medium carrots, peeled and coarsely diced (about 2 cups)

3 celery stalks, coarsely diced (about 2 cups)

1 large boiling potato, peeled and coarsely diced (about 2 cups)

1/2 small head Savoy cabbage, cored and coarsely chopped (about 2 1/2 cups)

1 bunch of Swiss chard, green leaves only, coarsely chopped (about 7 cups)

1 (28-ounce) can Italian plum tomatoes, preferably San Marzano (see note, page 35), with their juices, put through a food mill to remove the seeds

Salt and freshly ground black pepper to taste

5 thick slices 1- to 2-day-old crusty Italian bread, broken into small chunks

Put the beans in a medium pot, cover by 2 to 3 inches with cold water, and bring to a bubble over medium heat. As soon as the water begins to bubble, reduce the heat to low and simmer, uncovered, until the beans are tender, 45 minutes to 1 hour, stirring from time to time. The beans can be cooked a few hours ahead of time.

Heat $\frac{1}{3}$ cup of the oil in a large pot over medium heat. Add the onion and stir until it is pale yellow and soft, 8 to 10 minutes. Add the garlic and parsley, and stir for a minute or two. Add the kale, carrots, celery, potato, cabbage, and chard. Stir for a couple of minutes, then add the tomatoes, the beans and their cooking water. If needed, add just enough cold water to cover the vegetables by about 2 inches. Season with salt and pepper to taste, and bring the soup to a boil. Reduce the heat to low, cover the pan partially, and cook, stirring from time to time, until the vegetables are tender, about 45 minutes.

Turn off the heat. Stir in the bread and the remaining olive oil, and cool to room temperature. Cover and refrigerate overnight.

A few hours before serving, put the soup back on low heat and simmer for another 30 minutes, stirring often with a long wooden spoon to prevent sticking. At this point the soup will have "reboiled" twice (thus *ribollita*) and will have a thick consistency and a divine flavor. Taste, adjust the seasoning, and serve hot with a few drops of additional olive oil if desired.

RIBOLLITA, THE GEM OF ALL TUSCAN SOUPS

In Florence no respectable trattoria would be caught dead without this famous twice-boiled vegetable soup that combines winter vegetables, day-old bread, and luscious olive oil, transformed by long, slow cooking into a rustic delight. The vegetables change according to the area, the season, and the mood of the cook, but three ingredients—white beans, *cavolo nero* (black kale), and one- to two-day-old Tuscan bread—are essential. Fortunately for us, today we can easily find cannellini beans in most Italian and specialty food stores in the United States. And, thanks to Lucio Gomiero and Carlo Boscolo, founders of European Vegetable Specialties, today we can find true cavolo nero.

Tuscan Farro Soup

Zuppa di Farro

One of the most ancient grains of Italy is *farro*, a wheat with a nutty flavor that was once the staff of life for the Romans. Today farro is grown primarily in Tuscany and in the Abruzzi region and is, alone or in conjunction with other ingredients, the undisputed star of several rustic Tuscan soups. With the exception perhaps of bread soups, nothing gives Tuscans more satisfaction than a large bowl of thick farro or bean soup. In this country farro can be found in Italian specialty food stores or in health food stores. ◆ *serves 6 to 8*

$1/3$ cup extra-virgin olive oil, plus more for drizzling

3 garlic cloves, finely chopped

I small onion, finely minced (about I cup)

I medium carrot, minced (about $3/4$ cup)

I celery stalk, minced (about $3/4$ cup)

5 to 6 fresh sage leaves, shredded, or a pinch of crumbled dried sage

I (28-ounce) can Italian plum tomatoes, preferably San Marzano (see note, page 35), with their juices, put through a food mill to remove the seeds

Salt and freshly ground black pepper to taste

6 cups Chicken Broth (page 298) or canned low-sodium chicken broth

I pound farro (about $2^{1}/2$ cups), soaked in water to cover for 2 to 3 hours, then drained (see note, opposite)

Heat the $1/3$ cup oil in a medium saucepan over medium heat. Add the garlic, onion, carrot, and celery and cook, stirring, until lightly golden and soft, 8 to I0 minutes. Add the sage, stir for about I minute, then add the tomatoes. Season with salt and pepper and bring the sauce to a boil. Reduce the heat to medium low and cook, stirring from time to time, until the sauce has a medium-thick consistency, about I0 minutes.

In a large pot, bring the chicken broth to a boil. Drain the farro, rinse it under cold running water, and add to the broth. As soon as the broth comes back to a boil, stir the sauce into the broth, reduce the heat to low, and simmer, uncovered, until the farro is tender and the soup has a nice thick consistency, 30 to 40 minutes, stirring from time to time. Taste and adjust the seasoning.

Let the soup sit for 15 to 20 minutes, then serve with a drizzle of extra-virgin olive oil.

HOW TO USE FARRO

Cleaning and cooking farro is very much like cleaning and cooking dried beans:

• To clean, rinse the farro under cold running water and discard any pieces of husk or fragments. Put the farro in a large bowl, add cold water to cover generously, and let soak for 2 to 3 hours. Shake the bowl or stir the farro a few times with your hands so that any empty husks will come to the surface of the water. Drain, repeat this step one more time, and drain again.

• To cook, add farro to an already simmering soup or to simmering salted water, and cook over medium heat, uncovered, stirring from time to time, until tender. Keep in mind that even after farro is cooked, it will have a somewhat firm consistency.

This delightful grain can also be turned into cold or warm salads, or side dishes, or cooked in the manner of risotto, thus turning the dish into *farrotto*.

Ganino's Ricotta-Parmigiano-Spinach Dumplings

Gli Strozzapreti di Ganino

The people of Florence take a savory mixture of spinach or Swiss chard, ricotta, Parmigiano, and nutmeg, and turn it into large, delicious dumplings. These are known as either *strozzapreti* ("priest stranglers") or *ravioli nudi* ("naked ravioli") because they are not enveloped by pasta. At Osteria Ganino, a small but excellent trattoria that is patronized by a young, hip Florentine crowd, I had light-as-feathers strozzapreti that were bathed simply with sweet butter, aromatic sage, and freshly grated Parmigiano. These savory morsels are also terrific topped with a light, fresh tomato sauce. If you plan to visit Florence in spring, summer, or fall, go to Ganino, ask for an outdoor table that overlooks the small, charming Piazza dei Cimatori, and order the strozzapreti.

◆ *serves 4*

2 pounds fresh spinach, stems removed, washed in several changes of water

Salt

3/4 pound fresh ricotta

Pinch of freshly grated nutmeg

1 large egg, lightly beaten

1 1/3 cups freshly grated Parmigiano-Reggiano

1/2 cup all-purpose flour, plus more for shaping

Coarse salt

4 tablespoons unsalted butter

6 to 8 fresh sage leaves

Put a couple inches of water in a large pot over high heat; in a large bowl, prepare an ice-water bath. When the water begins to boil, add the spinach and a large pinch of salt, and boil for 1 to 2 minutes. Drain and plunge the spinach into the ice water. When cool, drain again. Squeeze the spinach with your hands to remove as much water as possible. Place the spinach on a clean kitchen towel or cloth napkin and wring the cloth to draw out as much water as possible. Chop the spinach very fine by hand or by pulsing in the bowl of a food processor, making sure not to purée it.

In a large bowl, combine the spinach with the ricotta, nutmeg, egg, and 1 cup of the Parmigiano. Season lightly with salt. Sprinkle in the flour a little at a time, and mix with your hands or with a wooden spoon until the ingredients are well incorporated and the mixture is moist but sticks together easily.

TEST THE CONSISTENCY OF YOUR DUMPLINGS

Bring a small saucepan of water to a boil. Take a large tablespoon of the spinach mixture, shape it into a ball about the size of a walnut, and drop it into the boiling water. If the dumpling keeps its shape and does not break up in the water, go ahead and shape the remaining mixture. If the dumpling falls apart, add a little more flour to the mixture.

Shape all the dumplings, then line them on a lightly floured baking sheet, making sure they do not touch one another. Refrigerate, uncovered, for up to several hours.

Bring a large pot of water to a boil over high heat and add a large pinch of coarse salt. Drop the dumplings gently into the boiling water. As soon as the water comes back to a boil, reduce the heat to medium and cook at a gentle simmer until the dumplings rise to the surface of the water, 3 to 4 minutes.

While the dumplings are cooking, melt the butter in a small skillet over medium heat. When it begins to foam, add the sage and stir a few times.

As the dumplings come to the surface of the water, remove them with a slotted spoon or a skimmer, draining the excess water back into the pot, and place on warm serving dishes. Spoon the butter-sage sauce over the dumplings and dust with the remaining Parmigiano. Serve at once.

WET RICOTTA

Cow's-milk ricotta is the most common type found in the United States, and it often has a larger amount of moisture than imported Italian ricotta. Since moisture in ricotta (or in the spinach) will make these dumplings fall apart in the water, this is what you do:

Line a strainer with two layers of cheesecloth. Add the ricotta and wrap it in the cheesecloth. Place the strainer over a large bowl and refrigerate for several hours or overnight to allow the liquid to drain. Or, to speed up the process, wrap the ricotta in the two layers of cheesecloth and gently squeeze out some of its liquid.

Rigatoni Dragged with Florentine Meat Ragù

Rigatoni Strascicati col Ragù

For the people of Tuscany, a slowly simmered meat ragù is much more than a simple meat sauce; it is soul food. This ragù probably originated centuries ago in peasant kitchens where cuts of inexpensive meat were simmered for hours to extract as much flavor as possible. The Tuscan ragù of today can be made with veal, beef, wild boar, pork, sausage, and mushrooms. It might have the addition of a few tomatoes, broth, wine, or just water. The people of Florence add finely minced chicken livers and chili peppers. Others prefer the addition of beef marrow. Despite these many variations, most agree that the base is always the same—chopped onion, carrot, and celery browned in oil—and that the ragù needs to cook for a considerable length of time. They also know that rigatoni and penne are the perfect vehicles, because these shapes can be tossed in the skillet and "dragged" with a large spoon until pasta and sauce are perfectly blended. The version here comes from La Baraonda Trattoria, an establishment that prides itself on keeping alive the flavors of genuine Florentine cooking. • *serves 6*

FOR THE RAGÙ

- 1/3 cup extra-virgin olive oil
- 1 small onion, finely minced (about 1 cup)
- 1 small carrot, minced (about 1/2 cup)
- 1 small celery stalk, minced (about 1/2 cup)
- 1 small sprig of fresh rosemary, leaves only, chopped (about 2 tablespoons)
- 1 tablespoon chopped fresh flat-leaf parsley
- 2 garlic cloves, peeled and minced
- 1 pound ground beef chuck
- 3 to 4 chicken livers, finely minced
- 1 cup medium-bodied red wine, such as Chianti Classico

- 2 large ripe tomatoes, or 3 canned plum tomatoes, peeled and minced
- 1/8 teaspoon freshly grated nutmeg
  Small pinch of crushed red pepper flakes
  Grated zest of 1/2 lemon
  Salt to taste
- 2 1/2 cups Chicken Broth (page 298) or canned low-sodium chicken broth

TO COMPLETE THE DISH

- 1 tablespoon coarse salt
- 1 pound dried rigatoni or penne
- 1 to 2 tablespoons unsalted butter
- 1/2 cup freshly grated Parmigiano-Reggiano

PREPARE THE FILLING

Heat the oil in a medium saucepan over medium heat. As soon as the oil is nice and hot, add the onion, carrot, and celery, and cook, stirring, until the vegetables begin to soften, about 5 minutes. Add the rosemary, parsley, and garlic, and stir until the mixture has a nice golden color, 3 to 4 minutes more.

Raise the heat to high. Add the beef and the chicken livers and cook, stirring from time to time and breaking up the meat with a wooden spoon, until the meat is golden brown, 10 to 12 minutes.

Add the wine and stir until half of it has evaporated. Add the tomatoes, nutmeg, red pepper flakes, and lemon zest. Season with salt. Add 2 cups of the chicken broth and bring to a fast simmer. Reduce the heat to very low, partially cover, and simmer, stirring from time to time, until the ragù has a rich brown color and dense consistency, about 2 hours. If the sauce reduces too much, add a little more broth. Taste, adjust the seasoning, and set aside until ready to use. The ragù can be prepared several hours or a few days ahead.

FINISH THE DISH

Bring a large pot of water to a boil over high heat. Add the coarse salt and the rigatoni and cook, stirring occasionally with a wooden spoon, until the pasta is tender but still firm to the bite. Scoop up and reserve 1 cup of the cooking water.

Meanwhile, reheat the ragù in a large skillet over medium heat. Drain the pasta and place it in the skillet with the ragù. Add the butter and about half of the Parmigiano and stir, dragging the pasta and the sauce together to combine. (Add just a little of the reserved pasta water if the sauce seems too dry.) Taste, adjust the seasoning, and serve with the remaining Parmigiano.

Penne with Porcini

Penne con Porcini Trifolati

In the fall and winter, when porcini mushrooms are plentiful, the restaurants and trattorie of Florence use them with abandon. One of the most classic preparations is simply to sauté these meaty, aromatic mushrooms in olive oil, garlic, and fresh herbs, then toss them with pasta. If you can get your hands on fresh porcini, which in this country is not an easy feat, you must try this dish. If not, use any wild or cultivated mushroom such as shiitake, chanterelle, oyster, or cremini. ◆ *serves 4 to 6*

1 pound fresh porcini mushrooms

1/3 cup extra-virgin olive oil

2 garlic cloves, minced

1 to 2 tablespoons chopped fresh flat-leaf parsley

3 fresh thyme sprigs

Salt and freshly ground black pepper to taste

1 tablespoon coarse salt

1 pound dried penne

2 tablespoons unsalted butter

Discard the mushrooms' stems, wipe the mushrooms clean with a damp towel, and thinly slice them.

Heat the oil in a large, heavy skillet over high heat. When the oil is hot but not yet smoking, add the mushrooms without crowding (you may need to sauté in 2 batches) and cook, stirring, until they have a nice golden color, 2 to 3 minutes. Reduce the heat to medium. Add the garlic, parsley, and thyme, and season with salt and pepper. Stir until the garlic begins to color, about 1 minute. Turn off the heat.

Meanwhile, bring a large pot of water to a boil over high heat. Add the coarse salt and the pasta and cook until the pasta is tender but still firm to the bite.

Scoop out and reserve about 1/2 cup of the pasta cooking water. Drain the pasta and place it in the skillet with the mushrooms. Add the butter and stir over medium heat until the pasta and mushrooms are well combined. Add a bit of the reserved cooking water if the pasta seems too dry. Taste, adjust the seasoning, and serve.

Risotto with Spinach

Risotto alla Fiorentina

Risotto alla Fiorentina is a delicious, straightforward recipe that cooks the risotto almost to its completion, then adds the fresh spinach only during the last 5 minutes. The last-minute addition of butter and Parmigiano gives the risotto the ideal creamy, moist consistency. ◆ *serves 4 to 6*

6 cups Chicken Broth (page 298) or low-sodium canned chicken broth

4 tablespoons (^{1}/$_2$ stick) unsalted butter

^{1}/$_2$ small onion, minced (about ^{1}/$_2$ cup)

2 cups Arborio, Carnaroli, or Vialone Nano rice

1 cup dry white wine

^{1}/$_2$ pound spinach, stemmed, washed, dried, and coarsely chopped

^{1}/$_2$ cup freshly grated Parmigiano-Reggiano

Heat the broth in a medium saucepan and keep warm over low heat. Melt 3 tablespoons of the butter in a large skillet over medium heat. When the butter foams, add the onion and cook, stirring, until the onion is pale yellow and soft, 4 to 5 minutes. Add the rice and stir until it is well coated with the butter and the onion and the grains begin to whiten, 2 to 3 minutes. Stir in the wine. When the wine is almost all evaporated, add 1 cup of the hot broth and cook, stirring, until most of the broth has been absorbed. Continue cooking and stirring the rice in this manner, adding a cup or so of broth at a time, for about 15 minutes.

Add the spinach and stir, adding small additions of broth, until the spinach is soft and the rice is tender but still a bit firm to the bite, 3 to 4 minutes.

Swirl in the remaining tablespoon of butter and about half of the Parmigiano. Stir until the cheese and butter are melted and the rice has a moist, creamy consistency. Taste and adjust the seasoning. Divide the risotto into serving bowls and serve with the remaining Parmigiano on the side.

THE FLORENTINE TABLE

APPETIZERS

Crostini: Small toasted bread slices topped with minced, creamy chicken liver, tuna fish, mixed seafood, mushrooms, or wild game.

Fettunta or Bruschetta: Slices of grilled country bread rubbed with garlic and dribbled with extra-virgin olive oil, often with the addition of ingredients such as black cabbage or tomatoes.

FIRST COURSES

Pappa al Pomodoro: A very thick tomato-bread soup.

Pappardelle al Cinghiale: Homemade egg pasta with wild boar ragù.

Penne Strascicate: Pasta that is "dragged" in a skillet with the sauce.

Ribollita: A super-delicious, very thick vegetable-bread soup.

Risotto alla Fiorentina: Risotto with meat ragù.

Strozzapreti: Ricotta-spinach dumplings often dressed with butter and fresh sage, or with a meat ragù.

Tortelli: Homemade pasta stuffed with potatoes or ricotta and spinach.

ENTRÉES

Arista: Roasted pork loin with garlic and rosemary.

Baccalà Fritto: Fried salt cod.

Bistecca alla Fiorentina: Two-inch-thick, charcoal-grilled T-bone.

Fricassea di Pollo: Pan-roasted chicken with wine, eggs, and lemon.

Rosticciana: Florentine grilled pork spareribs.

Scottiglia: A stew of mixed meats (poultry, game, veal, or lamb).

Trippa alla Fiorentina: Tripe simmered in tomatoes.

Zimino: Salt cod, squid, or cuttlefish cooked with tomatoes and Swiss chard.

VEGETABLES AND SALADS

Carciofi al Tegame: Pan-roasted artichokes with pancetta and garlic.

Fagioli all' Uccelletto: Small white beans cooked with tomatoes, sage, rosemary, and garlic.

Panzanella: A salad of summer tomatoes, bread, basil, onion, and cucumber with extra-virgin olive oil.

Pinzimonio: A mix of raw seasonal vegetables to dip in a mixture of extra-virgin olive oil, salt, and pepper.

Piselli alla Fiorentina: Spring peas with pancetta or prosciutto.

DESSERTS

Cenci: Deep-fried sweet pastry fritters.

Schiacciata: Flat, buttery, lemon-flavored cake.

Schiacciata con l'Uva: Flat sweetbread studded with red grapes and sugar.

Zuccotto: Dome-shaped cake stuffed with chocolate, almonds, and whipped cream.

SOME BASIC INGREDIENTS

Acciughe: Anchovies, fresh or preserved in salt.

Aglio: Garlic.

Cannellini: Small white Tuscan beans used in soups, stews, and salads.

Cavolo Nero: Black cabbage, a winter vegetable with long, somewhat curly, black to dark green leaves. It is used in vegetable soups such as ribollita, in fettunta, and in many other dishes.

Cipolle Rosse: Red onions, the variety mainly used in Tuscan cooking.

Erbe: Fresh herbs such as sage, rosemary, basil, oregano, thyme, and mint are synonymous with Tuscan cooking.

Farro: This nutty-tasting grain, also known as spelt, is one of the most ancient grains of Italy. It is the undisputed star of many Tuscan soups.

Fave: Fava beans are as popular in Tuscany as they are in Rome. A favorite Tuscan snack is to dip the raw beans in oil and salt and eat them with a slice of Pecorino cheese.

Finocchiona: A typical coarse Tuscan pork sausage seasoned with wild fennel seeds.

Lardo: Pork fat pickled in brine and used in cooking, or thinly sliced and topped on bread or grilled polenta.

Marzolino: Fresh, unripened, sheep's-milk cheese, made in spring.

Olio Vergine d'Oliva: Extra-virgin olive oil. Tuscany produces a wide range of extra-virgin oils and, just as with the grapes grown in the region, they have distinctive individual tastes that range from delicate and fruity to peppery.

Pane Toscano: Tuscan bread is indeed a valuable ingredient, used in innumerable dishes.

Pecorino: Pecorino is made with sheep's milk or with a blending of sheep's and cow's milk.

Pomodori: Tomatoes, fresh or canned.

Porcini: The common name of *boletus edulis,* the most loved wild mushroom of Italy. One of the favorite ways to cook porcini in Tuscany is to grill them, basted simply with extra-virgin olive oil.

Prosciutto: Salt-cured, air-dried hams, made from pork or wild boar.

Salsiccia: Sausages, fresh or dried.

Roasted Pork with Rosemary, Sage, and Garlic

Arista alla Fiorentina

Umberto, the owner of the quaint Osteria del Caffè Italiano, is a man with a mission: he wants his customers to enjoy his food and to have a good time. The night my daughter Paola and I were there, he took over the duties of the not-too-personable server assigned to us and proceeded to feed and charm us with his boundless energy. After I asked him to choose our dinner for us, he brought to the table an antipasto of mixed locally cured meats and assorted crostini. Then came the *arista,* a bone-in rack of pork loin roast. The roast was golden brown and succulent, and the potatoes that had been roasted in the same pan were crisp and fragrant with the taste of the pan juices. After talking with Umberto, this is what I learned: Leave the meat at room temperature for 20 to 30 minutes before roasting. Season the meat *generously* with salt and pepper (Tuscan people like no salt in their bread, but plenty on their roasts). Use only fresh herbs; dried won't do it. Don't overcook your roast. And finally, let the roast rest, loosely covered with foil, before slicing it. The arista can also be made by using a boneless center-cut loin. ◆ *serves 6*

6 medium boiling potatoes (2 to 2^1/$_2$ pounds)

2 garlic cloves, minced

2 tablespoons finely minced fresh rosemary

2 tablespoons finely minced fresh sage

1^1/$_2$ teaspoons salt plus more to taste

^{1}/$_2$ teaspoon freshly ground black pepper plus more to taste

1 bone-in pork rack roast, about 6 pounds, trimmed of excess fat and frenched

^{1}/$_2$ cup extra-virgin olive oil

Peel the potatoes, cut them into thick wedges, and place in a large bowl with enough cold water to cover. Set aside.

In a small bowl, combine the garlic, rosemary, and sage, and season with the salt and pepper. Loosen the fat around each bone slightly and pierce the meat in several places with a thin knife. Press some of the herb mixture into the cavities and inside the loosened skin around the bones, and rub a bit more all over the roast. Let the roast stand at room temperature for about 20 minutes.

Preheat the oven to 400°F.

Pour all but 2 or 3 tablespoons of the oil into a large, heavy roasting pan and place the roast in the pan, fat side down. Pour the remaining oil over the meat and season generously with salt and pepper. Place the pan on the middle rack of the oven and cook for about 20 minutes.

Drain the potatoes, pat dry with paper towels, and add to the roast. Cook, basting the meat every 15 minutes or so, until the roast is golden brown and registers 145°F on an instant-read thermometer, about 1 hour. At this point, the meat should be slightly pink.

Transfer the roast to a cutting board, cover loosely with foil, and let it rest for 10 to 15 minutes. Check the potatoes, which at this point should be tender and golden brown. If not, roast them a little longer.

Cut the pork between the bones and serve with some potatoes and a bit of the pan juices.

T-Bone alla Fiorentina

Bistecca alla Fiorentina

Steak dishes are not extremely popular with most Italians. In Florence, however, even the most reticent Italian will eagerly order a *Bistecca alla Fiorentina*. This great T-bone, which in Florence weights no less than 2 pounds and is about I^1/$_2$ inches thick, comes from the prized free-range *chianina* cows raised since the mid-nineteenth century in Tuscany's Val di Chiana. It is a perennial fixture in every restaurant and trattoria of the city. Ideally, a true Bistecca alla Fiorentina should be made with the chianina beef, but any fine T-bone will do. Massimo Masselli, the owner of the well-respected Osteria del Cinghiale Bianco, said to me, "The secret of good *bistecca* lies in the quality of its meat, so buy the best steak that money can buy. Make sure to have a very hot grill, and season the steak generously with salt only after it is grilled. No olive oil and no marinades, please." ◆ *serves 4*

4 T-bone steaks, cut I^1/$_2$ inches thick
Salt to taste

Finely ground black pepper to taste (optional)
Lemon wedges

Preheat the grill until very hot. Place the steaks on the grill and cook until charred on both sides, about I0 to I2 minutes for rare, and I7 to 20 minutes for medium rare.

When done, season liberally on both sides with salt and, if you wish, some black pepper. Serve with lemon wedges.

The Braised Beef of Florence

Stracotto di Manzo alla Fiorentina

Stracotto, meaning overcooked, is a typical Florentine dish that takes a large piece of beef, browns it in fruity olive oil, then braises it slowly for a few hours with vegetables, Chianti Classico, and tomatoes. The slow cooking over a low flame or in a moderate oven produces a fork-tender "overcooked" meat. This is not a dish for impatient people, since someone needs to be around to baste the meat every 30 minutes (although I believe even impatient people will be quickly converted by the taste and aroma of stracotto). An additional bonus here is that the flavorful sauce, which you should make sure to have plenty of, is so good that many trattorie in Florence have created a dish called Maccheroni allo Stracotto, which tosses rigatoni or penne with the thickened beef-vegetable sauce. (As with all pasta dishes, Maccheroni allo Stracotto is always served as a first course.) At the upscale Ristorante alle Murate the meat was cut into one thick slice, covered generously with the luscious sauce, and served with olive-oil-mashed potatoes. ◆ *serves 8*

3¹/₂ to 4 pounds beef rump roast or chuck

1 teaspoon salt plus more to taste

¹/₂ teaspoon freshly ground black pepper plus more to taste

¹/₂ cup extra-virgin olive oil

1 large carrot, diced (about 1 cup)

1 large celery stalk, diced (about 1 cup)

1 medium red onion, diced (1 to 1¹/₂ cups)

2 garlic cloves, finely minced

2 tablespoons chopped fresh flat-leaf parsley

1 teaspoon finely chopped fresh bay leaves

1 tablespoon finely chopped fresh sage

3 cups Chianti Classico or other medium-bodied red wine

1 (28-ounce) can Italian plum tomatoes, preferably San Marzano (see note, page 35), with their juices, put through a food mill to remove the seeds

Trim some of the fat from the meat. Season generously with the salt and pepper.

Heat the oil in a large, heavy pot or casserole over medium-high heat. When the oil is nice and hot but not yet smoking, add the meat and cook, turning it a few times, until it has a rich golden color on all sides, 10 to 12 minutes. Transfer the meat to a platter.

Reduce the heat to medium. Add the carrot, celery, and onion, and cook, stirring, until the vegetables are golden brown and begin to stick to the bottom of the pan, 10 to 12 minutes. Add the garlic, parsley, bay leaves, and sage, and stir until the herbs are lightly colored and fragrant, about 1 minute. Add 1 cup of the wine and stir quickly, lifting up the richly browned caramelized vegetables that stick to the bottom of the pan. When the wine is almost all evaporated and thickly coats the vegetables, return the meat to the pan and turn it over a few times to coat with the savory base.

Raise the heat to high, add the remaining wine and the tomatoes, and bring to a boil. Cover the pot, reduce the heat to low, and simmer, turning and basting the meat every 30 minutes or so, until the meat is very tender and flakes away when pierced with a fork, $2\frac{1}{2}$ to 3 hours. Turn off the heat and let the beef sit in its juices for an hour.

Place the meat on a cutting board and cover loosely with foil. If the sauce is too thin, bring it to a fast boil and stir until it has a nice medium-thick consistency. Taste and adjust the seasoning.

Cut the meat into thick slices (it will probably fall apart), and place on warm serving dishes. Spoon some sauce over the meat and serve hot, next to a mound of mashed potatoes or some soft, creamy Basic Polenta (page 306).

VARIATION

Maccheroni with Stracotto Sauce • If you have some leftover sauce, heat it up in a skillet. Add some cooked penne or rigatoni and a nice handful of Parmigiano-Reggiano, and stir over medium heat until pasta and sauce are well combined.

Rabbit Braised with Wine, Olives, and Sage

Coniglio con Olive e Salvia

The Tuscan way of preparing delicious home-cooked meals is straightforward and uncomplicated, and proves that you don't need to spend hours in the kitchen. This typical family fare can be made with rabbit, pheasant, or chicken, and is a staple of Florence's trattorie, where the rabbit is generally served with slices of fried or grilled polenta. ◆ *serves 4*

$^1/_3$ cup extra-virgin olive oil

1 cup all-purpose flour

2 (3-pound) rabbits, cut into serving pieces, washed and patted dry

$^1/_2$ teaspoon salt

$^1/_4$ teaspoon freshly ground black pepper

1 large onion, minced (about 1 to 1$^1/_2$ cups)

2 cups dry white wine

10 to 12 black Gaeta or Niçoise olives, pitted and quartered

10 fresh sage leaves, minced (about 2 tablespoons)

2 garlic cloves, minced

$^1/_4$ cup red-wine vinegar

Heat 4 tablespoons of the oil in a large skillet or casserole over high heat. Flour the rabbit pieces lightly. When the oil is very hot, add the rabbit to the skillet without crowding. (The rabbit can be browned in 2 batches.) Season with the salt and pepper and cook, turning once, until golden on both sides, 8 to 10 minutes. Transfer to a platter.

Discard the oil and place the skillet back over medium heat. Add the remaining oil. When it is hot but not yet smoking, add the onion. Cook, scraping the bottom of the pan to pick up the browned bits, until the onion is lightly golden and soft, 6 to 7 minutes. Return the rabbit to the pan, raise the heat to high, and add the wine. As soon as the wine begins to bubble, cover and reduce the heat to low. Simmer, stirring from time to time and turning the rabbit once, until the wine is almost all evaporated and the rabbit is tender when pierced with a fork, 45 to 50 minutes. Transfer the rabbit to a platter, cover loosely with foil, and keep warm in a low oven.

Add the olives, sage, and garlic to the pan, and stir over medium heat until the garlic is fragrant, about 1 minute. Add the vinegar and stir quickly until the pan juices have thickened, 2 to 3 minutes. Taste and adjust the seasoning. Spoon the pan juices over the rabbit and serve hot.

WHEN IN FLORENCE
Caffès, Pastry Shops, and Gelaterie

Caffè Giacosa
Via Tornabuoni 82
Tel. 239 6226
This venerable old caffè, established in 1815, is famous for pastries, chocolate, espresso, and delicious small sandwiches. It is also the place where the *negroni*, my very favorite Italian cocktail, was invented.

Caffè Pasticceria Gilli
Piazza della Repubblica 39/r
Tel. 213 896
The beautiful Piazza della Repubblica is the home of Gilli, one of the oldest caffès of Florence, established in 1733. Sit at one of the outdoor tables and choose from a large selection of superlative gelati, pastries, and chocolate. Or choose from a small selection of well-prepared cold dishes.

Caffè Pasticceria Rivoire
Piazza della Signoria 5/r
Tel. 214 412
Imagine sitting at a charming caffè facing Piazza della Signoria, the most beautiful square of Florence, leisurely sipping a frothy cappuccino and munching on delicious pastries. Caffè Rivoire, established in 1882, is such a spot, the perfect place to relax and watch people from all over the world stroll by.

Gelateria Carabé
Via Ricasoli 60/r
Tel. 289 476
Another superlative gelateria that is extremely popular with Florentines and tourists. Carabé's multiflavored gelatos and sorbettos are fantastic, but so is their coffee granita topped with sweet whipped cream.

Gelateria Vivoli
Via dell'Isola delle Stinche 7
Tel. 292 334
Perhaps the best and best-known gelateria of Florence. Their thick, creamy gelatos are impossible to resist.

Roasted Quail Wrapped in Pancetta

Quaglie Arrosto con la Pancetta

The many country trattorie scattered just outside Florence seem to specialize in little birds prepared in a variety of ways. These quails are stuffed with a savory mixture of mushrooms, and their somewhat dry meat is wrapped in pancetta and roasted in a medium-hot oven, so they remain soft and simply succulent. Serve over soft, creamy polenta. ◆ *serves 4*

FOR THE MUSHROOMS

- 1/2 pound mixed fresh mushrooms such as chanterelle, shiitake, cremini, and oyster
- 1/4 cup extra-virgin olive oil
- 1 garlic clove, minced
- 4 fresh sage leaves, minced
- 1 small sprig of fresh thyme, leaves only, chopped
- 1 tablespoon chopped fresh flat-leaf parsley

- 1/2 cup dry Marsala wine
- Salt and freshly ground black pepper to taste
- 1/2 cup freshly grated Parmigiano-Reggiano

FOR THE QUAILS

- 8 boned quails, thawed if frozen
- 8 slices pancetta or bacon
- 1/4 cup extra-virgin olive oil

PREPARE THE MUSHROOMS

Remove the mushrooms' stems and wipe the caps clean with a damp towel. Cut into thin slices, then mince.

Heat the oil in a large skillet over high heat. When the oil just begins to smoke, add the mushrooms and cook, stirring, until lightly golden, about 2 minutes. Add the garlic, sage, thyme, and parsley, and stir until the garlic begins to color, about 1 minute. Add the Marsala and season lightly with salt and pepper. Stir until the wine is almost all evaporated, 2 to 3 minutes. Place the mushrooms into a bowl, add the Parmigiano, and stir to combine. Set aside until ready to use.

PREPARE THE QUAILS

Preheat the oven to 375°F.

Rinse the quails inside and out, and pat dry with paper towels. Place on a work surface and season inside and out with salt and pepper. Thread the bottom of the quails with a toothpick securely, so the stuffing will not come out, then fill each with 2 tablespoons of the mushroom mixture.

Line up one slice of pancetta on a work surface and place one quail over the slice, breast side up. Tuck the wing tips behind the back of the bird, and wrap the pancetta all around the quail, covering the legs. (If the pancetta is not long enough to fully wrap the quail, use another half slice.) With a toothpick, secure the pancetta to the meat. Wrap the remaining quails.

Heat the oil in a large, heavy ovenproof pan or skillet over high heat. When the oil is hot and just begins to smoke, add the quails, breast side down, and cook until golden, about 2 minutes. Turn and brown the other side, 1 to 2 more minutes. Transfer the pan to the middle rack of the oven and roast until the pancetta is golden and crisp and the meat is cooked all the way through, 12 to 15 minutes. Transfer the quails to a large serving platter and cool for a few minutes. Remove the toothpicks and serve.

Grilled Spareribs

Rosticciana

The first time I went to Il Latini, one of the best trattorie of Florence, many years ago, I was blown away by the aroma that permeated the place. There on the large grill, in full view of customers who were coming and going, were enormous steaks, chickens, and meaty spare ribs, turned and basted by expert hands with oil-infused rosemary sprigs. The ribs that came to the table were richly browned, crisp, and tender. I remember asking the waiter for the secret of such a perfect, delicious dish. "Thirty years, Signora, the cooks here have been making them for over thirty years." ◆ *serves 4*

1/3 cup extra-virgin olive oil

Juice of 1 lemon

2 pounds pork spareribs

Salt and freshly ground black pepper

In a small bowl, combine the olive oil and lemon juice. Divide the spareribs into 4 equal portions and place on a large platter. Brush the oil-lemon juice over the meat generously, and season a bit recklessly with salt and several grinds of pepper. Marinate at room temperature for about 1 hour.

Heat up the grill or the barbecue. When it is quite hot, place the ribs on the grill and reserve the marinade. Cook, turning the ribs a few times and brushing them with the marinade, until they are cooked all the way through, 15 to 18 minutes on each side. (Make a small incision on the meat near the bone. If there is a trace of blood, cook the ribs a little longer.) When done, the ribs should be golden brown, a bit charred, and very crisp.

Place the ribs on individual serving dishes and serve hot.

VARIATIONS

Ribs Cooked in the Oven ◆ Marinate the ribs as instructed above. Preheat the oven to 425°F. Place the ribs in a lightly oiled baking pan. Put the pan on the middle rack of the oven and roast for 40 to 50 minutes, turning a few times, until the ribs are cooked all the way through and are nice and crisp. Check for doneness as explained above.

Grilled Trout with First-Pressed Olive Oil

Trote alla Griglia con Olio Novello

In spite of the many lakes and the Mediterranean sea that kisses the long Tuscan coast, the choices of seafood in Florence trattorie and restaurants are not many. Salt cod, squid, and cuttlefish are the undisputed favorites. There comes a time, however, when one yearns for something different. And so when a waiter of the well-known Osteria del Cinghiale Bianco, a restaurant that I have visited many times throughout the years, told me that one of the night's specials was grilled trout, I ordered it immediately. This is one of the simplest dishes, which relies on only three things: very fresh, plump trout; *olio novello*, first-pressed olive oil; and a good, hot grill. If you can't find olio novello, get the best extra-virgin olive oil you can afford, preferably one year old or less. Serve this delicious dish next to Deep-Fried Baby Artichokes (page 105) or with a nice radicchio or arugula salad. • *serves 4*

Olive oil for the grill

$^1/_2$ cup extra-virgin olive oil

2 lemons, I juiced, I cut into wedges

4 trouts, 10 to 12 ounces each, butterflied and boned, head and tail intact

I teaspoon salt plus more to taste

$^1/_4$ teaspoon freshly ground black pepper plus more to taste

4 very small sprigs of rosemary

4 small bay leaves

Preheat a grill or outdoor barbecue until very hot. Brush the grill with olive oil.

Put $^1/_3$ cup of the olive oil and the lemon juice in a small bowl and mix well to combine.

Place the trouts on a large cutting board and open them up like a book. Brush the inside with the oil-lemon mixture and season with salt and pepper. Fill the inside of each trout with a small sprig of rosemary and a bay leaf. Close them, brush the skin with the oil-lemon mixture, and season with salt and pepper.

Place the trouts on the hot grill and cook for 4 to 5 minutes on each side, or until the skin is golden and crisp. With a large spatula, scoop up each trout carefully (they fall apart easily) and place on serving plates. Open to remove bay leaf and reclose. Serve with a few drops of extra-virgin olive oil and a squeeze of lemon juice.

Braised Squid with Tomatoes, Chili, and Swiss Chard

Calamari in Inzimino

Tuscany has, besides hilly landscapes and luscious valleys, a formidable seacoast, where the seafood is generally prepared in a simple, straightforward manner. There are some exceptions, like this dish pairing squid, cuttlefish, or cod with tomatoes, Swiss chard, or spinach, seasoned generously with chili pepper and grated lemon zest. This dish seems to have roots in Livorno, one of Tuscany's most vibrant fishing centers, but it is also claimed by the people of Florence as their own. One of the best places to try this unusual dish is Cibrèo, perhaps Florence's most celebrated restaurant, whose chef prides himself on keeping alive the ancient traditions of Florentine cooking. ◆ *serves 4*

$1/2$ cup extra-virgin olive oil, plus more for drizzling

$1/2$ small red onion, minced (about $1/2$ cup)

I small carrot, minced (about $1/2$ cup)

I small celery stalk, minced (about $1/2$ cup)

3 garlic cloves, minced

$1/2$ cup dry white wine

I (28-ounce) can Italian plum tomatoes, preferably San Marzano (see note, page 35), with their juices, put through a food mill to remove the seeds

Salt to taste

Crushed red chili pepper to taste

2 pounds whole squid, cleaned as directed on page 199 and cut into $1/2$-inch rings, or $1^1/2$ pounds cleaned squid

2 bunches of Swiss chard (about I pound)

Grated zest of I lemon

4 ($1/2$-inch-thick) slices Italian country bread, grilled

Heat $1/3$ cup of the oil in a large sauté pan over medium heat. Add the onion, carrot, and celery, and cook, stirring, until the vegetables are soft and have a nice golden brown color, 8 to 10 minutes. Add half of the garlic, stir for about I minute, then add the wine. Cook, stirring, until the wine is reduced approximately by half. Add the tomatoes and bring to a fast simmer. Season with salt and with a generous pinch of chili pepper. Stir in the squid and bring the sauce to a boil. Cover the pan, reduce the heat to low, and cook at the lowest simmer, stirring from time to time, until the squid is tender, 45 to 50 minutes.

Meanwhile, remove the stalks from the Swiss chard leaves, and reserve the stalks for another use. Tear or cut the leaves into large pieces and wash them well under cold running water.

Bring 3 cups of water to a boil in a large pot over high heat. Add a generous pinch of salt and the chard leaves. Cover the pot and cook until soft, 2 to 3 minutes. Drain thoroughly, then press out the excess water with the back of a wooden spoon or with your hands.

Heat the remaining oil in a large skillet over medium heat. Add the remaining garlic and the lemon zest and stir for less than 1 minute. Add the reserved chard, season lightly with salt, and stir for a couple of minutes.

Add the chard to the calamari and simmer for 4 to 5 minutes longer. Turn off the heat, taste, and adjust the seasoning, adding more chili pepper if needed. (The sauce should be quite spicy.)

Let the dish rest for 10 to 15 minutes.

Place a slice of grilled bread into each serving bowl, top with the *inzimino*, and serve with a drizzle of olive oil.

Cucina Toscana
Via della Chiesa 7
Faith Willinger is a well-known cookbook author and cooking teacher who has been living in Florence for over twenty years. For information in the U.S., call Vivian at 847-432-1814.

Giuliano Bugialli's Cooking in Florence
Tuscan-born Giuliano Bugialli, an accomplished teacher and award-winning cookbook writer, has been teaching in Florence and in the Chianti area for many years. For information in the U.S., call 646-638-0883.

Italian Cuisine in Florence
Via Trieste 1
Tel. 480 041
General courses in Italian cooking, held in English.

Mercato di San Lorenzo
Piazza del Mercato Centrale
Another great food market that needs to be explored leisurely in order to see its richness and nuances. Walk slowly, inhale deeply, and let your senses tell you what you should buy for a picnic.

Mercato di Sant'Ambrogio
Piazza Ghiberti
If you want to know how Tuscan people eat, just visit Mercato di Sant'Ambrogio. Walk from stand to stand and delight in the sight and smell of freshly baked breads, cured meats, cheeses, sausages, fruits, vegetables, and herbs.

Toscana Saporita
For seven days, students are immersed in the traditional dishes of the region, with classes in the morning and wine and food touring in the afternoon. For information in the U.S., call 516-481-3677.

Classico Cooking: Cuisine and Life-Style of a Tuscan Villa
Chef Francesco Torre offers five-day hands-on cooking classes in an eleventh-century former abbey on a beautiful estate. For information in the U.S., call 214-373-1161.

Vivimarket
Via del Giglio 20-22/r
Tel. 294 911
A great specialty food store that imports food from all over the world.

Deep-Fried Baby Artichokes

Carciofini Fritti

An old saying of Florence states that "everything fried is good, even the sole of the shoes." Perhaps this is the reason small fried artichokes and other fried vegetables are so popular in the trattorie and wine bars of Florence. This is a dish that is quick to prepare, but it needs to be served at once, while the artichokes are still hot and crunchy. Serve them as an appetizer, or next to roasted or grilled lamb. ◆ *serves 4*

2 lemons, I juiced, I cut into wedges

2 pounds baby artichokes

I cup all-purpose flour

Vegetable oil for deep-frying

2 large eggs, beaten in a small bowl with a pinch of salt

Salt

Fill a large bowl with water and the lemon juice. Remove the artichokes' tough outer leaves by snapping them off at the base. Stop when you reach the pale yellow leaves. Slice off the tip of the artichokes, cut off the stem at the base, and, with a small knife, trim off any remaining green parts at the base. Cut each artichoke into thin wedges and drop them into the lemon water to prevent discoloring.

Drain the artichokes and dry thoroughly with paper towels. Place the artichokes on a sheet pan or large platter, and sprinkle both sides of the wedges with flour.

Heat 2 inches of oil in a medium saucepan over medium heat. When the oil is very hot and barely begins to smoke, dip 5 to 6 artichoke wedges quickly into the eggs and lower them into the hot oil. Fry until crisp and golden, 2 to 4 minutes. With a slotted spoon, transfer the artichokes to paper towels to drain. Place them on a warm plate, sprinkle with salt, and serve with lemon wedges, while they are still hot and crunchy.

VARIATION

Artichokes Coated with Bread Crumbs ◆ Clean and slice the artichokes as instructed above. Drain and dry on paper towels. Dip the wedges into the beaten eggs and coat with fine, dry bread crumbs. Fry until golden and crisp, then season with salt.

Green Beans with Garlic and Tomatoes

Fagiolini al Pomodoro

Long, narrow string beans, somewhat similar to Chinese string beans, are one of Florence's most popular vegetables. In this simple dish, the beans are cooked directly into the tomato sauce without the need to boil or blanch them. I generally make this dish several hours ahead, then reheat it and serve it next to any grilled or roasted meat.

• *serves 4*

1 pound green beans

1/3 cup extra-virgin olive oil

1/2 small onion, minced (about 1/2 cup)

2 garlic cloves, minced

4 large fresh tomatoes, peeled, seeded, and diced (about 2 1/2 cups) or 2 1/2 cups diced plum canned tomatoes with their juices

Salt and freshly ground black pepper to taste

6 to 8 leaves fresh basil, finely shredded

1 tablespoon chopped fresh flat-leaf parsley

Snap off both ends of the green beans, wash them under cold running water, and pat dry with paper towels.

Heat the oil in a large skillet over medium heat. Add the onion and cook, stirring, until lightly golden and soft, 6 to 7 minutes. Add the garlic and stir for about 1 minute. Add the fresh tomatoes and 1/2 cup water (if using canned tomatoes with juices, don't all water). Season with salt and several grindings of pepper and bring to a boil.

Add the beans to the sauce, cover the pan partially, and cook over low heat, stirring from time to time, until the beans are tender and the tomato juices have thickened, 15 to 20 minutes. Add a little more water if the sauce reduces too much.

Add the basil and the parsley and stir for a few minutes. Taste, adjust the seasoning, and serve.

Mushroom Salad with Celery and Pecorino

Insalata di Funghi, Sedano, e Pecorino

During a trip to Florence, after a long, delicious lunch at one of the city's top restaurants and hours of sightseeing and shopping, I returned to my hotel happy but absolutely exhausted. That night my husband and I opted to have a light dinner at the hotel. Our choice was a salad of cremini mushrooms, celery, and Pecorino cheese, complemented by a nice bottle of crisp, dry white wine. And the view of the Arno River down below made that impromptu dinner simply magical. ◆ *serves 4*

1 pound cremini mushrooms or white cultivated mushrooms

4 small white celery stalks, diced (1 to 1½ cups)

2 tablespoons minced fresh chives

Salt and freshly ground black pepper to taste

⅓ cup extra-virgin olive oil

Juice of 1 lemon

4 to 5 ounces Pecorino cheese, shredded

Remove the mushrooms' stems and clean the caps with a damp towel. Cut the mushrooms into thin slices and place in a salad bowl with the celery and chives. Season with salt and pepper, add the oil and lemon juice, and stir well to combine. Taste, and adjust the seasoning.

Divide the mushroom mixture among 4 serving dishes, shred the Pecorino cheese through the large holes of a cheese grater directly over the mushrooms, and serve.

VARIATION

This is a popular salad that I feature from time to time at my restaurant in Sacramento. One day when the cheese delivery did not arrive, I improvised and made the salad, minus the cheese and chives, with small chunks of perfectly ripe avocados. It was simply terrific!

Drunken Pears

Pere Ubriache

The first thing one notices when entering the cramped spaces of Buca dell'Orafo Trattoria in Florence is the very large platter of delectable, wrinkled, wine-glazed roasted pears displayed atop an old credenza. They were so tempting that I had the fleeting thought of beginning my meal with the pears. The practice of baking or poaching fruit is common all over Italy, and for most Italians it is the best way to end a meal. The ingredients are pretty standard: pears, which should be free of cuts or bruises; wine, which should be good enough to drink with your meal (don't buy cheap wine unless you want a sour-tasting syrup); sugar; and orange or lemon zest. Variables such as cinnamon, bay leaf, mint, or chopped roasted walnuts are up to the cook.

◆ *serves 6*

3 cups Chianti Classico wine, or any good, medium-bodied red wine

$^1/_2$ cup sugar

Grated zest of 2 oranges

6 equal-size Bosc pears, washed, with stems on

Preheat the oven to 325°F.

Put the wine, sugar, and orange zest in a medium saucepan and bring to a boil over medium heat. Stir until the sugar is completely dissolved, about 2 minutes.

Cut off one thin slice of the pears' bottoms and stand them close together in a deep baking dish. Add the wine mixture and place the dish on the middle rack of the oven. Bake, basting the pears from time to time, until they are tender and slightly wrinkled, and can be easily pierced with a thin knife, about 2 hours. Transfer the pears to a large serving dish and cool to room temperature.

Transfer the cooked-down wine to a small saucepan and bring to a gentle boil. Simmer over medium heat, stirring from time to time, until the wine has a thick, syrupy consistency. Spoon the wine glaze over the pears and serve.

A MATCH MADE IN HEAVEN

If you like the pairing of poached fruit with cheese, try these pears with a creamy, sweet Gorgonzola. Cut the baked pears in half lengthwise and arrange the halves cut side up on individual plates. Place a nice chunk of Gorgonzola on each plate and dribble the pears and cheese with the wine glaze.

Ponte Vecchio

Chocolate-Coated Zuccotto

Zuccotto alla Cioccolata

One of my favorite Italian desserts is *zuccotto*, a dome-shaped cake that is instantly associated with Florence. It requires no baking; it is made by lining a large bowl with slices of liqueur-soaked pound cake, and then filling the cake to capacity with chocolate, hazelnuts, almonds, and whipped cream. While the traditional zuccotto is topped only with confectioners' sugar, some pastry shops coat it with a rich, shiny chocolate glaze. This is the version I make at my restaurant in Sacramento, and it is consistently a best seller. ◆ *serves 10 to 12*

FOR THE ZUCCOTTO

- 6 ounces blanched hazelnuts
- 6 ounces blanched almonds
- 8 ounces semisweet chocolate, finely chopped
- 4 cups cold heavy whipping cream
- 1 cup confectioners' sugar

- $1^1/_2$ pounds pound cake, dark edges trimmed
- $1/_3$ cup rum
- $1/_3$ cup Grand Marnier liqueur

FOR THE CHOCOLATE GLAZE

- 8 ounces dark chocolate, dried
- $1^1/_2$ cups heavy cream

PREPARE THE ZUCCOTTO

Preheat the oven to 400°F.

Put the hazelnuts and almonds on a baking sheet and toast in the oven until lightly golden, 3 to 4 minutes. Let cool. Place the nuts in the bowl of a food processor and chop into very fine pieces, making sure not to process them into powder. Transfer to a large bowl, add half of the chocolate, and mix to combine.

Melt the remaining half of the chocolate in a double boiler over medium-low heat, or in a 200°F. oven, and cool.

Meanwhile, beat the cream with the confectioners' sugar until stiff. Fold the cream thoroughly into the chocolate-nut mixture. Refrigerate until ready to use.

Line a round 2-quart bowl with plastic wrap. Cut the pound cake lengthwise into $1/_4$-inch-thick slices. Cut a slice of pound cake into a square large enough to cover the bottom of the bowl. Line the inside of the bowl with slices of pound cake, reaching the top, and fill any gaps with more slices, trimming them to fit the gaps.

Combine the rum and liqueur in a small bowl or in a plastic squirt bottle, and brush or squirt the cake slices with the liquor.

Spoon the whipped cream–chocolate–nut mixture into the bowl, pressing it gently against the bottom and sides of the cake. With a tablespoon or a spatula, remove about I cup of the filling from the center of the cake, leaving a rounded cavity. Place the removed filling in a bowl and fold in the melted chocolate. Fill the cavity completely with this chocolate mixture and level the top with a spatula.

Cover the top of the cake with slices of pound cake, trimming the overhanging slices to the rim of the bowl. Brush or squirt the top of the cake with the liquors. Cover the bowl tightly with plastic wrap and refrigerate for I or 2 days.

PREPARE THE CHOCOLATE GLAZE

Combine the chocolate and cream on the top of a double boiler over simmering water. Stir until the chocolate is melted and well combined with the cream. Cool slightly.

Unwrap the cake and carefully invert it, flat side down, over a small cooling rack that can fit in your refrigerator. Pour about $1/3$ cup of the chocolate glaze over the cake, and with a small metal spatula, spread it lightly all over the cake. (This will seal the cracks and crumbs and ensure smooth glazing.) Refrigerate for 20 to 25 minutes, until firm. Pour the remaining chocolate over the cake in a circular motion, coating it evenly. (This time, do not use a spatula.) Refrigerate until the chocolate is set, about 30 minutes.

Remove the cake from the cooling rack with two warm large spatulas (warm the spatulas in hot water so they won't stick to the cake). Place the cake on a large, round serving plate. Refrigerate, uncovered, for several hours or overnight.

TIPS

- Freeze the cake for an hour before slicing for even, less crumbly slices.
- When pouring over the last coating of glaze, do not leave empty spots; dribble some glaze over the spot with a tablespoon. Do not use a spatula.
- Do not cover the cake with plastic wrap or it will mark the cake; cover with a dome.

Tuscan Pastry Fritters

Cenci

They are called *chiacchiere* in Lombardy, *sfrappole* in Emilia-Romagna, *crostoli* in the Veneto, and *cenci* in Tuscany. These delicious pastry fritters can be made with flour, butter or oil, eggs, sugar, sweet wine or liqueur, grappa, or rum. The dough is rolled out into a large, thin sheet, then is shaped into ribbons, rectangles, or squares and fried until the pastry turns golden and puffy. My variation comes from Tuscany and uses olive oil instead of butter; dough is flavored with lemon juice, lemon zest, and *vin santo*, a delightful Tuscan dessert wine. Pastry fritters are typically made at Carnival, Christmas, New Year's, and Easter, but can occasionally be found at other times in some of the most traditional trattorie of Florence. ◆ *serves 8 to 10*

2 cups all-purpose flour

1/3 cup granulated sugar

2 large eggs

4 tablespoons extra-virgin olive oil

Grated zest and juice of 1 lemon

3 to 4 tablespoons *vin santo* or Amaretto di Saronno liqueur

Vegetable oil for deep-frying

Confectioners' sugar for dusting

In the bowl of a food processor fitted with the metal blade, combine the flour with the granulated sugar. Add the eggs, oil, lemon zest and juice, and *vin santo* or Amaretto. Pulse until the dough is loosely gathered around the blade. Remove the dough from the bowl and, with your hands, work it into 2 disks. Flour the disks lightly, wrap them in plastic, and refrigerate for 1 hour or overnight.

Using a rolling pin or a pasta machine, roll out one disk of dough into an 1/8-inch-thick sheet. (For very crisp fritters, the dough should be rolled out very thin.) Dust the dough and the work surface lightly with flour as you stretch it out.

Using a pastry wheel, cut the sheet of dough into rectangles 5 inches long and 3 inches wide. With the pastry wheel make a slit in the center of each rectangle and place them on a lightly floured baking sheet. Roll out the remaining dough in the same fashion.

Pour 2 to 3 inches of oil into a large, deep skillet or saucepan and place on medium-high heat. When the oil is nice and hot but not yet smoking (drop a piece of dough in the oil, if the oil sizzles immediately around the dough, the oil is ready), lower 3 to 4 rectangles at a time into the oil. Fry, turning once, until the pastries are golden on both sides. Remove with metal tongs and drain on paper towels.

When done, pile the fritters on a large platter and sprinkle generously with confectioners' sugar. Serve at room temperature.

The fritters can be made a few days ahead. Keep them at room temperature, uncovered, until ready to use.

THE WINES OF TUSCANY

Situated on the banks of the Arno River at the northern end of Tuscany, Florence is the spirit and heart of this region as well as the Renaissance capital of Italy. Here are a few of my favorite Tuscan wines.

CHIANTI CLASSICO AND CHIANTI

The wine known as Chianti Classico must come from that area of Tuscany comprising parts of the provinces of Florence and Siena, bordered by the suburbs of Florence, east by the Chianti hills, Siena, and the valleys of the Pesa and Elsa rivers; this is the original Chianti region, hence the term Chianti Classico. A wider geographic area, simply called Chianti, extends farther. Wines from this latter zone may be called simply Chianti, or Chianti with a subappellation, but may not be labeled Chianti Classico.

The appellation Chianti Classico denotes not only a strict geographic location but also a strict production code determining the amount and type of grapes used, alcohol content, and yield per acre. Sangiovese, the major grape variety in all Chianti, may range from 80 percent to 100 percent. Other local varietals such as *colorino* and *canaiolo*, as well as international varietals such as cabernet sauvignon, merlot, and syrah, may be added up to a maximum of 20 percent. "Reserve" and "single-vineyard" designations allow for a wide range of tastes, from soft, medium-bodied, easy-drinking wines to more complex and structured wines with a backbone of tannin and a zing of acidity. All are good accompaniments to Tuscan meat and game dishes.

My personal favorites are Chianti Classico from Antinori, Fonterutoli, Castello di Rampolla, Isole e Olena, Badia a Coltibuono, Castello di Ama, and San Felice. A Chianti Classico Riserva is perfect with Bistecca alla Fiorentina.

BRUNELLO DI MONTALCINO

The commune of Montalcino, south of Siena, gives rise to this dark, full-bodied, tannic red wine made exclusively from sangiovese. The name *brunello*, which roughly translates as the "little brown one," is used for the local variety of the grape. Generally a powerful, concentrated, and fruity red wine, with hints of violets and leather on the nose, and packing plenty of tannin, it has a warm and peppery mouthfeel and ages well. Its younger brother, Rosso di Montalcino, also 100 percent sangiovese, is a bit less concentrated, more subdued, approachable, and affordable. While it lacks the star quality of Brunello di Montalcino, the Rosso can be a most enjoyable wine. Either is a fine accompaniment to most Tuscan red meat dishes, roasts, game, or stews. My favorite brunello, consistently year to year, is Castello Banfi. The Poggio alle Mura from Banfi is a gem. Other fine producers include Poggione, Barbi, Col d'Orcia, Mastrojanni, and Biondi Santi.

SUPER TUSCANS

In the late 1960s and early 1970s, some Tuscan wine producers began experimenting with nontraditional grape varieties (cabernet sauvignon, cabernet franc, merlot, syrah) and use of smaller, new oak casts. The first such wine was released in 1968 by Mario Incisa della Rocchetta and was called Sassicaia, a powerful cabernet sauvignon from grapes grown near the town of Bolgheri, a nontraditional wine-growing region south of Livorno (Leghorn) near the Mediterranean coast. The wine was a huge success and the phrase "Super Tuscan" was born. Others followed. In 1971, Piero Antinori released his first Tignanello, a pure sangiovese from grapes grown in the Chianti Classico area, without the addition of the white grape varieties that were required at that time. These wines were labeled as *Vino da tavola* (table wine) because they did not conform to the then existing wine regulations. And so it began.

My favorites of the Super Tuscans are Sassicaia from Tenuta San Guido; Ornellaia, a blend of cabernet sauvignon, merlot, and cabernet franc, from Tenuta dell'Ornellaia; Guado al Tasso, a blend of cabernet sauvignon, merlot, and syrah from Antinori vineyards in Bolgheri; Cepparello, a pure sangiovese from Isole e Olena; and Tignanello, now predominantly sangiovese with varying amounts of cabernet sauvignon, from Antinori.

These are all serious wines to accompany hearty red meat or game dishes.

VIN SANTO

This unique dessert wine is produced from partially dried grapes in practically all the wine-producing areas of the region. When vin santo is produced from red grapes it is called *occhio di pernice* ("partridge's eye") due to its rosy color. The drier versions are delicious as an aperitivo; the sweeter versions are perfect with the classic dry Tuscan cookies called *cantucci* or biscotti.

OTHER WINES

Tuscany is blessed with a wide variety of wines, both red and white, that I cannot attempt to describe in these brief paragraphs. Vino Nobile di Montepulciano, Morellino di Scansano, Carmignano, Val di Cornia, Monteregio di Massa Marittima, and Vernaccia di San Gimignano, to name a few, are all excellent. Try them if you have the opportunity.

BOLOGNA

APPETIZERS

Crostini with Creamy Mortadella Mousse {*Crostini con la Spuma di Mortadella*}

Prosciutto, Figs, and Parmigiano with Balsamic Vinegar
   {*Prosciutto con Fichi e Parmigiano all'Aceto Balsamico*}

FIRST COURSES

Ricotta–Swiss Chard Tortelloni with Gorgonzola Sauce {*Tortelloni al Gorgonzola*}

Spinach Tagliatelle with Pork Ragù {*Tagliatelle Verdi con Ragù Bianco*}

Tagliatelle with Prosciutto-Tomato Sauce {*Tagliatelle con Prosciutto e Pomodoro*}

Tagliolini in Capon Broth {*Tagliolini in Brodo di Cappone*}

Garganelli with Sausage, Porcini, and Cream {*Garganelli con Salsiccia, Porcini, e Panna*}

Garganelli with Spring Peas and Fresh Tomatoes {*Garganelli con Piselli Novelli e Pomodori*}

Dante's Vegetable Risotto {*Il Risotto di Verdure di Dante*}

Potato Gnocchi with Classic Bolognese Ragù {*Gnocchi di Patate con Ragù alla Bolognese*}

ENTRÉES

The Veal Cutlets of Trattoria Battibecco {*Lombatine di Vitello del Battibecco*}

Veal Stew with Vegetables and Tomatoes {*Spezzatino di Vitello con Sugo di Verdure e Pomodoro*}

Roasted Chicken with Pancetta, Potatoes, and Herbs {*Pollo al Forno con Pancetta, Patatine, e Aglione*}

Pork Shoulder Braised in Milk {*Stracotto di Maiale al Latte*}

Bologna's Stuffed Pork Chops {*Braciole di Maiale alla Vecchia Bologna*}

Zampone Sausage with Braised Lentils {*Zampone con Lenticchie in Umido*}

Braised Rabbit with Prosciutto and Tomatoes {*Stufato di Coniglio con Prosciutto e Pomodoro*}

Stewed Tripe Bologna-Style {*Trippa in Umido alla Bolognese*}

Monkfish with White Wine, Tomatoes, and Basil {*Rana Pescatrice al Pomodoro e Basilico*}

Poached Salmon with Bolognese Salsa Verde {*Salmone Lesso con Salsa Verde Bolognese*}

VEGETABLES

Mixed Vegetables with Prosciutto, Butter, and Parmigiano
   {*Verdure Miste con Prosciutto, Burro, e Parmigiano*}

Fava Beans with Mortadella {*Fave con Mortadella*}

Sautéed Swiss Chard with Hot Pepper {*Bietole in Padella con il Peperoncino*}

DESSERTS

Apple Cake with Raisins and Almonds {*Torta di Mele con Uvetta e Mandorle*}

Parmigiano-Reggiano Ice Cream with Balsamic Vinegar {*Gelato di Parmigiano-Reggiano al Balsamico*}

Ricotta-Mascarpone Fritters {*Frittelle di Ricotta e Mascarpone*}

I am sitting at Caffè Vittorio Emanuele overlooking the

magnificent thirteenth-century Piazza Maggiore in the heart of Bologna, slowly savoring a decadent gelato while looking at the people who stroll by. The thickly columned porticoes shelter me from the summer sun. A flock of pigeons dives low to catch small pieces of bread thrown by children whose mothers sport fashionable outfits. Seated on the steps of the recently refurbished fourteenth-century Gothic cathedral of San Petronio, Bologna's patron saint, clusters of teenagers are basking in the sun while taking in the view of this great square that for many years now has been devoid of cars. From my vantage point, I can see every angle of the square: Palazzo Comunale (the town hall), with its Renaissance tower and gigantic weather-beaten clock; the Loggia del Pavaglione, the most elegant stretch of arcades of Bologna, with its cozy caffès and stylish boutiques and the marvelous fountain of Neptune surrounded by mermaids. These sights lift and soothe my spirits.

Welcome to Bologna, the city where I was born and raised, a food lover's paradise where great eating is as essential to life as is breathing. Bologna, the capital of Emilia-Romagna, one of Italy's wealthiest regions, lies in a luscious valley surrounded by rich farmland and the soft, green hills of the Apennine mountains. Located halfway between Florence and Venice, Bologna, a major city of about half a million residents, was originally built on the site of an Etruscan town called Felsina. When Felsina became a military colony of Rome in 192 B.C. the name changed to Bononia, and it later evolved to its present name.

Bologna has many names: *Bologna la grassa* ("the fat") because of the scrumptiousness of its food; *Bologna la rossa* ("the red") because of the terra-cotta color of its buildings; and *Bologna la dotta* ("the learned") because of its nine-hundred-year-old university, the oldest in the Western world, a university that since its inception has drawn large numbers of scholars from all over Europe. Bologna is also known as the city of porticoes: twenty miles of arcaded streets, many of them centuries old, lined with fashionable stores, caffès, restaurants, hotels, banks, movie theaters, museums, and offices, shelter the Bolognesi from the heat of summer and the harsh, wet months of winter. By walking under these porticoes one has access to medieval and Renaissance buildings whose large, heavy front doors open into stunning, beautiful gardens that belong to time past. The longest uninterrupted stretch of porticoes—and by far the most imposing—is at the Madonna di San Luca sanctuary at the top of the Colle della Guardia hill, which stretches uphill for more than two miles. Some of these porticoes, built in different centuries, are in their own right works of art.

And so is the city's center architecture, whose great historic buildings, baroque churches, monasteries, patrician palaces and towers, from different periods, showcase a rare collection of styles. Around the thirteenth century, Bologna had more than a hundred towers that had been built by the city's patrician families, who constructed them as a sign of prosperity and power. Today there are just twenty visible towers. The two most famous and important brick towers, the ones instantly identified with the city, are the Garisenda, which is 150 feet high and sharply leaning, and the Asinelli, 320 feet tall and one of the oldest towers built in Europe; some of these towers still house artisan workshops in their bases. The stunningly preserved medieval city center radiates outward along twelve long arcaded avenues, spaced equally apart, until they reach the twelve large gates that, connected by long brick walls, used to protect medieval Bologna from invaders. Within the walls of old Bologna you will discover small, comfortable piazzas; ancient churches; beautifully preserved buildings; small parks; and dazzling food markets. You will also discover that all these places are, amazingly, practically free of tourists.

Bologna is an active, modern, dynamic city that is very much in tune with the demands of the twenty-first century. And yet unlike other major Italian cities, Bologna has a very palpable human quality that makes a visitor feel immediately at home. (Just patronize a caffè or trattoria for a few days and the waiter and bartenders will greet you as warmly as an old friend.)

Bologna, just like Florence, is a small, compact city and a walker's paradise. Begin, as I do when I am in Bologna, by sitting in one of the caffès on Piazza Maggiore. Walk around this large square, which is often the setting for night concerts, plays, art exhibitions, and special cultural events. Explore the majestic cathedral, whose sculpted portal, much admired by Michelangelo, was built in the fifteenth century. Observe the clusters of older Bolognesi men in the middle of the square, passionately discussing politics, sport, food, and women. Then take Via Rizzoli, one of the most elegant central streets of Bologna, until you reach the feet of the two towers. If you are in good shape, climb the 500 narrow, rickety, centuries-old, worn steps of the Asinelli tower. (Most Bolognesi will tell you, unabashedly, that they have never climbed the tower, and have absolutely no desire to do so.) Marvel at the distinctive russet redbrick color of the city at your feet, a city that has expanded almost to reach the feet of the Apennine mountains.

On your second day, when your tired legs have regained their strength, take a leisurely walk under the porticoes until you reach the church and square of Santo Stefano, a compelling sight of seven churches tightly cloistered together by an architectural design that took centuries to complete. Check out the many museums, artisan shops, art galleries, and elegant boutiques in the center of town. Stroll under the Loggia del Pavaglione and stop at Zanarini, the most beautiful, historical caffè of the city, and order a gelato. Seek out the stunning "secret" hidden courtyards of Renaissance buildings that can take you magically back in time. When you are tired, sit in one of the small parks in the center of the city and observe the pulse and rhythm of a very beautiful, modern, human city.

And then there is the food, a food that is instantly associated with richness and succulence. I am very grateful for the good fortune to have been born and raised in Bologna, a city with a heritage of great food. If Bologna's cuisine had a symbol, it would be a large, thin, golden sheet of homemade pasta, a sheet so large that it would embrace and feed the whole region. This is the land of great stuffed pasta dishes such as tortellini, spinach lasagne, tortelloni, and tortelli. In many trattorie and restaurants of Bologna, these pastas are still made by the expert hands of the *sfoglina*, the restaurant's pasta maker, and are stuffed with a variety of hams, other meats, cheeses, or vegetables. It is also the land of homemade string pasta such as tagliolini, pappardelle, and golden tagliatelle, which are combined in a blissful union with rich, complex ragùs or with butter sauces lightly tinged with the sweet, locally produced tomato paste.

The first thing I want when I am in Bologna (after eating at my brother's house) is to head straight to Ristorante Diana or Ristorante Da Cesari for a plate of traditional pasta. Tortellini in capon broth, tagliatelle with Bolognese meat ragù, or succulent spinach lasagne will do. For my entrée, I must have the *cotoletta alla Bolognese,* a large slice of pale tender veal coated with bread crumbs, sautéed in butter until crisp, topped with prosciutto and Parmigiano, and simmered in wine and broth until the cheese is melted. And, if truffles are in season, I will ask for a generous shaving of white truffle over my cutlet.

Another dish that I must eat in Bologna is *bollito misto,* mixed boiled meats. A generation or so ago, this dish was standard fare in the restaurants, trattorie, and homes of the region, but today it can be found in only a handful of Bologna's traditional restaurants and trattorie. A waiter will come to your table pushing a steam trolley filled with a large variety of hot, mixed boiled meats—veal rump, beef brisket, capon, calf's tongue, *cotechino* sausage, and more—served with an array of traditional condiments and sauces.

Eating in Bologna is a voyage of endless discovery. The food can be hearty or delicate, complex or simple, and relies heavily on its generous use of butter and pork products, which find their way into innumerable dishes. Ingredients such as prosciutto di Parma, mortadella di Bologna, pancetta, sausages, balsamic vinegar, and Parmigiano-Reggiano are the undisputed jewels and the basic staples of the Bolognese kitchen. The best way to see all that Bologna's gastronomy has to offer is to take a long, leisurely stroll through its much-acclaimed food markets, especially Mercato delle Erbe, a large, enclosed market in the center of the city, and Mercato di Mezzo, the oldest and most important open market, probably the most beautiful in Italy.

(Today in several Italian cities the food markets often share spaces with merchants of trinkets, but in Bologna the food markets are all about food.) This is where my mother used to shop, every morning at dawn, for we lived in a two-hundred-year-old apartment building just a few blocks away. Nothing seems to have changed. Stall after stall is filled to capacity with splendid produce, fresh seafood still moving in their watery tanks, exotic fruits, fresh herbs and spices. There are cheese stores, fresh pasta and bread stores, butcher shops, poultry shops, and nice caffès where you can stop for a quick espresso and a sweet *cornetto*.

Then there is Tamburini, Bologna's most celebrated specialty food store, which entices you in with the powerful aroma of its food and the marvelous display of mouthwatering preparations.

Every time I am in Bologna I visit Tamburini and buy enough food to feed an army: seafood salads, roasted or stuffed vegetables, roasted lamb, homemade sausage, rosy mortadella, creamy *stracchino* cheese, and my very favorite treat, *crema fritta* (deep-fried cream), which I then carry to my brother's or sister's house for our noon meal. And I reconnect with Bologna, the city of my youth.

WHEN IN BOLOGNA
Food Markets, Specialty Food Stores, and Cooking Schools

From the U.S., dial 011, followed by the country code of 39. The area code for all numbers below is 051.

Al Regno della Forma
Via Oberdan 45
Tel. 233 609
A small shop that is a shrine to the large wheels of perfectly aged Parmigiano-Reggiano cheese of the region.

The International Cooking School of Italian Food and Wine, Bologna, Italy
201 East 28th Street, New York, NY 10016
Tel. 212-779-1921, fax 212-779-3248
For information in the United States, contact Mary Beth Clark.

Mercato delle Erbe
Via Ugo Bassi
The enclosed, cavernous Mercato delle Erbe, a great place to shop during the cold winter months, has a high concentration of free-standing stalls that offer a staggering abundance of food. Packed with Bolognesi, many of whom still shop daily to pick, smell, sort, and argue before buying. Closed Thursday afternoons.

Mercato di Mezzo or Mercato Centrale
Via Pescherie Vecchie
This is the oldest, most important open-air food market of Bologna. Situated in the heart of the city and nestled among the magnificent Piazza Maggiore, Via Clavature, Via Caprarie, and Via Orefici, this gorgeous medieval marketplace is a culinary mecca: stall after stall offers seasonal fresh produce and vegetables, and small specialty stores

showcase all kinds of meats, cheeses, hams, fish, breads, pastas, pastries, spices, and coffee. This is a magical, exuberant place, permeated by aromas that seduce you instantly. Closed Thursday afternoons.

Paolo Atti e Figli
Via Caprarie 7
Tel. 220 425
and
Via Drapperie 6
Tel. 233 349
Two locations, one name, and a family that in Bologna is an institution. For over 120 years, these two bread shops, with their legendary fresh pasta corners, their bakeries, and their gastronomic specialties, have delighted generations of Bolognesi.

Tamburini
Via Caprarie 1
Tel. 234 726
Tamburini is Bologna's most prominent specialty food store, and has been in the same family since 1932 nourishing the heart, soul, and belly of generations of Bolognesi with all kinds of prepared food, from hot and cold entrées to stuffed vegetables and a large assortment of salads, seafood salads, and glorious roasted meats. At one end of the store, rabbits, chickens, pork loin, leg of lamb, and a variety of birds are slowly cooked on a large spit, basted with aromatic branches of rosemary or sage. Elsewhere, you'll find rosy prosciutto di Parma, divine mortadella di Bologna, aged Parmigiano-Reggiano, ultra-creamy mascarpone, or fresh buffalo mozzarella. And don't forget to pick up some delicious *crema fritta*. For me, paradise is a shopping spree at Tamburini.

Crostini with Creamy Mortadella Mousse

Crostini con la Spuma di Mortadella

Ristorante Diana is a bastion of authentic Bolognese cuisine. It has been in the same location for over a century, serving tiny handmade tortellini in a rich capon broth, spinach tagliatelle paired with the classic Bolognese meat ragù, and *bollito misto* (mixed boiled meats), sliced steaming hot from a large cart and served with the classic *salsa verde*. Another delightful, traditional dish at Diana is the *spuma di mortadella*, a creamy mortadella mousse that is spread on crostini and served to greet customers as they sit down. Serve with white wine, sparkling wine, or a light aperitivo. ◆ *makes about 20 crostini*

1/2 pound mortadella, cut into 1 or 2 thick slices and diced

1/3 cup freshly grated Parmigiano-Reggiano

1/4 teaspoon freshly grated nutmeg

2/3 cup heavy cream

Salt to taste

20 slices crusty bread such as baguette

1/4 cup extra-virgin olive oil

2 tablespoons capers, coarsely chopped

2 tablespoons finely minced fresh chives

Put the mortadella, Parmigiano, and nutmeg in the bowl of a food processor fitted with the metal blade. Pulse until the mortadella is completely puréed. With the machine running, pour in the cream.

Place the mixture in a medium bowl, taste and adjust the seasoning, then cover with plastic wrap and refrigerate for an hour or two. Leave the mousse at room temperature for a half hour or so before serving.

Preheat the oven to 400°F. Brush the bread slices lightly on both sides with the oil and place on a baking sheet. Bake on the middle rack of the oven until the bread is golden. Turn and brown the other side, 3 to 4 minutes. (The bread can be toasted several hours ahead.)

Spread the mousse on the crostini and top with a bit of chopped capers and chives. (The capers and the chives can also be stirred into the mousse.)

Prosciutto, Figs, and Parmigiano with Balsamic Vinegar

Prosciutto con Fichi e Parmigiano all'Aceto Balsamico

This simple yet luscious appetizer pairs three of Emilia-Romagna's most loved ingredients: prosciutto di Parma, perhaps the world's finest ham; Parmigiano-Reggiano cheese, the king of the Italian cheeses; and luscious artisan-made balsamic vinegar. The mild saltiness of the prosciutto and the Parmigiano is tamed by the balsamic and fresh, ripe figs. In Bologna, this appetizing, hassle-free dish can be found in most eating establishments. ◆ *serves 4*

1/4 pound Parmigiano-Reggiano, cut into small chunks

1 tablespoon artisan-made balsamic vinegar (see note)

12 thin slices prosciutto di Parma

12 fresh figs, washed, dried, and halved or quartered

Place the Parmigiano in a bowl and toss with the balsamic. Arrange the prosciutto slices, slightly overlapping, on salad plates. Place a small mound of balsamic-coated Parmigiano in the center of each plate, fan 3 figs around it, and serve.

BALSAMIC VINEGAR

Balsamic vinegar is an aromatic, concentrated, nectar-like vinegar made from the boiled-down juices of the white trebbiano grape. It is a specialty of Modena and Reggio-Emilia, and its production and aging take decades. The boiled-down must of the grapes is reduced in a series of barrels of diminishing size and different woods, all of which gives a difference fragrance to the vinegar. During the aging process, the vinegar evaporates and concentrates, giving the balsamic its thick, velvety, highly aromatic quality. True artisanal balsamic bears the Modena consortium seal that reads *"Aceto Balsamico Tradizionale di Modena"* or *"di Reggio Emilia,"* and can be found in specialty food stores. While artisan-made balsamic is expensive, it should be used as a condiment, sparingly: a few drops added to grilled meats, Parmigiano, berries, or gelato. This product has absolutely nothing to do with commercially produced balsamic vinegar, which in many cases is made outside the designated area of Emilia-Romagna.

Ricotta–Swiss Chard Tortelloni with Gorgonzola Sauce

Tortelloni al Gorgonzola

One of the most delightful pasta dishes of Bologna is tortelloni: large pillows of handmade pasta stuffed with creamy ricotta cheese, nutmeg, Parmigiano-Reggiano, and chopped parsley, spinach, or chard. The traditional sauce for tortelloni, called *burro e oro*, is a lightly simmered mixture of tomatoes, butter, and cream.

However, at Anna Maria, a well-established trattoria in the center of Bologna, the plump tortelloni come to the table in a creamy, luscious sauce of sweet Gorgonzola cheese. I simply love them. ◆ *serves 4 to 6*

FOR THE TORTELLONI

2 cups fresh ricotta cheese, drained if needed (see note)

1 cup cooked, drained Swiss chard or spinach, finely chopped

$1/2$ cup freshly grated Parmigiano-Reggiano

1 large egg, lightly beaten

$1/2$ teaspoon freshly grated nutmeg

Salt to taste

$1/2$ recipe Basic Pasta Dough (page 301)

FOR THE SAUCE AND TO SERVE

$1/4$ pound sweet Gorgonzola cheese

$1 1/2$ cups heavy cream

$1/2$ cup Chicken Broth (page 298) or low-sodium canned chicken broth

1 tablespoon chopped fresh flat-leaf parsley

Salt to taste

1 tablespoon coarse salt

$1/2$ cup freshly grated Parmigiano-Reggiano

PREPARE THE TORTELLONI

In a large bowl, thoroughly combine the ricotta, Swiss chard, Parmigiano, egg, nutmeg, and salt. Taste and adjust the seasoning. Cover the bowl with plastic wrap and refrigerate until ready to use. (The filling can be prepared up to a day ahead.)

Cut a thin sheet of the dough into 3-inch squares. Place the filling into a pastry bag and pipe about 1 tablespoon in the center of each square. Fold the dough in half over the filling to form a triangle. Seal the dough around the filling, pressing the edges firmly together to seal. Combine the two pointed corners together and press to seal. Continue until all the filling and the pasta have been used up.

Cover a large tray with a clean kitchen towel and sprinkle some flour over it. Line the tortelloni in a single layer, leaving some space between them. The tortelloni can be used immediately or can be refrigerated, uncovered, for several hours.

PREPARE THE SAUCE

Put the Gorgonzola, cream, and broth in a 14-inch skillet over high heat. As soon as the cream begins to bubble, reduce the heat to medium high and cook, stirring with a wooden spoon, until the Gorgonzola is melted and the sauce has a medium-thick consistency, 5 to 7 minutes. Stir in the parsley and season with salt. Turn off the heat.

Meanwhile, bring a large pot of water to a boil over high heat. Add the coarse salt and the tortelloni and cook, stirring a few times with a wooden spoon, until the tortelloni are tender but still firm to the bite, 2 to 3 minutes.

Scoop up and reserve about ½ cup of the pasta cooking water. Carefully drain the tortelloni and place them in the skillet. Mix gently over medium heat until the pasta and sauce are well combined. If the sauce is too thick, add some of the cooking water. Taste, adjust the seasoning, and serve at once with a light sprinkle of Parmigiano.

RICOTTA

Ricotta, meaning "re-cooked," is a by-product of cow's, goat's, or sheep's milk. Leftover whey from daily cheese making is turned into a soft, lumpy, delicious cheese. The ricotta of Bologna and Emilia-Romagna is particularly sweet and creamy. American-made cow's-milk ricotta is often more watery than the Italian counterpart. In that case, place a strainer over a deep bowl. Line it with two layers of cheesecloth, and add the ricotta. Tie the cheesecloth to enclose the ricotta. Place some weight, such as two or three small plates, over the ricotta. Refrigerate overnight to drain.

Spinach Tagliatelle with Pork Ragù

Tagliatelle Verdi con Ragù Bianco

This delicious white-meat ragù, a lighter version of the traditional tomato-tinged Bolognese ragù, was a few decades ago quite popular in several of Bologna's oldest trattorie. Today it seems to have been almost completely forgotten. So when I found Spinach Tagliatelle with White Ragù on the menu of Sandro al Navile, a well-known restaurant on the outskirts of Bologna, I ordered it immediately. The tagliatelle had that special porous texture typical of pasta made by hand, and were coated with a delicious, light creamy ragù and topped with two-year-old grated Parmigiano-Reggiano. It was love at first bite. This recipe makes about twice as much ragù as you'll need for the pasta; freeze the rest for another time. ◆ *serves 4 to 6*

5 tablespoons unsalted butter

2 ounces sliced pancetta, chopped

1/2 cup finely minced yellow onion

1/2 cup finely minced carrot

1/2 cup finely minced celery stalk

2 pounds ground pork butt or pork shoulder

1/4 pound sliced prosciutto, chopped
Salt and freshly ground black pepper to taste

1/2 cup dry white wine

1 tablespoon double-concentrated Italian tomato paste

1 cup Chicken Broth (page 298) or low-sodium canned chicken broth

2 to 3 cups whole milk

1 tablespoon coarse salt

1 recipe Basic Spinach Pasta Dough (page 303), rolled out and cut into tagliatelle, or 1 pound imported dried tagliatelle

1/2 to 3/4 cup freshly grated Parmigiano-Reggiano

Heat 4 tablespoons of the butter in a heavy, wide-bottomed saucepan over medium heat. When the butter begins to foam, add the pancetta, onion, carrot, and celery and cook, stirring with a wooden spoon, until the mixture is soft and lightly golden, about 10 minutes.

Raise the heat to high. Add the pork and prosciutto and season with salt and pepper. Cook, breaking up the meat with the wooden spoon, until the meat is lightly golden, 8 to 10 minutes. Add the wine. Cook and stir, scraping the bottom of the pan with a wooden spoon, until the wine is reduced approximately by half. In a medium bowl, combine the tomato paste with the broth, and whisk to combine. Add this mixture to the saucepan with just enough milk to barely cover the meat; set aside the remaining milk. As soon as the liquid begins to bubble, reduce the heat to the barest simmer, partially cover the pan, and cook, stirring from time to time and checking the ragù every 30 minutes or so, for 1½ to 2 hours. At the end of cooking, the sauce should be thick and creamy, with a moist but not liquid consistency. If the sauce reduces too much during cooking, add a little more milk. Taste, adjust the seasoning, and turn off the heat. (The ragù can be prepared several hours or a day ahead. Refrigerate tightly covered.)

Bring a large pot of water to a boil over high heat. Add the coarse salt and the tagliatelle, and cook until the pasta is tender but still firm to the bite. Drain and place in a large heated bowl. Add the remaining tablespoon of butter, about half of the sauce, and a nice handful of the Parmigiano. Toss quickly until the pasta and sauce are well combined. Place the pasta in serving bowls and top it with a tablespoon or two of additional ragù. Serve at once with the remaining Parmigiano on the side.

AN ADDITIONAL BURST OF FLAVOR

In Bologna, pasta that is served with a meat sauce is occasionally boiled in an aromatic meat or chicken broth instead of water. When the pasta is drained and tossed with the sauce, the dish takes on a whole new, delicious dimension.

Tagliatelle with Prosciutto-Tomato Sauce

Tagliatelle con Prosciutto e Pomodoro

This is a traditional sauce of Bologna that will never go out of style, because it is thick and absolutely delicious. Butter, prosciutto, tomatoes, and just a touch of cream cook together for a short amount of time and become the perfect creamy accompaniment for fresh pasta. If you are using homemade pasta, be sure to undercook it a little, because it will continue cooking when it is tossed in the skillet with the sauce.

• *serves 4 to 6*

4 tablespoons ($^{1}/_{2}$ stick) unsalted butter

5 ounces thickly sliced prosciutto, diced

1 (28-ounce) can Italian plum tomatoes, preferably San Marzano (see note, page 35), with their juices, put through a food mill to remove the seeds

Salt to taste

2 to 3 tablespoons heavy cream

1 tablespoon coarse salt

1 recipe Basic Pasta Dough (page 301), rolled out and cut into tagliatelle, or 1 pound imported dried tagliatelle

$^{1}/_{2}$ cup freshly grated Parmigiano-Reggiano

Heat 3 tablespoons of the butter in a large skillet over medium heat. When the butter begins to foam, add the prosciutto and cook, stirring, until it turns lightly golden, 2 to 3 minutes. Add the tomatoes and season with salt. As soon as the tomatoes come to a boil, reduce the heat to low and simmer, uncovered, until the sauce has a medium-thick consistency, 8 to 10 minutes. Add the cream and the remaining tablespoon of butter, stir for a minute or two, then turn off the heat.

Meanwhile, bring a large pot of water to a boil over high heat. Add the coarse salt and the tagliatelle and cook until the pasta is tender but still firm to the bite. Drain the pasta and add it to the skillet. Add about half of the Parmigiano and stir quickly over medium heat until the pasta and sauce are well combined. Taste, adjust the seasoning, and serve with the remaining Parmigiano on the side.

Tagliolini in Capon Broth

Tagliolini in Brodo di Cappone

If you walk into a restaurant or trattoria in Bologna that serves tortellini or tagliolini in broth, please order it. You will have stumbled upon one of the most remarkable, traditional soups of the city—and a soup that can be prepared completely ahead: Make the broth a few days ahead, and the tagliolini the day before. Then, at the last minute, cook the tagliolini in this fragrant, homemade broth. ◆ *serves 4 to 6*

10 cups Capon Broth (page 297) or Chicken Broth (page 298)

$^1/_2$ recipe Basic Pasta Dough (page 301) rolled out and cut into tagliolini, or $^1/_2$ pound imported dried tagliolini

$^1/_2$ cup freshly grated Parmigiano-Reggiano

Put the broth in a large pot and bring to a gentle boil over medium heat. Add the tagliolini and cook, uncovered, until the pasta is tender but still a bit firm to the bite. Turn off the heat and let the soup rest for a few minutes.

Ladle the soup into individual serving bowls and serve with a sprinkle of freshly grated Parmigiano.

Garganelli with Sausage, Porcini, and Cream

Garganelli con Salsiccia, Porcini, e Panna

The entrance of Ristorante Da Nello is so small that if the glass door didn't showcase a large table full of fresh seasonal ingredients, you could pass by and completely miss this centrally located, quaint restaurant, which has been in the same family for several generations. This humble place is a favorite of the Bolognesi; its food is as traditionally Bolognese as possible, except for one dish, *gramigna* with sausage and cream. Gramigna, a short, somewhat curly fresh Bolognese egg pasta (made by pressing the dough through a small hand-operated extruder), is paired with a sauce of sausage, dried porcini mushrooms, and lots of cream. The owners created this dish in 1948, just a few years after the Second World War, so that after years of deprivation, diners could luxuriate without guilt in a rich, decadent dish. Cream is used sparingly in Bolognese cooking, but this dish still draws legions of fans. Because gramigna is not available in the United States, *garganelli*, a small grooved maccheroni, is used for this dish. ◆ *serves 4 to 6*

I ounce dried porcini mushrooms, soaked in 2 cups lukewarm water for 20 minutes

4 tablespoons ($^1/_2$ stick) unsalted butter

3 medium shallots, finely minced

$^1/_2$ pound mild Italian pork sausage (containing no fennel seeds, chili pepper, or other spices)

$^1/_2$ cup dry white wine

I to I$^1/_2$ cups heavy cream

Salt and white pepper to taste

I tablespoon coarse salt

I pound imported dried *garganelli* or penne rigate

$^1/_2$ cup freshly grated Parmigiano-Reggiano

I tablespoon chopped fresh flat-leaf parsley

Strain the mushrooms and reserve the soaking water for another use. Rinse the mushrooms well under cold running water, then chop them into small pieces.

Heat 3 tablespoons of the butter in a large skillet over medium heat. As soon as the butter begins to foam, add the shallots and cook, stirring, until lightly golden and soft, 5 to 6 minutes. Raise the heat to high and add the sausage. Cook, stirring and breaking up the sausage with a wooden spoon, until it is lightly golden, 7 to 8 minutes. Add the porcini mushrooms, and stir with the sausage for 2 to 3 minutes.

Add the wine. When the wine is almost all evaporated, add the cream. Season with salt and a bit of white pepper. When the cream begins to bubble, reduce the heat to medium low and simmer, uncovered, stirring occasionally, until the sauce has a medium-thick consistency, about 10 minutes.

Meanwhile, bring a large pot of water to a boil over high heat. Add the coarse salt and the *garganelli,* and cook until the pasta is tender but still firm to the bite. Scoop up and reserve about $1/2$ cup of the pasta cooking water.

Drain the pasta and add it to the sauce. Add the remaining tablespoon of butter, a nice handful of Parmigiano, and the parsley. Stir quickly over medium heat until the pasta and sauce are well combined. If the pasta seems a bit dry, stir in some of the reserved pasta water. Taste, adjust the seasoning, and serve with the remaining Parmigiano on the side.

THE BOLOGNESE TABLE

APPETIZERS

Insalata di Porcini: Fresh porcini salad.

Spuma di Mortadella: A creamy mortadella mousse spread over crostini.

Parmigiano al Balsamico: Chunks of Parmigiano-Reggiano sprinkled with a few drops of aged balsamic vinegar, served alone or in conjunction with cured meats.

Salumi Misti: Mixed, cured meats such as prosciutto di Parma, mortadella di Bologna, culatello, or other cured sausages are traditionally served alone or in combination as the opening of a Bolognese meal.

FIRST COURSES

Gramigna: A short, somewhat curly homemade pasta that is traditionally paired with a luscious sauce of sausage, cream, butter, and tomatoes.

Lasagne Verdi: Spinach pasta layered with Bolognese meat sauce, béchamel sauce, and Parmigiano.

Passatelli: Strand-shaped pieces of an egg-Parmigiano bread-crumb dough.

Tagliatelle Verdi: Homemade string-shaped spinach pasta often topped with a Bolognese meat ragù.

Tortellini: Very small rings of homemade pasta stuffed with ground pork, veal, prosciutto, mortadella, Parmigiano, and nutmeg. Served in a flavorful broth or with a sauce.

Tortelloni: Large pillows of homemade pasta stuffed with spinach or Swiss chard, ricotta, and Parmigiano.

ENTRÉES

Bollito Misto: Mixed boiled meats, sliced thin and served with *salsa verde*.

Carrello degli Arrosti: Mixed roasted meats carved at the table.

Coniglio alla Cacciatora: Rabbit braised with prosciutto, wine, and tomatoes.

Cotechino: A large, boiled pork sausage served with mashed potatoes or stewed lentils. Cotechino is also served with mixed boiled meats.

Cotoletta alla Bolognese: Breaded veal cutlet topped with prosciutto and Parmigiano.

Grigliata Mista: Mixed grill of fish or meats.

Trippa alla Parmigiana: Stewed tripe cooked with tomatoes and Parmigiano.

Zampone: Pig's-foot sausage, stuffed with minced pork and spices and boiled. Served with mashed potatoes or lentils.

VEGETABLES AND SALADS

Insalate Miste di Stagione: Mixed seasonal greens.

Piselli al Prosciutto: Peas with prosciutto.

Pomodoro e Melanzane Gratinate: Baked tomatoes and eggplant with butter and Parmigiano.

Verdure alla Griglia: Grilled vegetables.

DESSERTS

Carrello dei Dolci: Assorted desserts and pastries presented on a rolling cart.

Macedonia: Mixed fruit salad.

Torta di Mele: Apple cake.

Torta di Riso: Rice cake.

SOME BASIC INGREDIENTS

Aceto Balsamico: Luscious artisan-made Balsamic Vinegar from the provinces of Modena and Reggio-Emilia.

Burro: The creamy, unsalted butter of Bologna is a vital ingredient to the many pasta sauces of the region and to luscious dishes such as the Cotoletta alla Bolognese.

Concentrato di Pomodoro: The intensely flavored, locally produced sweet tomato paste is used for Bologna's faintly red-colored sauces.

Culatello: The most prized ham of the region, used mainly as a delectable antipasto.

Erbe: In the cooking of Bologna, fresh herbs are used frugally as an accent, and they seldom dominate a dish.

Formaggio di Fossa: A cheese of Romagna that is aged in ditches lined with straw.

Mortadella: The most famous Bolognese pork sausage. Served thinly sliced, alone or with other cured meats. It is a vital ingredient in the filling of Bologna's famed tortellini.

Olio Vergine d'Oliva: When butter is not used, extra-virgin olive oil is the fat of choice.

Pancetta: Unsmoked, cured Italian bacon whose importance in the Bolognese kitchen is surpassed only by that of prosciutto and butter.

Parmigiano-Reggiano: A cow's-milk cheese that has been made by artisans for seven centuries. It is impossible to imagine the cooking of the region without it.

Pomodori: Tomatoes, fresh or canned, are used for sauces.

Porcini Freschi: In Bologna fresh, wild porcini are used in pasta stuffings, risottos, sauces, stews, and salads.

Porcini Secchi: Dry porcini have a highly concentrated, musky aroma and flavor. A handful of reconstituted dried porcini can enrich pasta sauces and pasta stuffings, risottos, soups, stews, and braised meats.

Prosciutto di Parma: Unsmoked, salted, air-cured ham made in the Parma region's hills and used extensively in the cooking of Bologna.

Strutto: Lard. In the countryside of Bologna, some traditional dishes are still made with lard. It is firm and can even be sliced.

Garganelli with Spring Peas and Fresh Tomatoes

Garganelli con Piselli Novelli e Pomodori

Garganelli are small, grooved maccheroni that are typical of Emilia-Romagna. Once, this lovely pasta was made religiously by hand at home and in restaurants and trattorie. In Bologna the most typical restaurants would have their *sfoglina*, pasta maker, make pasta such as garganelli, tagliatelle, and tiny tortellini in full view of their patrons. Today these priceless women have almost all disappeared, and only a handful of restaurants in Bologna pride themselves on having a sfoglina in their kitchens. Luckily, though, this type of pasta is now commercially made by Barilla and other large pasta companies, and it can be found in Italian specialty food stores. This is one of the delicious dishes of Trattoria Battibecco in Bologna that highlights their simple cooking philosophy: get the best, freshest ingredients, and use them in a simple, uncluttered way. This dish is very simple and very, very good. ◆ *serves 4*

Salt

1 pound unshelled fresh peas, or a 10-ounce package frozen peas

4 tablespoons ($^1/_2$ stick) unsalted butter

$^1/_4$ pound thickly sliced pancetta, diced

$^1/_2$ small yellow onion, minced (about $^1/_2$ cup)

$^1/_2$ cup dry white wine

1 pound ripe plum tomatoes, peeled, seeded, and diced (see note, page 27), or 2 cups canned plum tomatoes, minced with their juices

Freshly ground black pepper to taste

$^1/_2$ pound dried garganelli (see note, opposite) or penne rigate

$^1/_2$ cup freshly grated Parmigiano-Reggiano

Bring a small saucepan with salted water to a boil and add the peas. Cook until the peas are tender but still a bit firm to the bite, 2 to 4 minutes, depending on size. Drain and set aside.

Heat 3 tablespoons of the butter in a large skillet over medium heat. When the butter begins to foam, add the pancetta and the onion and cook, stirring, until lightly golden and soft, 4 to 5 minutes. Add the wine and cook, stirring, until the wine is reduced approximately by half. Add the tomatoes, season with salt and pepper, and cook, stirring, until the tomatoes have softened and their juices have thickened, 5 to

6 minutes. Add the peas and the remaining tablespoon of butter and stir for a minute or two. Taste and adjust the seasoning.

Meanwhile, bring a large pot of water to a boil. Add 1 tablespoon of salt and the garganelli and cook, uncovered, until the pasta is tender but still firm to the bite. Scoop up about $1/2$ cup of the pasta cooking water and set aside. Drain the pasta and add it to the sauce. Add a small handful of Parmigiano and stir for a minute or two, until the pasta and sauce are well combined. Add a bit of the reserved pasta water if the sauce seems a bit dry. Taste, adjust the seasoning, and serve with the remaining Parmigiano on the side.

NOTE

Garganelli seem to have a penchant for multiplying after they are cooked. For this reason I have listed here only $1/2$ pound of pasta, which gives 4 nice servings of cooked pasta.

Dante's Vegetable Risotto

Il Risotto di Verdure di Dante

Once upon a time Bologna had Dante, a great restaurant that served not only the traditional food of the city possibly better than anybody else, but also dishes of fantasia. Dante's creativity in the kitchen was matched only by that of his wife, Vittoria. After twenty or so years of successful partnership, Vittoria got seriously ill. Dante, to be close to her, closed the restaurant. After several years, Dante reemerged solo on Bologna's restaurant scene and opened Papa Rè. When I visited him in his new establishment, it was as if time had stood still: we were two old friends sharing stories, drinking, eating, and reminiscing about the old days. This is one of Dante's splendid risottos, originally created by Vittoria. In her honor, he keeps it consistently on his menu. ✦ *serves 4 to 6*

FOR THE VEGETABLES

Salt

1 small carrot, diced (about $1/3$ cup)

1 small celery stalk, diced (about $1/3$ cup)

$1/2$ cup fresh shelled green peas, or frozen small peas, thawed

$1/4$ pound fresh spinach, stems and bruised leaves discarded, thoroughly washed

FOR THE RISOTTO

6 cups Vegetable Broth (page 299) or canned low-sodium chicken broth

$1/2$ ounce dried porcini mushrooms, soaked in lukewarm water for 20 minutes

4 tablespoons ($1/2$ stick) unsalted butter

2 medium shallots, finely minced

1 ($1/8$-inch-thick) slice of prosciutto, finely diced

2 cups Arborio, Carnaroli, or Vialone Nano rice

1 cup dry white wine

3 tablespoons heavy cream

$1/2$ cup freshly grated Parmigiano-Reggiano

PREPARE THE VEGETABLES

Fill a small saucepan halfway with water and bring to a boil. Add a pinch of salt with the carrot and celery, and cook over medium heat until tender, 3 to 5 minutes. Drain, cool under cold running water, and set aside

If using fresh peas, cook them in another small saucepan halfway filled with salted boiling water until tender but still firm to the bite, 3 to 5 minutes depending on size. Drain, cool under cold running water, and set aside.

Bring 1 cup of water to a boil in a medium pot. Add a pinch of salt and the spinach and cook, uncovered, until the spinach is thoroughly wilted, 2 to 3 minutes. Drain in a colander and cool under cold running water. Purée the spinach in a food processor with a few tablespoons of water if needed. Set aside. (The vegetables can be prepared up to this point several hours ahead.)

PREPARE THE RISOTTO

Heat the broth in a medium saucepan and keep warm over low heat. Drain and rinse the mushrooms. Chop them into small pieces and set aside.

Melt 3 tablespoons of the butter in a large skillet over medium heat. When the butter begins to foam, add the shallots and cook, stirring, until lightly golden and soft, 5 to 6 minutes. Add the prosciutto and reserved mushrooms, stir for a couple of minutes, then add the rice. Cook, stirring constantly, until the rice is translucent and well coated with the savory base, 2 to 3 minutes. Add the wine and stir until the wine is almost all evaporated.

Now begin adding the broth, 1 cup or so at a time, or just enough to barely cover the rice. Stir until most of the broth has been absorbed. Continue cooking and stirring in this manner, adding a small ladle of broth at a time, for about 15 minutes.

Add the reserved carrot, celery, peas, and puréed spinach to the rice. Stir for a couple of minutes. Add the remaining tablespoon of butter, the cream, and about ¼ cup of the Parmigiano. Mix quickly for a few minutes, until the butter and cheese have melted and the rice has a moist, creamy consistency. Taste, adjust the seasoning, and serve at once, with the remaining Parmigiano on the side.

Potato Gnocchi with Classic Bolognese Ragù

Gnocchi di Patate con Ragù alla Bolognese

Potato gnocchi, a classic dish of many Italian regions, is very much at home in Bologna, where it is combined with a variety of luscious sauces. One of the best combinations—and a favorite of mine—is the pairing of plump yet light gnocchi with a rich Bolognese ragù. While the making of the potato gnocchi is basic, and traditionally does not change much from area to area, the making of the Bolognese ragù has many permutations. Although the Accademia della Cucina Italiana issued a decree of what constitutes the most typical Bolognese ragù, each Bolognese loves to think he or she is the only maker of the real ragù. The base of chopped onion, carrot, and celery that browns slowly in butter and oil is always the same, but the type of meat and liquid used changes from cook to cook. At Caminetto d'Oro, a very small trattoria in the center of town, I was served gnocchi that were tossed with a lusciously rich ragù of pork, veal, chicken livers, pancetta, and prosciutto. The addition of a little milk in the sauce gave the ragù a velvety, delicate taste.

In Bologna, this ragù is also paired with spinach tagliatelle (the most classic combination), garganelli, penne, and rigatoni. This recipe makes about twice as much ragù as you'll need for the gnocchi; freeze the rest. ◆ *serves 4 to 6*

2 tablespoons extra-virgin olive oil

3 tablespoons unsalted butter

2 ounces sliced pancetta, finely chopped

1 small onion, finely minced (about 1/2 cup)

1 small carrot, finely minced (about 1/2 cup)

1 small celery stalk, finely minced (about 1/2 cup)

1/4 pound chicken livers, finely chopped

1 pound ground pork butt or pork shoulder

1 pound lean ground veal

1/4 pound sliced prosciutto di Parma, finely chopped

Salt and freshly ground black pepper to taste

1/2 cup dry white wine

1 cup whole milk

3 cups Meat Broth (page 298) or canned low-sodium chicken broth

3 tablespoons double-concentrated Italian tomato paste

1 tablespoon coarse salt

1 recipe Basic Potato Gnocchi (page 304)

1/2 cup freshly grated Parmigiano-Reggiano

Heat the oil and 2 tablespoons of the butter in a large, heavy, wide-bottomed saucepan over medium heat. When the butter begins to foam, add the pancetta, onion, carrot, and celery and cook, stirring with a wooden spoon, until the mixture is soft and lightly golden, about 10 minutes.

Raise the heat to high and add the chicken livers. Stir for about 1 minute, then add the pork, veal, and prosciutto. Season with salt and pepper, and cook, breaking up the meat with the wooden spoon, until the meat is lightly golden, 8 to 10 minutes.

Add the wine and cook, stirring and scraping the bottom of the pan with the wooden spoon, until the wine is almost all evaporated. Add the milk and bring to a simmer. Cook, stirring, until the milk is reduced by approximately half.

In a large bowl, whisk together the broth and tomato paste. Add to the saucepan as soon as the liquid begins to bubble, reduce the heat to the barest simmer, partially cover the pan, and cook, stirring from time to time, checking the ragù every 30 minutes or so, for $1\frac{1}{2}$ to 2 hours. At the end of cooking, the sauce should be thick with a rich brown color. If the sauce reduces too much, add a little more milk, broth, or water. Taste, adjust the seasoning, and turn off the heat. (The ragù can be prepared several hours or a day ahead. Refrigerate, tightly covered.)

Bring a large pot of water to a boil over high heat. Add the coarse salt and the gnocchi. Cook, uncovered, until the gnocchi rise to the surface, about 2 minutes. After another 30 seconds or so, remove the gnocchi with a large slotted spoon, draining the excess water back into the pot. Place the gnocchi in a large, heated bowl.

Add the remaining tablespoon of butter, about half of the ragù, and a nice handful of the Parmigiano. Toss quickly until the gnocchi and sauce are well combined. Place the gnocchi in serving bowls and top with a tablespoon or two of additional ragù. Serve at once with the remaining Parmigiano on the side.

The Via Emilia, or state highway 9 (SS 9), cuts a straight line across Emilia-Romagna, from Piacenza in the northwest tip, southeast over 250 kilometers, to Rimini on the Adriatic coast. It geographically divides the region into two distinct areas: to the north, the fertile flatlands or plains of the Po River valley; and to the south, the hill country renowned for prosciutto and Parmigiano, and home to most of the major vineyards. I shall briefly describe several major wines and wine areas, starting from Piacenza in the Emilia side and ending in the Romagna hills.

Many wines from Emilia-Romagna, both white and red, can be still or slightly bubbly (*frizzante*), dry or off-dry (*amabile*), or even sweet. The majority of these regional wines are consumed locally, although some make it to the United States.

COLLI PIACENTI

Under this appellation are a variety of reds and whites, including cabernet sauvignon, chardonnay, barbera, ortrugo, pinot grigio, and pinot nero. The wine I think typifies the best from this area is Gutturnio, a dry red made from two grape varieties, barbera and croatina. A medium-bodied wine, it is soft, smooth, and velvety, and accompanies most red meat and game dishes; some prefer a Gutturnio with pasta. La Tosa is an excellent producer, and the Gutturnio Vignamorello is exceptionally good.

LAMBRUSCO

The frothy, purplish beverage known as Lambrusco to most Americans is sweet and cola-like, while in Italy it is usually dry and frizzante. Lambrusco vineyards, found mainly in the flatlands in the provinces of Reggio Emilia and Modena, provide the four varieties: Lambrusco di Sorbara, Grasparossa di Castelvetro, Salamino di Santacroce, and Reggiano. Usually consumed with antipasti, *salumi*, or white meats, Lambrusco is a wonderful accompaniment to *bolliti misti* or *tortellini al ragù*.

COLLI BOLOGNESI

In the hills to the southwest of Bologna, the Colli Bolognesi appellation includes both reds and whites ranging from albana and chardonnay to barbera and merlot. Many of these wines are simple and straightforward, meant for early consumption. Some are exceptionally good: I particularly enjoy the cabernet sauvignon from this area, especially the Rosso di Enrico Vallania from the Vigneto delle Terre Rosse, located in Zola Predosa, the outskirts of Bologna. The wine is unoaked, a rare treat nowadays, and can accompany almost any pasta or meat dish from Bologna.

SANGIOVESE DI ROMAGNA

This is the red wine of the region—both the everyday red and the special-occasion *riserva*. Sangiovese di Romagna is generally a tad lighter in flavor and body than the Tuscan variety, but in recent years, many wine producers, working with different clones, have made outstanding wines to rival those of the neighboring region to the south. In Bologna, one drinks sangiovese with either pasta or meat dishes. Although many sangiovese-based wines can be pedestrian, some are truly divine: I particularly enjoy the Sangiovese di Romagna Le More (unoaked) from Castelluccio, and the slightly oaked Ronco delle Ginestre from the same producer. My husband and I don't always agree on wine, but we consistently find the Umberto Cesari Sangiovese wines to be right on the mark— varietally fresh, well balanced, and with a solid structure. The Liano, a blend of sangiovese (70 percent) and cabernet sauvignon (30 percent), is also one of our favorites. Other fine producers include Fattoria Paradiso and Fattoria Zerbina.

ALBANA DI ROMAGNA

This white wine has a straw color, a hint of almonds on the nose, and a brisk acidity. The dry version is best suited for fish-based antipasti. An Albana *passito*, a dessert wine called the Scacco Matto from Fattoria Zerbina, is really a treat.

The Veal Cutlets of Trattoria Battibecco

Lombatine di Vitello del Battibecco

One of my favorite eating places in Bologna is Trattoria Battibecco, an understated, elegant establishment that serves terrific food. The chef-owner is Nico Costa, a fifty-something dynamo who cooks like an angel. His wife, Giuliana, tends to the front of the house and pampers her clients just like a doting mother would. When I asked Nico if he could contribute a recipe for my new book, he gladly gave me this one, which, he said, was his adaptation of the classic *cotoletta alla Bolognese.* His variation takes a thick slice of milk-fed veal, dredges it in grated Parmigiano, dips it in beaten eggs, coats it with bread crumbs, and fries it until crisp. He then covers it with prosciutto di Parma and fontina cheese and simmers it for a few minutes in a reduction of cream, butter, and broth until the cheese is melted. A luscious, delicious Bolognese dish that takes only a few minutes to prepare. ◆ *serves 4*

I pound boneless veal loin, cut into 4 thick slices

I cup freshly grated Parmigiano-Reggiano

I 1/2 cups fine dried bread crumbs

2 large eggs, beaten in a bowl with a pinch of salt

1/3 cup extra-virgin olive oil

2 tablespoons unsalted butter

1/4 cup heavy cream

1/4 cup Chicken Broth (page 298) or low-sodium canned chicken broth

4 thin slices prosciutto di Parma (about 1/4 pound)

4 thin slices Fontina cheese (2 to 3 ounces)

Place the veal slices between 2 pieces of plastic wrap. With a meat mallet, pound the slices until they are approximately 1/4 inch thick.

Spread the Parmigiano and bread crumbs on 2 sheets of aluminum foil. Coat the veal slices with the Parmigiano, pressing the cheese into the meat with the palms of your hands. Dip the cutlets quickly into the beaten eggs, then coat with the bread crumbs. Press the crumbs into the meat with your hands. Place the cutlets on a large platter and refrigerate, uncovered, for I hour.

Heat the oil in a large nonstick pan over medium-high heat. When the oil is nice and hot, add the cutlets without crowding. Cook, turning once, until they have a nice golden crust, about 2 minutes on each side. Drain on paper towels.

Discard the oil in the skillet, wipe it clean with paper towels, and return it to medium-low heat. Add the butter, cream, and broth, season lightly with salt, and simmer until it begins to thicken, 1 to 2 minutes.

Meanwhile place a slice of prosciutto and a slice of Fontina over each cutlet. Add the cutlets to the simmering sauce, prosciutto-fontina facing up. Cover the skillet and cook for a minute or two, or until the cheese is melted.

Place the cutlets on serving dishes. If needed, reduce the sauce over high heat until thick. Dribble a little sauce over each cutlet and serve hot.

PREPARING AHEAD

One hour before you want to serve, bread and fry the cutlets, top them with the Parmigiano and the Fontina, and lay them on a sheet pan. Finish the dish at the very last moment.

Veal Stew with Vegetables and Tomatoes

Spezzatino di Vitello con Sugo di Verdure e Pomodoro

In Bologna, veal, pork, or lamb are often cooked with a savory base of onion, pancetta or prosciutto, wine, broth, and occasionally tomatoes. Often, other ingredients are added to a stew (my mother used to add leftover roasted potatoes during the last minutes of cooking). But no matter what goes into the pot, the most important trick for making this delightful winter dish lies in its slow, long cooking, which allows the meat to become fork-tender. A great homey dish that can be found in one variation or another in many of Bologna's trattorie. • *serves 4*

3 tablespoons unsalted butter

3 tablespoons extra-virgin olive oil

1 small yellow onion, minced (about 1 cup)

2 to 3 ounces thickly sliced pancetta, diced

2 medium carrots, peeled and cut into $^1/_2$-inch rounds

2 celery stalks, washed and cut into $^1/_2$-inch pieces

2 pounds boneless veal cross ribs or shoulder, trimmed of fat and cut into 2-inch pieces

1 cup all-purpose flour

   Salt and freshly ground black pepper to taste

1 cup dry white wine

$^1/_2$ cup canned Italian plum tomatoes, preferably San Marzano (see note, page 35), with their juices, put through a food mill to remove the seeds

2 cups Chicken Broth (page 298) or low-sodium canned chicken broth

Preheat the oven to 350°F.

Heat the butter and oil in a large ovenproof skillet or wide-bottomed heat-proof casserole (one with a lid) over medium heat. When the butter begins to foam, add the onion and cook, stirring, until lightly golden and soft, about 5 minutes. Add the pancetta, carrots, and celery and stir until the pancetta and vegetables begin to color, 2 to 3 minutes. With a slotted spoon, scoop up the vegetables, draining the fat back into the skillet, and transfer to a bowl.

Return the skillet to medium-high heat. Place the veal in a large, fine-meshed strainer over a bowl. Sprinkle the meat with the flour, shaking the strainer to distribute the flour evenly. Working in batches, add the veal to the skillet and brown on all sides, 6 to 7 minutes. Season with salt and pepper.

With a slotted spoon, transfer the veal to the vegetable bowl. Discard most of the fat in the skillet and return it to high heat. Add the wine. Cook, stirring and scraping the bottom of the pan with a wooden spoon to pick up the flavorful brown bits attached to the bottom. When the wine is reduced approximately by half, return the veal and vegetables to the pan and stir for a minute or two. Add the tomatoes and broth and bring to a boil. Turn off the heat, cover the skillet with aluminum foil and its lid, and place it on the center rack of the oven. Cook, stirring, and turning the meat from time to time, until the veal is tender and begins to flake when pricked with a fork, about 1½ hours. Taste and adjust the seasoning. Let the stew sit for 15 to 20 minutes before serving.

Roasted Chicken with Pancetta, Potatoes, and Herbs

Pollo al Forno con Pancetta, Patatine, e Aglione

Nothing could be simpler than this roasted chicken, which becomes absolutely outstanding when roasted at a high temperature, which gives the chicken a crisp skin and a moist meat. The *aglione,* a mixture of fresh chopped rosemary, sage, and garlic with salt, is rubbed over the chicken before roasting, giving the bird a tremendous flavor boost. (Pheasant or rabbit can also be used instead of chicken.) This is a typical dish of Bologna's countryside trattorie, such as the ever popular Gigina, which keeps serving the traditional dishes of the area. When I am in Bologna and yearn for the flavors of my mother's cooking, I head straight to Gigina. ◆ *serves 4*

1 large (5- or 6-pound) chicken, cut into 8 serving pieces

$^1/_3$ to $^1/_2$ cup extra-virgin olive oil

2 tablespoons chopped fresh rosemary

2 tablespoons chopped fresh sage

2 garlic cloves, finely chopped

$^1/_2$ teaspoon salt

$^1/_4$ teaspoon freshly ground black pepper

3 large boiling potatoes (about 1$^1/_2$ pounds)

2 to 3 ounces thickly sliced pancetta, diced

Wash the chicken thoroughly under cold running water and pat dry with paper towels. Put the pieces in a large bowl and add the oil. In a small bowl, combine the rosemary, sage, and garlic. Add this herb mixture to the chicken and season with the salt and pepper. Mix everything well with your hands. Cover and refrigerate for a few hours. Remove the chicken from the refrigerator and leave at room temperature for about $^1/_2$ hour before roasting.

Preheat the oven to 450°F.

When the oven is nice and hot, peel and cut the potatoes into 1-inch pieces. Add them to the bowl with the chicken and mix well to coat with the herb mixture.

Transfer the chicken, potatoes, and any herbs and oil left at the bottom of the bowl into a large roasting pan. Place the pan on the middle rack of the oven and roast for 35 to 40 minutes. At this point the chicken and potatoes should be richly browned and crisp, and should stick a bit to the bottom of the pan. Stir the pancetta into the pan and return to the oven, cooking 3 to 4 minutes longer. Serve with a little dribbling of the pan's flavorful oil.

TO KEEP *AGLIONE*

Chop all the herbs with the garlic and the salt and place in a jar. Close the jar tightly with its lid and refrigerate for up to 2 weeks.

Pork Shoulder Braised in Milk

Stracotto di Maiale al Latte

The cuisine of Bologna and Emilia-Romagna would not exist without pork, whose delicate taste and rich golden color make it the undisputed star of Bologna's best-loved dishes. One of the most traditional dishes of Bologna is a loin of pork braised gently in milk on top of the stove, until the meat is tender and the milk has thickened and browned into glazed clusters of sauce. The last time I was in Bologna I discovered a variation that produced an even more tender meat, made with a boneless pork shoulder, a fattier meat, which was slowly braised in the oven, not on top of the stove. I loved it. ◆ *serves 6*

$^1/_3$ cup plus 2 tablespoons extra-virgin olive oil

4 pounds boneless pork shoulder, trimmed of excess fat

$^1/_2$ teaspoon salt

$^1/_4$ teaspoon freshly ground black pepper

2 tablespoons unsalted butter

2 small onions, minced (about 2 cups)

4 to 5 cups whole milk

Preheat the oven to 300°F.

Heat the oil in a large, heavy, ovenproof skillet (one with a lid) over medium-high heat. Season the pork on all sides with the salt and pepper, and add to the pan, fat side down. Cook, turning, until the meat has a nice golden color, about 10 minutes. Transfer to a large platter.

Discard the fat from the pan and wipe clean with paper towels. Return the pan to medium-low heat and add the butter. As soon as the butter begins to foam, add the onions and cook, stirring, until soft and pale yellow, 6 to 7 minutes. Place the pork over the onions and add enough milk to come about one third of the way up the sides of the meat. As soon as the milk comes to a boil, turn off the heat, cover the pan with heavy-duty foil, and top with the lid. Place the pan on the middle rack of the oven and cook, basting and turning the meat every 30 or 40 minutes, until it easily flakes when pierced with a fork, about 3 hours.

Transfer the meat to a cutting board and cover loosely with foil. Place the pot on medium-high heat and cook, stirring, until the remaining milk has reduced and coagulated into thick, brown clusters. Cut the meat (it will probably fall apart), and place on warm serving dishes. Top with the browned milk clusters and serve hot.

THE GLORIES OF BRAISING

Braising is my favorite way of cooking: with a little effort, I can prepare a deeply flavored dish that will feed many. The braising technique of moist-heat cooking takes an inexpensive, tough cut of meat and cooks it slowly with liquid in a tightly covered pot. Italians love to brown the meat on top of the stove before placing it in the oven with a variety of vegetables and just enough liquid to come about one third of the way up the sides of the meat. Here are some braising tips:

- Choose a nice, heavy pot that will fit the meat, liquid, and vegetables a little snugly.
- Cover the pot tightly with aluminum foil, then cover the foil with a tight-fitting lid, so moisture will not escape.
- Make sure that the liquid in the pot simmers lightly, and baste and turn the meat several times during cooking.
- At the end of cooking, the meat will have shriveled considerably and will basically fall apart.

Bologna's Stuffed Pork Chops

Braciole di Maiale alla Vecchia Bologna

Emilia-Romagna is famous throughout Italy for its superlative pasta and the quality of its pork. One of my favorites of Bologna's traditional pork dishes is a thick, well-marbled chop that is stuffed with prosciutto and fontina cheese, then cooked over high heat just long enough for the cheese to melt. In winter, this delicious dish appears on the menu of several of Bologna's trattorie, often served with crisp, fried polenta. • *serves 4*

4 bone-in center-cut pork chops, 1 1/2 inches thick

1/2 teaspoon salt

1/4 teaspoon freshly ground black pepper

4 thin slices prosciutto (about 1/4 pound)

1/3 cup freshly grated Parmigiano-Reggiano

1/3 cup extra-virgin olive oil

1 cup dry white wine

1/2 cup Chicken Broth (page 298) or low-sodium canned chicken broth

3 fresh sage leaves

1 tablespoon unsalted butter

Trim the extra fat from the pork chops. Make a pocket in each chop by cutting the meat horizontally, on one side only, until you reach the bone. Open the chops just like you would a book, and season with the salt and pepper inside and out. Fill each chop with 1 slice of prosciutto and 1 or 2 tablespoons of Parmigiano. Close the chops and secure them with several toothpicks. (Make sure the stuffing is well secured inside the chops, so the cheese will not leak.)

Heat the oil in a large skillet over medium heat. When the oil is hot but not smoking, add the chops without crowding. Brown them gently, 4 to 5 minutes on each side. Transfer to a platter.

Discard some of the fat in the skillet and return it to high heat. Add the wine, broth, sage, and butter. Bring the liquid to a boil while scraping the bottom of the pan with a wooden spoon. Return the chops to the skillet, cover the pan, and reduce the heat to medium low. Cook gently until the chops are cooked all the way through, 7 to 8 minutes longer. Add a little more wine if the pan juices reduce too much.

Remove the toothpicks and transfer the chops to warm serving plates. Dribble some of the pan juices over the chops and serve.

FOR A JUICY PORK CHOP

- Choose chops that are 1 to 1½ inches thick, for they are less prone to dry out.
- Brown chops to a rich color over medium heat. A very high heat can dry out the meat.
- Do not crowd the pan or the chops will not brown properly. A 12-inch skillet will hold 4 chops perfectly.
- Check for doneness by making a small slit in the meat, preferably near the bone. If the meat is barely pink, the chops are done.

Zampone Sausage with Braised Lentils

Zampone con Lenticchie in Umido

If your traveling should take you to Modena and Bologna, go to Fini restaurant in Modena, or Diana restaurant in Bologna, and ask for *zampone* (see note). This succulent sausage stuffed into the skin of a pig's-foot will arrive in a steam trolley, pushed by a waiter who will cut thick slices of rosy, moist zampone and serve it with either mashed potatoes or braised lentils. If you are lucky, he will drizzle a few drops of precious balsamic vinegar over the zampone. This is heartwarming winter food, best enjoyed with family and friends. ♦ *serves 10*

I *zampone* sausage (6 to 8 pounds)

3 tablespoons unsalted butter

3 tablespoons extra-virgin olive oil

I small yellow onion, minced (about I cup)

I small carrot, minced (about ¹/₂ cup)

I small celery stalk, minced (about ¹/₂ cup)

I garlic clove, finely minced

I tablespoon chopped fresh flat-leaf parsley

I tablespoon chopped fresh rosemary

I pound brown lentils, picked over and washed in several changes of cold water

2 cups canned Italian plum tomatoes. preferably San Marzano (see note, page 35) with their juices, put through a food mill to remove the seeds

Salt and freshly ground black pepper to taste

The night before you are planning to cook the *zampone*, place it in a large bowl, cover generously with cold water, and refrigerate overnight. (The soaking will soften the sausage and remove the salt.)

Drain and dry the sausage. With a needle, prick the skin in several places so that the sausage will not burst as it cooks. Wrap the sausage tightly in cheesecloth and tie it with kitchen string just as you would tie a roast. Place the sausage in a stockpot large enough to hold it comfortably, or place it in a fish poacher. Add enough cold water to cover generously, and bring to a boil over medium-high heat. Reduce the heat to medium low and cook at a gentle simmer for 2¹/₂ to 3 hours. Turn off the heat. Scoop up and reserve 3 cups of the cooking broth. Leave the zampone in the rest of the hot broth for an hour or two.

While the zampone is resting, prepare the lentils. Heat the butter and oil in a large skillet over medium heat. Add the onion, carrot, and celery, and cook, stirring, until the vegetables are soft, 8 to 10 minutes. Add the garlic, parsley, and rosemary, and stir for a minute or two. Add the lentils, and stir for a few minutes until they are coated with the savory base. Add half of the reserved cooking broth and the tomatoes. Bring to a gentle bubble, then reduce the heat to medium low and partially cover the skillet. Cook at a gentle simmer, stirring from time to time and adding a bit more broth or water if needed, until the lentils are tender, about 40 minutes. At the end of cooking, the lentils should be tender but still a bit firm to the bite, and most of the liquid in the skillet should have evaporated. Season with salt and pepper to taste. (The lentils can be prepared several hours ahead and reheated gently just before serving.)

Carefully lift the zampone from the pot and place on a cutting board. Remove the string and cheesecloth, and cut and discard the pig's foot. Slice into $^1/_2$-inch-thick rounds, arrange on a serving platter, and serve warm with the lentils.

ITALIAN *ZAMPONE*

Zampone, a specialty of the city of Modena, is a lightly cured sausage stuffed into the skin of a pig's-foot. The best-quality zampone has a mild, delicate taste, a gelatinous consistency, and an exquisitely tender texture. In Modena and in Bologna, zampone is always part of a great *bollito misto,* mixed boiled meats; or it can be served sliced by itself. *Cotechino* sausage can be substituted for zampone. Prick the skin of $1^1/_2$ pounds cotechino in several places and simmer in water to cover until tender, 1 to $1^1/_2$ hours. Serve sliced cotechino with lentils or mashed potatoes.

Braised Rabbit with Prosciutto and Tomatoes

Stufato di Coniglio con Prosciutto e Pomodoro

This dish begins with the deep browning of the rabbit, followed by the addition of flavorful, homey onion, celery, and carrot. After a slow braise with wine, tomatoes, and broth, grated lemon zest and minced garlic are stirred into the sauce during the last few minutes of cooking. I particularly love this in winter, when it is generally served with soft, creamy polenta (which in Bologna has the addition of Parmigiano). If you are in Bologna's city center during the fall and winter, check out Trattoria Anna Maria and Trattoria Della Santa, both of which often prepare this delectable dish.

◆ *serves 4 to 6*

1/3 to 1/2 cup extra-virgin olive oil

2 rabbits, 3 to 3 1/2 pounds each, cut into 6 serving pieces each, washed and dried with paper towels

1 teaspoon salt plus more to taste

1/4 teaspoon freshly ground black pepper plus more to taste

1 small yellow onion, minced (about 1 cup)

1 small carrot, minced (about 1/2 cup)

1 small celery stalk, minced (about 1/2 cup)

2 ounces thickly sliced prosciutto, diced

1 cup dry white wine

1 cup canned Italian plum tomatoes, preferably San Marzano (see note, page 35), with their juices, put through a food mill to remove the seeds

1 cup Chicken Broth (page 298) or low-sodium canned chicken broth

1 garlic clove, minced

Grated zest of 1 lemon

Preheat the oven to 375°F.

Heat the oil in a wide-bottomed skillet (one with a lid) over high heat. Season the rabbit pieces with the salt and pepper. When the oil is very hot, add the rabbit pieces in batches, without crowding. Cook until the pieces are golden on all sides, 6 to 8 minutes, then transfer to a large platter.

Discard some of the fat in the skillet and return the skillet to medium heat. Add the onion, carrot, and celery, and cook, stirring, until the vegetables are lightly golden and soft, 5 to 6 minutes. Add the prosciutto, stir for a minute or two until it is lightly golden, then add the wine. Cook, stirring with a wooden spoon and scraping the bottom of the pan, until most of the wine has evaporated. Add the tomatoes and broth. As soon as the sauce begins to bubble, return the rabbit to the skillet and cover with aluminum foil and the lid. Place the skillet on the center rack of the oven and cook, stirring a few times, until the rabbit is tender, 40 to 50 minutes, and the sauce is thick and has reduced approximately by half.

Remove the skillet from the oven and transfer the rabbit to serving dishes. Place the pan over medium-low heat. Add the garlic and lemon zest and stir for a minute or two, until well combined with the sauce. Taste, adjust the seasoning, and spoon over the rabbit. Serve hot.

ABOUT RABBIT

Rabbit's lean, somewhat sweet meat is low in fat and calories and rich in protein, vitamins, and minerals, and is a favorite of many Italians. In buying rabbit, look for a young, 3- to $3^{1}/_{2}$ -pound rabbit, which has more tender meat than an older, larger rabbit. If fresh rabbit is not available, look for a frozen young rabbit, which comes already cut up. In cooking rabbit, be sure to brown the meat on medium-high or high heat until golden; do not crowd the pan, so the rabbit will brown quickly and evenly; and, if you are braising or stewing the rabbit, cover the pan and cook the rabbit over gentle heat, basting and turning the pieces a few times.

Stewed Tripe Bologna-Style

Trippa in Umido alla Bolognese

Tripe was my mother's favorite dish. She would wash, scrub, and soak the tripe for hours, then simmer it in a large earthenware pot for yet more hours. Tripe comes from the stomach of ruminants such as calves and cows, and it used to be a staple in the homes and restaurants of the region. Today, however, only a handful of eating places in Bologna prepare it. This version braises the tripe slowly in the oven with vegetables, wine, broth, and tomatoes, then finishes it with the addition of butter and Parmigiano. Honeycomb tripe can be found in supermarkets, butcher shops, and Italian specialty food stores, cleaned and partially precooked. ◆ *serves 4 to 6*

FOR THE TRIPE

- 2 pounds fresh or frozen honeycomb veal tripe
- 1/2 cup white-wine vinegar
- 1 medium yellow onion, peeled and quartered
- 1 carrot, washed and cut into 1-inch pieces
- 1 bay leaf

FOR THE STEW

- 3 tablespoons unsalted butter
- 1/3 cup extra-virgin olive oil
- 1/2 small onion, minced (about 1/2 cup)
- 1 small carrot, minced (about 1/2 cup)
- 1 small celery stalk, minced (about 1/2 cup)
- 2 tablespoons chopped fresh flat-leaf parsley
- 2 ounces thickly sliced pancetta, minced
  Salt and freshly ground black pepper to taste
- 1 cup dry white wine
- 2 cups canned Italian plum tomatoes, preferably San Marzano (see note, page 35), with their juices, put through a food mill to remove the seeds
- 1 cup Chicken Broth (page 301) or low-sodium canned chicken broth
- 3/4 cup freshly grated Parmigiano-Reggiano

PREPARE THE TRIPE

Rinse the tripe thoroughly under cold running water and place in a large pot. Add the vinegar, onion, carrot, and bay leaf and enough cold water to cover by 2 inches. Bring to a boil, reduce the heat to medium, and simmer for 20 to 30 minutes. Drain and set aside to cool. Cut the tripe into $1/2$-inch-wide, 3-inch-long strips, and set aside.

FINISH THE DISH

Preheat the oven to 325°F.

Heat 2 tablespoons of the butter and the oil in a large, heavy sauté pan or heatproof casserole (one with a lid) over medium heat. As soon as the butter begins to foam, add the minced onion, carrot, and celery; I tablespoon of the parsley; and the pancetta. Cook, stirring, until the vegetables and pancetta are lightly golden and soft, 5 to 6 minutes. Add the tripe and season with salt and pepper. Stir for 3 to 4 minutes, until the tripe is well coated with the savory base. Raise the heat to high and add the wine. Stir until the wine has reduced approximately by half. Add the tomatoes and the broth, and bring to a boil. Cover the pan, place on the middle rack of the oven, and cook gently until the tripe is tender, 2 to $2^{1}/2$ hours. Check and stir the tripe every 30 minutes or so, adding a little more broth or water if the sauce thickens too much.

When the tripe is nice and tender, remove from the oven and stir in the remaining butter, parsley, and about half of the Parmigiano. Taste and adjust the seasoning, and serve hot with the remaining Parmigiano on the side.

NOTE

Because honeycomb tripe comes from the cow's stomach, it may remain slightly chewy even after it has been cooked for hours; this is a characteristic of tripe. This dish is even better when made ahead; reheat gently just before serving.

Monkfish with White Wine, Tomatoes, and Basil

Rana Pescatrice al Pomodoro e Basilico

Nico Costa, the owner of Trattoria Battibecco in Bologna, loves monkfish and cooks it as simply as possible to allow the fish's own flavor to shine. In this preparation, Nico browns the monkfish quickly in olive oil, then cooks it in a reduction of white wine and tomatoes that is seasoned simply by a bit of garlic, salt, red pepper flakes, and basil. The result is a flavorful dish that yields a moist fish, and can be prepared on the spur of the moment. ◆ *serves 4*

I boneless monkfish tail, about 2 pounds, cut into 8 thick pieces, trimmed of all dark skin

$1/3$ to $1/2$ cup extra-virgin olive oil

$1/2$ teaspoon salt plus more to taste

I cup all-purpose flour

2 garlic cloves, minced

2 anchovy fillets packed in salt or oil, minced

I cup dry white wine

I (28-ounce) can Italian plum tomatoes, preferably San Marzano (see note, page 35), with their juices, put through a food mill to remove the seeds

$1/4$ teaspoon crushed red pepper flakes plus more to taste

8 fresh basil leaves, finely shredded

I tablespoon unsalted butter

Wash the monkfish under cold water and pat dry with paper towels.

Heat the oil in a large skillet over medium-high heat. Season the monkfish with the salt and flour it lightly. Place the monkfish in the skillet without crowding. Cook, turning once, until the fish has a nice golden color, about 2 minutes on each side. Transfer to a plate.

Discard half of the fat in the skillet and return it to medium heat. Add the garlic and anchovies and stir for 20 to 30 seconds. Add the wine and cook, stirring and scraping the bottom of the skillet with a wooden spoon, until the wine is reduced approximately by half. Add the tomatoes, season with salt and the red pepper flakes, and bring the sauce to a fast simmer.

Return the monkfish and all its juices to the skillet. Cover the pan and reduce the heat to low. Simmer, stirring and basting once or twice, until the fish is cooked through, 7 to 8 minutes. Place the fish on warm serving dishes.

Add the basil and butter to the skillet, raise the heat to high, and stir quickly for a minute or two, to thicken up the sauce. Taste and adjust the seasoning. Spoon the sauce over the fish and serve immediately.

ABOUT MONKFISH

Monkfish is a large, homely, bottom-feeding scavenger, considered by many "the poor man's lobster" because its white, lean meat resembles cooked lobster tail meat. Boneless monkfish tails of varying sizes can be found in most fish markets.

Poached Salmon with Bolognese Salsa Verde

Salmone Lesso con Salsa Verde Bolognese

On a hot summer day, there is no food that pleases me more than a perfectly grilled, roasted, poached, or steamed fish, topped simply by a bit of green olive oil and a few drops of lemon juice—a dish that can be prepared with a minimal amount of fat (or none at all). Such a fish dish is typical of good home cooking and of the many unpretentious restaurants and trattorie of Bologna such as Diana, Rodrigo, Battibecco, and Cesari. ◆ *serves 4*

FOR THE SALSA VERDE

Yolks of 2 hard-boiled eggs

2 loosely packed cups fresh flat-leaf parsley, washed and dried on paper towels

1 tablespoon capers, rinsed

1 garlic clove, peeled

4 anchovy fillets

3 small pickled gherkins, drained and cut into large pieces

2 small cipolline onions pickled in wine vinegar, rinsed (optional)

1 teaspoon Dijon mustard

1 teaspoon grated lemon zest and juice of 1 lemon

1/2 cup extra-virgin olive oil, or more if needed

Salt to taste

FOR THE SALMON

1 cup dry white wine

1 medium carrot, cut into 1-inch pieces

1/2 small onion, peeled and quartered

1 celery stalk, cut into 1-inch pieces

1 tablespoon black peppercorns

4 sprigs of fresh flat-leaf parsley

Salt to taste

4 salmon fillets, each 1 inch thick (about 8 ounces each)

Olive oil, for drizzling

1 lemon, cut into wedges

PREPARE THE SALSA VERDE

Put all the ingredients except the lemon juice, oil, and salt in the bowl of a food processor fitted with the metal blade. Pulse until the ingredients are finely chopped but not puréed. Transfer to a bowl. Add the lemon juice and oil and stir energetically to blend; the sauce should have a medium-thick consistency and a slightly piquant taste. Add a bit of salt and more oil, if needed. Cover the bowl and refrigerate. Salsa verde can be refrigerated up to 3 days. Bring to room temperature before serving.

PREPARE THE SALMON

Fill a large skillet halfway with water. Add the wine, carrot, onion, celery, peppercorns, parsley, and salt. Bring to a boil, reduce the heat to medium low, and simmer for about 30 minutes.

Slip the salmon into the pan without overlapping, making sure that each piece is completely covered by the broth (add a bit of water if needed). As soon as the broth comes back to a boil, reduce the heat to low and simmer gently for 4 to 5 minutes. Turn off the heat and let the salmon sit in the flavorful broth until its inside is no longer translucent, 6 to 7 minutes longer.

Pick up the salmon with a large metal spatula, pat dry with paper towels, and place on serving plates. Season with salt to taste, drizzle with olive oil and lemon juice, and serve with a couple of tablespoons of salsa verde.

NOTE

If you prefer serving chilled salmon, leave the salmon in its broth and place it in the refrigerator for several hours or overnight. It will be incredibly moist and flavorful.

Mixed Vegetables with Prosciutto, Butter, and Parmigiano

Verdure Miste con Prosciutto, Burro, e Parmigiano

Many Northern Italian restaurants and trattorie have on their menu mixed vegetables, which often consist of cauliflower, broccoli, carrots, string beans, fennel, and onions. The vegetables are either boiled or steamed, and turned into colorful salads or a delicious sauté. Rodrigo in Bologna prepares them both ways. I love this version's addition of rosy, sweet prosciutto; Parmigiano; and just a touch of heavy cream.

◆ *serves* 8

1 small cauliflower, 1¹/₂ to 2 pounds

1¹/₂ pounds broccoli

2 medium carrots

Salt

4 tablespoons (¹/₂ stick) unsalted butter

3 ounces prosciutto, cut into 2 thick slices, diced

¹/₄ cup heavy cream (optional)

¹/₄ to ¹/₃ cup finely grated Parmigiano-Reggiano

Freshly ground black pepper

Remove all the leaves from the cauliflower, cut in half through the stem, and separate into equal-size florets; wash. Trim the broccoli into equal-size florets; wash. Peel the carrots and slice into ¹/₃-inch-thick rounds.

To boil the vegetables: Bring a large pot of salted water to a boil and prepare an ice-water bath in a large bowl. Add the vegetables by type and cook until tender but still firm to the bite, 4 to 5 minutes for each type. Drain, then plunge into the ice bath to stop the cooking. Drain again and set aside.

To steam the vegetables: Steam them by type, covered, over boiling water until tender but still firm to the bite, 4 to 5 minutes. Plunge into an ice-water bath to stop the cooking. Drain again and set aside.

Heat the butter in a large skillet over medium heat. When the butter begins to foam, add the prosciutto and cook, stirring, for a couple of minutes. Add the cream and simmer for 1 minute. Add the vegetables and the Parmigiano and season lightly with salt and pepper. Cook and stir for 4 to 5 minutes, until the vegetables are hot and thoroughly coated. Taste, adjust the seasoning, and serve.

WHEN IN BOLOGNA
Caffès, Pastry Shops, and Gelaterie

All the below are centrally located, and serve wonderful espresso, cappuccino, pastries, chocolate, and multiflavored *gelati;* most have outdoor tables.

Bricco d'Oro
Via Farini 6
Tel. 236 231
Great, central location to stop for a good espresso or cappuccino, and to indulge in a golden *bomboloni* (a large yeast doughnut) or brioche. Try the hot chocolate topped with whipped cream.

Caffè' dei Commercianti
Strada Maggiore 23/c
Tel. 266 539

Gelateria Ugo
Via San Felice 24
Tel. 263 849

Pasticceria Impero
Via Indipendenza 39
Tel. 232 337

Pasticceria Majani
Via dei Carbonesi 5
Tel. 234 302

Zanarini
Piazza Galvani I
Tel. 222 717
This historic caffè, which opened in 1919, has been for generations of Bolognesi a home away from home. Zanarini is located in the Pavaglione, the premier shopping area of Bologna. The large, stunning bar is where the action is: beautiful, elegant people stopping in for their daily dosage of caffeine, pastries, or cocktails. For the more leisured life, just sit at one of the outdoor tables, order a large gelato, and watch the parade of Bolognesi go by.

Fava Beans with Mortadella

Fave con Mortadella

Fresh tender fava beans are one of the favorite springtime vegetables in Italy. In Rome fava beans are sautéed with *guanciale* (pork jowl), garlic, and olive oil. In Florence they are dipped into salt and eaten raw. And in Bologna they are sautéed with butter, onion, and mortadella, Bologna's prized cured pork sausage. In country trattorie this preparation is often served over sliced bread that has been grilled or fried in butter. In Bologna, however, it is served as a side dish to roasted meats. ◆ *serves 4 to 6*

Salt

3 pounds fresh unshelled fava beans

3 tablespoons unsalted butter

I small shallot, finely minced

2 ounces mortadella, in I thick slice, cubed

2 ounces prosciutto, in I thick slice, cubed

$1/2$ teaspoon sugar

Freshly ground black pepper to taste

Bring a large pot of salted water to a boil and prepare an ice-water bath in a large bowl. Shell the fava beans and discard the pods. Drop the beans in the boiling water and cook for 1 to 2 minutes, depending on size. Drain and plunge in the ice water to stop the cooking. When cool, drain again. Pinch the skin of each bean, breaking it at one end, and squeeze the bean out of its skin. Set aside.

Heat the butter in a medium skillet over medium heat. When the butter begins to foam, add the shallot and cook, stirring, until pale yellow and soft, 4 to 5 minutes. Add the mortadella and prosciutto and stir for a couple of minutes. Add the reserved fava beans and the sugar, and season with salt and several grinds of pepper. Cook and stir for 2 to 3 minutes, or until the beans are heated through. Serve hot.

NOTE

The season for fresh fava beans is spring. When the beans are very small, young, and tender, their skin doesn't need to be removed. As the season progresses and the beans become larger, their skin is tougher and needs to be peeled off.

Sautéed Swiss Chard with Hot Pepper

Bietole in Padella con il Peperoncino

Swiss chard's green leaves can be used in soups, in pasta fillings, in salads, in sautés, and even in savory pies; its broad, creamy stalks are best when gratinéed (see note). At Trattoria Gigina on the outskirts of Bologna, the leaves are blanched, then sautéed with oil, garlic, anchovies, and plenty of peperoncino (small, hot chili pepper). ♦

serves 4 to 6

3 pounds Swiss chard
Salt
⅓ cup extra-virgin olive oil
2 garlic cloves, minced

2 anchovy fillets packed in salt or in oil
Fresh red chili pepper, minced, or crushed red pepper flakes to taste

Remove the stalks from the Swiss chard leaves and reserve. Wash the leaves thoroughly in several changes of cold water, then put them in a large pot with 2 cups water and a pinch of salt. Cook over medium heat until the leaves are tender, 5 to 6 minutes. Drain well and set aside.

Heat the oil in a large skillet over medium heat. Add the garlic, anchovies, and minced peperoncino or pepper flakes. Stir for about 1 minute, then add the chard. Season with salt and cook, stirring, for 3 to 4 minutes, or until the chard is heated through. Taste, adjust the seasoning, and serve.

HOW TO GRATINÉE SWISS CHARD STALKS

Wash the stalks under cold running water, add them to a pot of salted boiling water, and cook for a couple of minutes. Drain dry with paper towels, and place in a buttered baking dish, with the stalks slightly overlapping. Dot with butter and sprinkle generously with Parmigiano-Reggiano. Bake in a 350°F. oven until the cheese is melted.

Apple Cake with Raisins and Almonds

Torta di Mele con Uvetta e Mandorle

One of the most common homey desserts of Bologna is *torta di mele*, a dense, moist apple cake. Every cook seems to have a personal version and many of the trattorie and *osterie* serve it with a glass of sweet wine. This version comes from Antica Trattoria del Pontelungo. • *serves 8 to 10*

5 tablespoons unsalted butter at room temperature, plus more for greasing the pan

5 to 6 Amaretti di Saronno (almond cookies)

1 package active dry yeast

1/3 cup warm whole milk

2/3 cup plus 2 tablespoons granulated sugar

4 large eggs

2 cups all-purpose flour

3/4 cup golden raisins or dried cherries, soaked in dry Marsala wine for 20 minutes, then drained

1/2 cup slivered almonds

Grated zest of 1 lemon

4 large Pippin or Granny Smith apples, peeled, cored, and thinly sliced

Confectioners' sugar for dusting

Preheat the oven to 375°F. Butter a 10-inch springform baking pan.

Place the amaretti cookies in a large plastic bag and seal. With a rolling pin, crush the amaretti into small crumbs. Press the crumbs into the bottom and sides of the pan.

Stir the yeast into the warm milk until dissolved.

In a large bowl or in the bowl of an electric mixer, beat the butter with 2/3 cup of the granulated sugar. Add the eggs, one at a time, and beat until they are pale yellow and thick. Beat in the flour and the yeast mixture. When well incorporated, add the plumped raisins or cherries, the almonds, and the lemon zest. With a large spatula, fold in three quarters of the apples.

Pour the batter into the buttered pan and smooth the top evenly with the spatula. Arrange the remaining apples over the batter, and sprinkle with the remaining granulated sugar.

Bake for 40 to 50 minutes, or until the cake is golden brown and the sides begin to come away from the pan. Cool to room temperature. Remove the cake from the pan, place on a nice serving dish, and sprinkle the top with confectioners' sugar.

Parmigiano-Reggiano Ice Cream with Balsamic Vinegar

Gelato di Parmigiano-Reggiano al Balsamico

In spite of its name, this is not a *gelato*, it is a cheese course. Heavy cream and grated Parmigiano are cooked together into a thick, luscious cream, chilled overnight, and served cold, either as an appetizer or at the end of the meal. A few years ago, when I had it at Ristorante Diana in Bologna, the waiter brought to the table a very small bottle of aged artisan-made balsamic, and drizzled it on the gelato. It was absolutely delicious. Today when I serve it at my restaurant in Sacramento, I like to embellish the dish with a few slices of grilled crostini, some roasted walnuts, and some dried figs.

◆ *serves 6 to 8*

4 cups heavy cream

2¾ cups (about 22 ounces) very finely grated fresh Parmigiano-Reggiano

Pinch of white pepper

Balsamic vinegar, preferably artisan-made or well-aged

Put the cream in a medium saucepan and bring to a gentle simmer over medium heat. Add the Parmigiano and the pepper, reduce the heat to low, and simmer until the cheese is melted and the cream has thickened, about 2 minutes.

Transfer to a 10 x 12-inch baking pan (the cream should be about 1 inch thick) and smooth the top with a spatula. Chill in the refrigerator without covering, then cover with plastic wrap and refrigerate overnight, or until the cream is nice and firm.

When you are ready to serve, scoop up a nice-size ball of cream with an ice cream scoop, place on dessert plates, and drizzle with balsamic vinegar.

Ricotta-Mascarpone Fritters

Frittelle di Ricotta e Mascarpone

One of the first places I go for dinner when I am in Bologna is Rodrigo, a quaint, friendly restaurant in the center of town. The food is consistently wonderful, especially the tiny homemade tortellini swimming in a golden capon broth, the fish risottos, and the mixed grill of absolutely fresh fish. From time to time Rodrigo also serves special homey desserts—simple concoctions that Italian grandmothers used to make. This is one of those treats. Serve the fritters immediately, while they are puffy and hot, or they will deflate somewhat. • *makes 20 to 25 fritters*

4 large eggs	1 tablespoon finely grated orange zest
1/2 cup granulated sugar	1 tablespoon finely grated lemon zest
1 pound ricotta	3 tablespoons Amaretto di Saronno liqueur
1/4 pound mascarpone	Vegetable oil for deep-frying
1 cup all-purpose flour	Confectioners' sugar for dusting
3 teaspoons baking powder	

FOR BATTER MADE BY HAND

In a large bowl, beat the eggs with the granulated sugar until soft and fluffy. Add the ricotta, mascarpone, flour, baking powder, orange and lemon zests, and Amaretto. Mix until the ingredients are well incorporated and the batter has a smooth consistency. Cover the bowl and refrigerate for a few hours, which will allow the batter to settle and thicken. Bring to room temperature before frying.

FOR BATTER IN A FOOD PROCESSOR

Put the eggs and the granulated sugar in the bowl of a food processor fitted with the metal blade and pulse until incorporated. Add the ricotta and mascarpone, flour, baking powder, orange and lemon zest, and Amaretto. Pulse until the mixture has a smooth, creamy consistency. Place in a large bowl, cover with plastic wrap, and refrigerate for a few hours. Bring to room temperature before frying.

Pour 2 to 3 inches of oil in a medium saucepan over medium-high heat. When the oil is very hot, and a bit of batter added to the oil turns golden almost immediately, drop a few tablespoons of batter at a time into the hot oil. Cook until the bottoms of the fritters are golden brown. Turn with a slotted spoon and fry the other side. Drain on paper towels.

When all the fritters are done, place them on a large platter, sprinkle with confectioners' sugar, and serve while hot.

Gigina
Via Stendhal 1/b
Tel. 322 132

Antica Trattoria del Cacciatore
Via Caduti di Casteldebole 25
Tel. 564 203
A wonderful restaurant on the outskirts that is run and operated by the Ferrari family. Stefano is the brilliant chef, Eugenio is the sommelier, and their sister runs the dining room. A waiter will come to your table with a large cart of appetizers and you will find yourself asking for a taste of this and a taste of that, and often you will be too full to order anything more. So restrain yourself, because the other food here is very delicious, especially their game dishes.

Da Cesari
Via dei Carbonesi 8
Tel. 237 710
The food in this very pleasant restaurant is traditional and seasonal. Classic dishes such as Tortellini in Capon Broth, Veal Cutlets with Prosciutto and Parmigiano, and Calf's Liver with Balsamic Vinegar are always on the menu. Seasonal dishes might include a delectable, thick fresh porcini soup and thin, homemade noodles with fresh white truffle. One of the dishes I love—a dish my mother used to make quite often—is *trippa alla parmigiana*, slowly braised tripe in the manner of Parma. If you like tripe, you must go to Cesari.

Diana
Via Indipendenza 24
Tel. 231 302
I love this restaurant! Not because the food is better than at other places, and not because the décor is enchanting. I love it because it has consistently retained its unique, old-fashioned personality and has not yielded to new food trends. Diana's purpose is simply to retain what is old and good. And so if you should find yourself in Bologna, you *must* go to this temple of traditional Bolognese cuisine and experience food that, unfortunately, is slowly disappearing.

I Carracci
Via Manzoni 2
Tel. 225 445
I Carracci, the stylish restaurant of the opulent Grand Hotel Baglioni, first grabs your attention with the stunning sixteenth-century frescoes on the ceilings, then wins you over with its food and superlative service. This is a place where you want to dress up and linger while sipping a Bellini. The menu changes daily, taking advantage of the season. I still have memories of a great porcini mushroom risotto.

Osteria de' Poeti
Via de' Poeti 1/b
Tel. 236 166
Located in a medieval building on the narrow, central street of Via de' Poeti, this *osteria* has come a long way from its humble beginnings as the gathering place of blue-collar workers who would meet to play cards and drink cheap wine. Today it has become a hip place. Modernized and

embellished, with soft lights and piano music, Osteria de' Poeti offers pretty good food and a large number of wines, with many offered by the glass. Their appetizers are so varied and so good that you can make a whole meal out of them.

Papa Rè
Piazza dell'Unità 6
Tel. 356 120

A small, pleasant restaurant a few miles from the city center. Dante, the owner, has been in the restaurant business all his life and serves a mixture of traditional and creative dishes. One of his signature dishes, and by far my favorite, is the splendid Dante's Vegetable Risotto (page 138).

Pappagallo
Piazza della Mercanzia 3/c
Tel. 231 200

Restaurant Pappagallo is without any doubt the best-known and oldest restaurant of Bologna, located on the ground floor of a majestic thirteenth-century building smack in the center of the city. Pappagallo owes its reputation to the succulent Bolognese cooking of the original chef, Bruno Tasselli, who presided over the kitchen for more than forty years. Today Ezio Salsini, who has owned Pappagallo for the last fifteen years, prepares the same type of food. Dishes not to be missed are Lasagne Verdi alla Bolognese, Fritto Misto di Pesce, and Veal Chop alla Bolognese.

Ristorante al Cambio
Via Stalingrado 150
Tel. 328 118

Ristorante al Cambio is the domain of Massimiliano Poggi, a talented young chef. The restaurant has two menus: One featuring the traditional dishes of Bologna, and the other offering the innovative dishes that Massimiliano creates daily. Try the very, very small Tortellini in Capon Broth, the Pheasant Breast Stuffed with White Truffle, or the Lasagne del Cambio, a delicious lighter version of the traditional lasagne alla Bolognese.

Rodrigo
Via della Zecca 2/h
Tel. 235 536

A charming restaurant that for the last forty years has consistently served wonderful food. This is a place where the Bolognesi go to eat. Enzo and Gilberto, the owners, who began working at Rodrigo when they were in their teens, are always on hand to greet customers. The restaurant serves great homemade pastas, wonderful fresh seafood, and delectable, homey desserts.

Trattoria Anna Maria
Via Belle Arti 17
Tel. 266 894

Anna Maria, the owner of this trattoria, has not changed her menu for more than fifteen years, and the reason is simple: her customers seem to be happy to eat food that is highly flavorful, traditional, and abundant. The menu offers homemade fluffy gnocchi or delicate tortelloni with Gorgonzola cheese sauce, tagliolini in capon broth, roasted veal shank, roasted lamb, calf's liver, and slowly stewed tripe.

Trattoria Battibecco
Via Battibecco 4
Tel. 223 298

Even though the sign on the door says *trattoria*, Battibecco is in fact a very stylish restaurant that serves the classic food of Emilia-Romagna as well as signature dishes from other regions. Nico Costa is the brilliant chef-owner, and Giuliana, his wife, tends to the dining room. Some of their best sellers are homemade Garganelli with Prosciutto and Peas, Lobster Risotto, and Rack of Veal with Fresh Porcini.

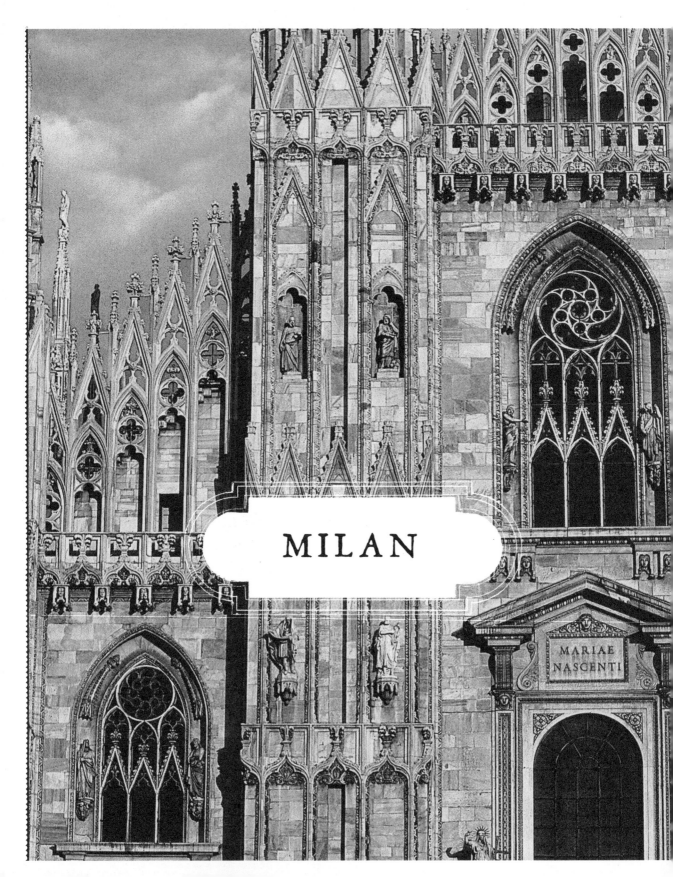

MILAN

MARIAE
NASCENTI

APPETIZERS

Crisp Risotto Cakes with Mushrooms {*Risotto al Salto con Funghi*}

Bresaola with Oil, Parmigiano, and Artichokes {*Bresaola con Olio, Parmigiano, e Carciofini*}

Prawns with Cannellini, Rosemary, and Hot Pepper
    {*Gamberi in Padella con Cannellini, Rosmarino, e Peperoncino*}

FIRST COURSES

Milanese Saffron Risotto {*Risotto alla Milanese*}

Risotto with Gorgonzola and Pears {*Risotto con Gorgonzola e Pere*}

Risotto with Chanterelles, Fontina, and Sparkling Wine {*Risotto con Finferli, Fontina, e Spumante*}

Milanese Squash Tortelli {*Tortelli di Zucca e Mostarda alla Milanese*}

Chestnut-Flour Tagliatelle with Mushrooms {*Tagliatelle di Farina di Castagne ai Funghi Misti*}

Garganelli with Spring Peas, Crisp Pancetta, and Pecorino
    {*Garganelli con Piselli, Pancetta Tostata, e Pecorino*}

Potato Gnocchi with Shrimp, Squid, and Clams
    {*Gnocchetti di Patate con Scampi, Calamari, e Vongole*}

Minestrone with Beans and Rice Milan-Style {*Minestrone alla Milanese*}

ENTRÉES

Old-Fashioned Milanese Veal Shanks {*Ossobuco alla Milanese di una Volta*}

Sautéed Breaded Milanese Veal Chops {*Costolette di Vitello alla Milanese*}

Stuffed Roasted Veal {*Vitello Arrosto Imbottito*}

Roasted Capon with Pancetta, Sage, and Rosemary {*Cappone Arrosto alla Pancetta, Salvia, e Rosmarino*}

Pheasant Hunter-Style {*Fagiano alla Cacciatora*}

Milanese Meatballs Wrapped in Cabbage {*Mondeghili nella Verza*}

Cuttlefish and Warm Potato Salad {*Insalata di Seppie e Patate*}

Asparagus with Parmigiano and Fried Eggs {*Asparagi con Parmigiano e Uova Fritte alla Milanese*}

VEGETABLES AND SALADS

Celery Root and Green Apple Salad {*Insalata di Sedano di Verona e Mele*}

Marinated Artichoke Hearts {*Carciofini Marinati*}

Peppers, Onions, and Tomatoes in a Skillet, Milan-Style {*La Peperonata Milanese*}

DESSERTS

Milan's Crumbly Cake {*Torta Sbrisolona*}

Rice, Almond, and Raisin Cake {*Torta di Riso, Mandorle, e Uvetta Sultanina*}

Cherries Poached in Red Wine and Spices {*Ciliege Cotte nel Vino Rosso*}

Milan l'è un gran Milan ("Milan is a great Milan"):

This is how generations of true Milanese refer to their beloved city. The first thing that comes to mind when talking about Milan is the city's great achievements. Milan, the most international city of Italy and one of the world's trendsetters, is the capital of design, fashion, business, high finance, commerce, culture, and technology. And, during the last few years, Milan seems to have also become Italy's dining capital.

Milan is the city that, together with New York and Paris, every year tells the rest of the world what to wear. It is the city for the best and the brightest, for dreamers and for achievers. Fast-moving, dynamic Milan, with more than 1,300,000 people, is the second largest Italian city, after Rome. It is, without any doubt, the New York of Italy. And, like New York, Milan is a melting pot of people from all over the world.

While some will argue that Milan is not one of the most beautiful cities of Italy, I think it is a beautiful, sexy, modern city, one that needs to be discovered layer by layer. For me the image of Piazza del Duomo at night—wrapped in a blanket of fog, with the dazzlingly gorgeous cathedral barely visible—is as beautiful and romantic as anything I have ever seen.

The history of Milan and its region is a complex one. Beginning in the eleventh century, the region was occupied by hordes of invaders—Roman, German, Spanish,

Austrian, and French—who came, conquered, and left behind uncommon gastronomic and cultural legacies. Milan is the capital of landlocked Lombardy, one of the largest and wealthiest of all Italian regions, stretching from the Alps in the north to the Po Valley in the south. The city offers majestic buildings, magnificent churches, hidden medieval courtyards, and districts such as Brera and the Navigli, considered by many the most Parisian, bohemian, laid-back areas of Milan: Brera has the famous Piccolo Teatro, and the even more famous Pinacoteca, one of the most important museums of Europe; the Navigli has a network of canals and waterways created centuries ago to supply water to the countryside, plus an abundance of quaint restaurants, trattorie, caffès, artisans and art shops, and boutiques. These districts are magical places, where old and new mingle in perfect harmony.

I discovered Milan in my late teens. My older brother, some friends, and I took a train from Bologna to spend a weekend there. It was a humid, hot day, a day when only tourists seemed interested to roam the city. We visited as many churches, museums, and libraries as we could because they were cool and comfortable. We nibbled on divine gelatos and on panettone topped with whipped cream at Caffè Motta, one of the city's oldest caffès, in Piazza del Duomo, and surveyed the animated activity of the piazza. (Unfortunately, Caffè Motta is now a fast-food place, Milan-style.) We attended the Sunday mass at the Duomo, the spectacular Gothic marbled cathedral on the square that bears its name. After the service, we climbed the stairs to the terraces on the roof where, speechless, we stared at the stunning square below and at the amazing artistry of the *guglie*—the ornate, spiked towers of the church that seemed to stretch as if trying to touch the sky. This cathedral, the third largest church in the world, has the statue of the *madonnina,* as the Milanese call their Madonna, on top of the highest guglia. The Duomo is the symbol of Milan, a symbol that took four and a half centuries to build.

Another symbol of the city is La Scala, the most famous opera house in the world, which came to life in August 1778 and has since been the home of some of the world's best singers, composers, and dancers: Verdi, Puccini, Callas, Pavarotti, Tebaldi, and Nureyev have been immortalized in this magnificent *teatro.* Sit at one of the historic caffès under the magnificent Galleria Vittorio Emanuele II next to the Duomo, which was built in 1867 and is considered by the Milanese their own outdoor living room, and observe the smartly, casually dressed people who stroll. Walk through the most fashionable streets of Milan—Via Montenapoleone, Via Manzoni, Via Sant'Andrea, and Via Spiga in the heart of the city—where art boutiques and the biggest names of the fashion world display the triumph of "Made in Italy," and you will feel the pulse of the city.

And then, as always, there is the food, made succulent by the rich agriculture of the region: sweet butter, cheeses, cream, hams, salami, veal, pork, vegetables, rice, and cornmeal are used with abandon. If olive oil, beef, bread, and wine define the cuisine of Florence, butter, cheese, rice, and polenta define Milanese cooking.

The best place to experience the richness of the Milanese table, as well as food specialties from other cities and regions, is at Peck, the most incredible specialty food store of Italy, located only a few blocks from Piazza del Duomo. I never stop marveling at the mind-boggling selections of wines, cheeses, cured meats, freshly made egg pastas, desserts, vegetables, and, best of all, platter after platter of beautifully prepared, succulent-looking dishes to go. During one of our many trips to Milan, my husband and I were given a nice room with a large terrace overlooking the square and the cathedral. So we went to Peck and bought a bottle of wine, a loaf of bread, *vitello tonnato* (thinly sliced cold veal covered with a divine tuna-mayonnaise sauce), and *mozzarella di bufala* (fresh mozzarella made from buffalo milk) tossed with cherry tomatoes and a voluptuous green olive oil. We took the food to our terrace and improvised a memorable picnic.

The second best place to experience the traditional food of Milan is to eat in a trattoria. I still remember a meal I had many years ago at the venerable Trattoria della Pesa while I was researching one of my first books. I had been told that for authentic, classic Milanese food, nobody could beat this little trattoria. I was somewhat disappointed by the modest dining room, and by the cold, almost bored attitude of the waiter. But then the food arrived, preceded by a most divine aroma, and everything else became irrelevant. The golden, absolutely perfect risotto was one of the best I had ever eaten, and the *cassouela*, a unique pork and cabbage stew, was simply memorable.

Because the food of Milan is today multi-ethnic, some people are convinced that Milanese cooking is slowly disappearing. But in Milan's venerable trattorie such as Masuelli San Marco, La Piola, Alfredo, Gran San Bernardo, and Casa Fontana true Milanese cooking is still prepared daily: Risotto alla Milanese served next to ossobuco, braised veal shanks; *mondeghili,* Milanese meatballs wrapped in cabbage; *brasato,* a slowly braised beef pot roast served next to soft, creamy polenta; *costoletta alla Milanese,* breaded, crisp veal chop; minestrone, a super-thick vegetable-rice soup; delicate squash-stuffed tortelli, bathed in butter, Parmigiano, and sage; *risotto al salto,* leftover risotto that is flattened into a small skillet and fried in plenty of butter; and *rostin negaa,* veal chops oven-braised in plenty of wine.

And then there is the food of the elegant restaurants of the city, which are as good as the best in New York, London, or Paris, and are the domain of celebrity chefs. After three or four days of sampling the traditional dishes of Milan, my husband and I dress in our best and treat ourselves to a deluxe restaurant. One of our very favorites is Sadler, located in the Navigli district, with modern, refined cuisine, a mellow mood, soothing décor, outstanding service, and memorable food. And so we linger at the table, sipping great wine while savoring light-as-air homemade *pizzoccheri* (buckwheat noodles) with black truffle, black risotto with a ragù of scallops, slices of succulent suckling pig with tiny white beans, roasted rack of lamb with crisp deep-fried squash blossoms, and panettone pudding with white chocolate.

It is time to leave. So we opt to have a cognac at one of the beautiful caffès in the Galleria. With glass in hand, we toast Milan, perhaps the most vibrant city of Italy.

Tomorrow, during the long flight back to the United States, when the flight attendant will place that sad-looking tray of food in front of me, I will longingly remember the wonderful meals we had in this great city. Now, more than ever, I am convinced that this high-fashion, high-tech, sophisticated, fast-moving city is the place to go for great food.

Crisp Risotto Cakes with Mushrooms

Risotto al Salto con Funghi

In Milan, leftover saffron risotto is turned into delicious, crisp rice cakes called *risotto al salto*. At Trattoria Casa Fontana they make small, golden cakes; top them with sautéed mixed mushrooms; and serve them as a delicious appetizer. ◆ *serves 4*

FOR THE RISOTTO CAKES

- 2 cups leftover Milanese Saffron Risotto (page 184)
- 1 large egg, lightly beaten
- 2 tablespoons unsalted butter

FOR THE MUSHROOMS

- 3 to 4 tablespoons extra-virgin olive oil
- 1/2 pound mixed mushrooms (shiitake, cremini, chanterelles), wiped clean and thinly sliced
- Salt and freshly ground black pepper to taste
- 1 garlic clove, finely minced
- 1 tablespoon chopped fresh flat-leaf parsley

MAKE THE RISOTTO CAKES

In a bowl, combine the risotto with the beaten egg.

Heat 1/2 tablespoon of the butter in a 6-inch nonstick skillet over medium heat. When the butter begins to bubble, add about 1/2 cup of the risotto and spread it over the bottom of the skillet with a spatula, pressing the rice down to form a pancake. When the bottom is golden and crisp, 4 to 5 minutes, turn the cake onto a plate, then slide it back into the pan to brown the other side, about 4 minutes. Repeat with the remaining butter and risotto. Keep the pancakes warm in a low heated oven.

MAKE THE MUSHROOMS

Heat the oil in a large skillet over medium-high heat. Add the mushrooms and cook, stirring, until they are lightly golden and soft, 4 to 5 minutes. Season with salt and pepper to taste. Add the garlic and parsley, and stir until the garlic is lightly colored, 1 to 2 minutes. Taste and adjust the seasoning.

Place the risotto cakes on individual dishes, top with a small mound of mushrooms, and serve.

Bresaola with Oil, Parmigiano, and Artichoke

Bresaola con Olio, Parmigiano, e Carciofini

Il Verdi is a hip trattoria-restaurant-wine bar that is always crowded with a young clientele who are perhaps more interested in showing off than eating. It is a great place for nibbling, tasting some wine, and connecting with your fellow man. The last time I was there, several years ago, I had one of my favorite appetizers made with *bresaola*: (dried, salted beef): it was very thin, topped by marinated baby artichokes, oil, lemon, black pepper, and slivers of Parmigiano. It was absolutely delicious. Serve with small slices of bread or with breadsticks. ◆ *serves 4*

6 ounces bresaola, cut into thin slices

Freshly ground black pepper to taste

¼ cup extra-virgin olive oil

Juice of 1 lemon

16 marinated baby artichokes (see note, page 225) or store-bought artichokes marinated in olive-oil

3 ounces Parmigiano-Reggiano, shredded into thin slivers

Drape the sliced bresaola on individual plates. Season with black pepper and sprinkle with oil and lemon juice. Place 4 small artichokes in the center of each plate, and top with slivers of Parmigiano.

BRESAOLA

Bresaola is a filet of beef that is cured in salt and dried. This delicious product is a specialty of the Valtellina, a beautiful, sunny valley in the northern part of Lombardy. Bresaola is now quite popular in the United States and is often served as a component of an antipasto misto. It can be found in Italian markets and specialty food stores.

Prawns with Cannellini, Rosemary, and Hot Pepper

Gamberi in Padella con Cannellini, Rosmarino, e Peperoncino

Claudio Sadler is without a doubt one of the most prominent Italian chefs, a modern, intelligent chef who cooks with his soul. Sadler restaurant is one of the first places I go when I am in Milan. His food is unique, elegant, unfussy, and absolutely delicious. This is one of his simplest dishes, which relies entirely on the ingredients and the expert eye of the cook. It can be served as an appetizer or, by doubling the recipe, as an entrée. ◆ *serves 4*

FOR THE BEANS

- 1 1/2 cups dried cannellini beans or white kidney beans, picked over and soaked overnight in cold water to cover
- 1 garlic clove, peeled and lightly mashed
- 1 bay leaf
- 1/3 to 1/2 cup extra-virgin olive oil
- 1 large shallot, minced (about 1/2 cup)
- 6 large fresh tomatoes, diced (about 4 cups)
- 1/2 teaspoon salt plus more to taste
- 1/4 pound thickly sliced pancetta, cut into 1/2-inch pieces
- 1 cup dry white wine
- 1 tablespoon chopped fresh flat-leaf parsley
- 1/2 teaspoon chopped fresh red chili pepper or hot red pepper flakes plus more to taste

FOR THE PRAWNS

- 8 jumbo prawns, shelled and deveined
  Salt to taste
- 1 tablespoon chopped fresh rosemary
- 1/3 cup extra-virgin olive oil

PREPARE THE BEANS

Discard any beans that come to the surface of the water. Drain and rinse the beans under cold running water and put them in a large pot. Cover generously with cold water, add the garlic and bay leaf, and bring to a gentle boil. Cook uncovered over medium heat, until the beans are tender, 30 to 40 minutes. Drain the beans, discard the garlic and bay leaf, and set aside. (The beans can be cooked ahead. Transfer them to a bowl with their liquid and cool. Cover and refrigerate for a day or two.)

Heat half of the oil in a large skillet over medium heat. Add half of the shallot and cook, stirring, until soft, 4 to 5 minutes. Add the tomatoes and season with the salt. Cook uncovered over medium heat, stirring occasionally, until the tomatoes are soft, 10 to 15 minutes. Purée the tomatoes and their juices in a food processor, then press the mixture through a fine sieve and into a bowl.

Heat the remaining oil in another large skillet. Add the remaining shallot and cook until soft, 4 to 5 minutes. Add the pancetta and stir until it is lightly golden and crisp, 2 to 3 minutes. Add the reserved beans and the wine, season lightly with salt, and stir until the wine is almost all evaporated, 5 to 6 minutes. Stir the puréed tomatoes into the beans, and simmer uncovered over low heat until the juices in the pan have thickened, 8 to 10 minutes. Add the parsley and the chili pepper, taste, and correct the seasoning. Keep the sauce warm over very low heat.

FINISH THE DISH

Meanwhile, put the prawns in a large bowl. Season with salt, add the chopped rosemary and the olive oil, and mix to combine.

Heat a large nonstick skillet over medium-high heat. When hot, add the prawns and all the oil in the bowl. Cook until the prawns are golden on both sides, 3 to 4 minutes.

Spoon the beans and sauce in the center of serving dishes, arrange the prawns over the beans, and serve hot.

Milanese Saffron Risotto

Risotto alla Milanese

For me one of the great joys of eating regionally is to order local, traditional dishes. When I am in Milan, what I crave is the creamy, golden Risotto alla Milanese. Even though this seductive dish is now served in Italian restaurants all over the world, I maintain that the risottos of Milan's traditional establishments are in a class by themselves. Alfredo Valli, the esteemed eighty-year-old owner of Alfredo, Gran San Bernardo restaurant, believes that a properly cooked risotto relies on several things: slowly simmered homemade meat broth; Vialone, a short-grain rice (a Milanese favorite) that releases the right amount of starch as it cooks and becomes plump while keeping the bite; sweet butter; saffron threads; and the best Parmigiano-Reggiano that money can buy. To all of this I add: patience, since the risotto needs to be stirred and watched for about 20 minutes. The result, however, is incredibly satisfying. ◆ *serves 4 to 6*

7 cups Meat Broth (page 298) or canned low-sodium beef broth

$^1/_2$ teaspoon crumbled saffron threads

4 tablespoons ($^1/_2$ stick) unsalted butter

$^1/_2$ small yellow onion, minced (about $^1/_2$ cup)

2 cups Vialone Nano, Arborio, or Carnaroli rice

$^1/_2$ cup dry white wine

$^1/_2$ cup freshly grated Parmigiano-Reggiano

Salt to taste

Heat the broth in a medium saucepan and keep warm over low heat. Transfer 1 cup of the hot broth to a bowl, stir in the saffron, and set aside.

Melt 3 tablespoons of the butter in a large, heavy skillet over medium heat. When the butter begins to foam, add the onion and cook, stirring, until pale yellow and soft, 4 to 5 minutes. Add the rice and stir until it is well coated with the butter and onion, and begins to whiten, about 2 minutes. Stir in the wine. When the wine is almost all evaporated, add 1 cup of the hot broth. Cook and stir until most of the broth has been absorbed. Continue cooking and stirring the rice in this manner, adding 1 cup or so of broth at a time, for about 15 minutes.

Add the 1 cup of saffron broth and continue cooking and stirring until most of the broth has been absorbed and the rice is tender but still a bit firm to the bite, 3 to 4 minutes.

Swirl in the remaining tablespoon of butter and about half of the Parmigiano. Stir quickly until the cheese and butter are melted and the rice has a creamy, moist consistency. Taste, adjust the seasoning, and serve with the remaining Parmigiano on the side.

GOLDEN-ORANGE SAFFRON

The botanical name of saffron is *Crocus sativus*, and from the stigmas of this prized bud come the world's most expensive spice: 75,000 stigmas are need to produce a pound of saffron. In Sardinia, Tuscany, and Abruzzo, saffron is harvested by hand in the fall, when the crocuses are in full bloom.

When buying saffron, choose saffron in threads. Do not buy powdered saffron, because it is often mixed with other spices. Store saffron in a cool, dark place, in a sealed plastic bag. It will keep well for several months. Keep in mind that saffron is very aromatic, and its flavor, when released by soaking in warm or hot broth, is unmistakable.

Risotto with Gorgonzola and Pears

Risotto con Gorgonzola e Pere

I had this delicious risotto at La Piola, one of the oldest traditional trattorie of Milan. When I asked the waiter about the unusual combination of pears and Gorgonzola, he smiled and said, "What is so unusual about pears and cheese?" I can't even tell you how wonderful this dish is. Buy pears that are just barely soft (if too ripe they will break apart during cooking). Choose a mild, sweet Gorgonzola. And, if at all possible, make a nice, light chicken broth from scratch. Then your risotto will taste as good as the one I had at this quaint trattoria. ◆ *serves 4 to 6*

7 cups Chicken Broth (page 298) or canned low-sodium chicken broth

3 tablespoons unsalted butter

1/2 small yellow onion, minced (about 1/2 cup)

2 cups Arborio, Carnaroli, or Vialone Nano rice

2 large, barely ripe Anjou pears, peeled and diced

1 cup dry white wine

2 ounces mild, sweet Gorgonzola, cut into small pieces

1 tablespoon chopped fresh flat-leaf parsley

Heat the broth in a medium saucepan and keep warm over low heat.

Melt the butter in a large, heavy skillet over medium heat. When the butter begins to foam, add the onion and cook until pale yellow and soft, 4 to 5 minutes. Add the rice and stir until it is coated with the butter and the onion, and begins to whiten, 2 to 3 minutes. Add the pears, stir for a minute or two, then add the wine. Stir until most of the wine has evaporated. Add about 1 cup of the hot broth, or just enough to barely cover the rice. Cook, stirring, until the broth has been almost completely absorbed. Continue cooking and stirring the rice in this manner, adding broth 1 cup or so at a time, for about 17 minutes. At this point the rice should be tender but still a bit firm to the bite.

When most of the last addition of broth is incorporated, add the Gorgonzola. Stir quickly until the cheese is completely melted and the rice has a thick, creamy consistency, 2 to 3 minutes. If the risotto seems a bit dry, stir in a little more broth. Stir in the parsley, taste, adjust the seasoning, and serve.

ABOUT GORGONZOLA

Gorgonzola is the Italian version of a naturally fermented blue cheese made from cow's milk, and is produced primarily in the regions of Piedmont and Lombardy. While a mature Gorgonzola, aged five to six months, has a pungent, direct taste, a two- to three-month-old Gorgonzola is milder, sweeter, and creamier. Serve Gorgonzola at the end of a meal with grapes or pears, or use it as a component of risotto and pasta sauces.

Vittorio Emanuele II Gallery

Risotto with Chanterelles, Fontina, and Sparkling Wine

Risotto con Finferli, Fontina, e Spumante

In a city that has a high number of fashionable and trendy restaurants with dazzling prices, one occasionally finds a gem such as Trattoria Casa Fontana, the home of 23 types of risottos. I discovered this classic trattoria several years ago while researching another book. I was intrigued by and a bit skeptical of such a large number of risottos. But as my husband and I sat down and the waiter suggested starting the meal with an antipasto, "because the risotto will take a minimum of a half hour to prepare," I knew that risotto was taken very seriously. This is one of them. ◆ *serves 4 to 6*

7 cups Vegetable Broth (page 299) or canned low-sodium chicken broth

3 tablespoons unsalted butter

$1/2$ small yellow onion, minced (about $1/2$ cup)

$1/2$ pound chanterelle or shiitake mushrooms, wiped clean and diced (about 3 cups)

2 cups Arborio, Carnaroli, or Vialone Nano rice

1 cup sparkling wine or dry white wine

$1/4$ pound Fontina cheese, finely diced

1 tablespoon chopped fresh flat-leaf parsley

Heat the broth in a medium saucepan and keep warm over low heat.

Melt the butter in a large, heavy skillet over medium heat. Add the onion and cook until it is pale yellow and soft, 4 to 5 minutes. Add the mushrooms and stir until lightly golden, 2 to 3 minutes. Add the rice and cook until it is coated with the savory base and begins to whiten, 2 to 3 minutes. Add the wine and stir until most of it has evaporated. Add about 1 cup of the hot broth, or just enough to barely cover the rice. Cook, stirring, until the broth has been almost completely absorbed. Continue cooking and stirring the rice in this manner, adding broth 1 cup or so at a time, until the rice is tender but still a bit firm to the bite, about 17 minutes.

When most of the last addition of broth is incorporated, add the Fontina. Stir quickly until the cheese is completely melted and the rice has a thick, creamy consistency, 2 to 3 minutes. Stir in the parsley, taste, adjust the seasoning, and serve.

WHEN IN MILAN
Restaurants, Trattorie, and Wine Bars

From the U.S. dial 011, followed by the country code of 39. The area code for all numbers below is 02.

Bacco Wine Bar
Via Marcona 1
Tel. 546 0697
Bacco offers 350 choices of wines and simple, tasty dishes such as pastas, risottos, hams, cheeses, and pâtés.

Bice
Via Borgospesso 12
Tel. 7600 2572
This classic restaurant opened its doors in 1926 and through the decades has been a favorite of fashion and design moguls. Bice serves traditional Milanese dishes as well as Tuscan specialties such as *ribollita*, *arista* (roasted pork loin), and *stracotto* (beef braised in wine and served with polenta).

Cracco-Peck
Via Victor Hugo 4
Tel. 876 774
An elegant, fine-dining establishment that belongs to the Peck family. The young chef Carlo Cracco presides over the modern and creative food. Dress up in your best garb and get ready to be pampered by faultless service.

Da Giacomo
Via Pasquale Sottocorno 6
Tel. 7602 3313
Walking into Da Giacomo, with its turn-of-the-century high-ceilinged dining rooms, is like being transported back in time. This warm, inviting restaurant, about ten minutes from the center of town, caters primarily to Milanesi. The food is a mixture of Milanese and Tuscan, with a strong emphasis on seafood. My favorite dish was *gnocchetti allo scoglio*, small, ridgeless potato gnocchi tossed in a delightful ragù of prawns, calamari, and clams.

Don Lisander
Via Manzoni 12/a
Tel. 760 201 30
Very centrally located, this restaurant is favored by Milanesi and out-of-towners alike. Don Lisander serves traditional Milanese dishes as well as those of other regions. Melt-in-the-mouth ossobuco and saffron-tinted risotto are his trademarks. You will probably be seated in an interior garden covered by a large tent. Very romantic.

Il Luogo di Aimo e Nadia
Via Montecuccoli 6
Tel. 416 886
My husband and I discovered Aimo and Nadia over twenty years ago, and have been consistently in love with this terrific, elegant place ever since. Aimo, the cherubic looking chef, is an immaculately clad presence in the two dining rooms, chatting and tempting his customers with descriptions of the specials of the day. His wife, Nadia, is in the kitchen preparing some of the most splendid food in Milan. This restaurant is about a fifteen-minute drive from the center of town.

La Cantina di Manuela
Via Cadore 30
Tel. 5518 4931
This enoteca has one of the largest selections of Italian wines and a great assortment of regional hams, cheeses, and homemade sweet condiments.

La Piola
Viale Abruzzi 23
Tel. 29 53 12 71
La Piola is a seriously traditional trattoria where you can find dishes hardly seen on other menus. The place is small and is generally filled with locals. One of my favorite dishes was the *cassoeula*, a very rich, very flavorful pork stew that is traditionally made with many parts of the pig and served mostly in winter.

Masuelli San Marco
Viale Umbria 80
Tel. 55 18 41 38
Every single time I am in Milan I make a stop at Masuelli, a trattoria that has been in the same family for over eighty years; for me, eating at Masuelli is like eating in a Milanese home. And, just as in an Italian home, the kitchen is the domain of Tina Masuelli and her son Massimiliano, while the front of the house is left in the capable hands of Pino, Tina's congenial husband. Try their incomparable *bollito misto*, an array of assorted meats simmered for hours and served with succulent condiments.

Ombre Rosse
Via Plinio 29
Tel. 2952 4734
Large selections of wines, delicious pâtés, cold dishes, and regional cheeses.

Osteria del Binari
Via Tortona 1
Tel. 894 094 28
A charming small restaurant, with a hip clientele, that serves the food of the area as well as dishes from other regions. Don't miss the many mouthwatering appetizers.

Ristorante al Porto
Piazzale Cantore 3
Porta Genova
Tel. 8321 1481
One of the best, perennially busy, seafood restaurants of Milan, catering to a fashionable clientele. Don't miss the *antipasto misto di pesce*, the *spaghettini con vongole veraci*, or the risotto with mixed seafood.

Ristorante a Santa Lucia
Via San Pietro all'Orto 3
Tel. 7602 3155
This rustic, very popular restaurant, within walking distance of Piazza del Duomo, has been in operation since 1929. The food here has a strong Neapolitan influence, which makes it the perfect place for a hearty pasta dish, a great pizza, or a delightful seafood salad.

Rosy e Gabriele
Via Sirtori 26
Tel. 295 25930
This traditional pizzeria is open until 2 A.M., serving typical Neapolitan pizzas as well as calzoni, savory breads, and *insalatone* (large, creative salads).

Sadler
Via Troilo 14 (Angolo Via Conchetta)
Tel. 5810 4451
Claudio Sadler is one of the hottest chefs of Italy. The restaurant, which is located in the hip area of the Navigli, is generally packed with a serious assortment of food lovers from all over the world. Sadler's food is seasonal and creative, but still grounded in regional traditions. The restaurant has a romantic and relaxed feeling, the service is attentive and unobtrusive, and the food is terrific.

Salumeria Armandola
Via della Spiga 50
Tel. 7602 1657
This is a fast-food place Italian-style, where you can take out or can eat while standing. Try their roast chicken, rabbit, or pork; baked pastas; and delicious vegetables.

Trattoria Casa Fontana 23 Risotti
Piazza Carbonari 5
Tel. 67 04 710
If risotto is one of your favorite dishes, then you shouldn't miss Casa Fontana, the home of twenty-three risottos made the old-fashioned way, slowly and with tender, loving care. So be prepared to wait for thirty to forty minutes, since each risotto is made completely from scratch. Casa Fontana is about a fifteen-minute drive from the center of town.

Trattoria Milanese
Via Santa Marta 11
Tel. 8645 1991
Since 1919, this casual trattoria in the heart of town has served genuine Milanese dishes, and it is one of the few places left in Milan where the waiters still speak the local dialect. The food here is traditional to the core: *mondeghili* (Milanese meatballs) and *foiolo in umido* (stewed tripe) were two of my favorites.

The Castello Sforzesco

Milanese Squash Tortelli

Tortelli di Zucca e Mostarda alla Milanese

One of my very favorite pasta dishes of Milan is squash tortelli, a specialty pasta that used to be prepared mostly on Christmas Eve. While pasta stuffed with squash is typical of several Northern Italian regions, the Milanese version adds Amaretti di Saronno cookies (see note, page 229), Parmigiano, and the incomparable *mostarda di Cremona* (see note), producing a filling that is subtly sweet, complex, and unique at the same time. Make this dish in the fall, when squash is at its very best. ◆ *serves 8*

FOR THE TORTELLI

- 1 medium butternut squash, about 2 pounds
- 1/4 pound imported *Mostarda di Cremona*, very finely chopped
- 3 Amaretti di Saronno (imported Italian almond cookies), finely chopped
- Grated zest of 1 lemon
- 1/2 cup freshly grated Parmigiano-Reggiano
- 2 tablespoons fine, dried, unseasoned bread crumbs
- 1/8 teaspoon freshly grated nutmeg
- Salt to taste
- 1 recipe Basic Pasta Dough (page 301)

TO COOK AND SERVE

- 1 tablespoon coarse salt, plus more to taste
- 3 to 4 tablespoons unsalted butter
- 1 small sprig of fresh rosemary
- 1/3 to 1/2 cup freshly grated Parmigiano-Reggiano

PREPARE THE FILLING AND TORTELLI

Preheat the oven to 350°F.

Cut the squash in half lengthwise and discard the seeds. Wrap each half in foil, place on a sheet pan, and bake on the middle rack of the oven until it is tender and can be easily pierced with a knife, about 1 hour. Remove from the oven and let cool in its wrapping.

Scoop out the pulp of the squash and place it in a large, clean kitchen cloth napkin (do not put the pulp in a porous kitchen towel, for it will stick to the towel). Wrap the napkin around the squash and squeeze out 1/3 to 1/2 cup of the watery juices. Reserve the juices (see note). Purée the squash through a food mill directly into a bowl. Add the chopped *mostarda di Cremona*, the almond cookies, lemon zest,

Parmigiano, bread crumbs, and nutmeg. Season lightly with salt and mix thoroughly. Cover and refrigerate for several hours or overnight.

Roll out one thin sheet of dough at a time (see page 302) and trim so it has straight edges and is about 6 inches wide. Place 1 tablespoon of the filling every 3 inches on the sheet of dough, putting the filling closer to the edge near you. Fold the sheet in half over the filling and seal around each mound, pressing out air pockets with your fingertips. Cut between the filling and press the edges to seal.

Cover a tray with a kitchen towel and sprinkle with flour. Line the tortelli in a single layer, leaving space between them. Repeat until all the dough and filling are used. The tortelli can be used immediately or refrigerated, uncovered, for several hours.

COOK AND SERVE

Bring a large pot of water to a boil. Add the tablespoon of coarse salt and the tortelli, and cook until the pasta is tender but still a bit firm to the bite, 2 to 3 minutes.

While the pasta is cooking, melt the butter in a large skillet over medium heat. Add the sprig of rosemary, stir for a minute or two, then discard the rosemary.

Scoop out and reserve about $1/2$ cup of the pasta cooking water. Drain the tortelli gently and place them in the skillet with the butter. Add about half of the Parmigiano and season lightly with salt. Mix gently over medium heat until the tortelli and sauce are well combined. Stir in a little bit of the cooking water if the tortelli seem a bit dry. Serve at once with the remaining Parmigiano on the side.

NOTE

Since squash has a high water content, resist the temptation to squeeze out more watery juices than is indicated in the recipe, for you will be left with a small ball of very dry pulp. If that should happen, boil down the reserved squash juice until it is a very thick glaze, then stir a tablespoon or two into the puréed squash.

Mostarda di Cremona, which is made with large pieces of plump, mixed fruit that are preserved in a sweet, mustardy syrup, is a specialty of Cremona, Lombardy.

Chestnut-Flour Tagliatelle with Mushrooms

Tagliatelle di Farina di Castagne ai Funghi Misti

I have been eating pasta all my life, so when I come across something that is just a little bit unusual, I order it. The very polished waiter of the Four Seasons Hotel in Milan described this pasta as tasting, "good enough for an angel." Later, when I looked with regret at my empty plate, I had to agree. The almost sweet taste of the chestnut tagliatelle paired with the meaty, woodsy taste of the fresh wild porcini was a delightful experience. Even though fresh porcini are sometimes available in American markets, most of the time they are not. So I prepare this dish with a mixture of assorted fresh mushrooms. ◆ *serves 4*

FOR THE CHESTNUT TAGLIATELLE

- I cup unbleached all-purpose flour
- I cup finely milled chestnut flour
- 3 extra-large eggs
- I to 2 tablespoons whole milk

FOR THE MUSHROOMS

- $^{1}/_{3}$ cup extra-virgin olive oil
- $^{1}/_{2}$ pound mixed mushrooms, such as chanterelles, shiitake, and oyster, wiped clean and thinly sliced
- 2 garlic cloves, minced
- $^{1}/_{2}$ cup dry white wine

  Salt and freshly ground black pepper to taste
- I tablespoon chopped fresh flat-leaf parsley
- 2 tablespoons unsalted butter

PREPARE THE TAGLIATELLE

Prepare the pasta as instructed on page 301, using the flours, eggs, and milk in this recipe. Roll out the dough and cut into tagliatelle as instructed on page 303. (The pasta can be made several hours or a day or two ahead.)

FINISH THE DISH

Heat the oil in a large skillet over high heat. When the oil just begins to smoke, add the mushrooms without crowding (sauté in 2 batches if needed) and cook, stirring, until the mushrooms are lightly golden, 2 to 3 minutes. Add the garlic and stir until it begins to color, about 1 minute. Add the wine, season with salt and pepper, and cook, stirring, until the wine is almost all evaporated, 2 to 3 minutes. Add the parsley, stir once or twice, and turn off the heat.

Meanwhile, bring a large pot of water to a boil. Add 1 tablespoon of salt and the pasta. Cook uncovered over high heat, stirring a few times, until the pasta is tender but still a bit firm to the bite. Scoop up and reserve $1/2$ cup of the cooking water.

Drain the pasta and add it to the mushrooms. Season with salt and add the butter and a few tablespoons of the reserved cooking water. Mix quickly over medium heat until the butter is melted and the pasta and mushrooms are well combined. Taste, adjust the seasoning, and serve.

Garganelli with Spring Peas, Crisp Pancetta, and Pecorino

Garganelli con Piselli, Pancetta Tostata, e Pecorino

Claudio Sadler, chef owner of the superlative Milanese restaurant that bears his name, takes a traditional Roman dish such as pasta *carbonara* and elevates it to new heights. The starring ingredients in this dish are superlative pasta, spring peas or fava beans, perfectly aged cheese, and crisp pancetta. This is one of the favorite dishes of Andrew, my six-year-old grandson, who consistently asks for more. ◆ *serves 4*

I   pound unshelled fresh peas,
     or 5 ounces frozen peas, thawed

3   large egg yolks

I   large egg

$1/3$ cup heavy cream

     Salt to taste

2   tablespoons unsalted butter

2   tablespoons extra-virgin olive oil

$1/2$ very small yellow onion, minced
     (about $1/3$ cup)

     Chopped fresh red chili pepper or
     crushed red pepper flakes to taste

$1/4$ pound thickly sliced pancetta,
     cut into $1/2$-inch pieces

$1/2$ pound dried *garganelli* or penne rigate

$1/2$ cup freshly grated Pecorino Romano
     or Parmigiano-Reggiano

Bring a small saucepan of water to a boil. Shell the peas and add to the water. Cook over medium heat until the peas are tender but still a bit firm to the bite, 2 to 3 minutes, depending on size.

In a large, shallow serving dish that can later accommodate the pasta, beat the egg yolks and whole egg with the cream. Season with salt and set aside.

Heat the butter and oil in a large skillet over medium heat. When the butter begins to foam, add the onion and cook, stirring, until lightly golden and soft, about 5 minutes. Add the chili pepper and pancetta and cook, stirring, until the pancetta is golden and crisp, 2 to 3 minutes. Add the peas and stir just long enough to coat them with the savory base, 1 to 2 minutes.

Meanwhile, bring a large pot of water to a boil. Add 1 tablespoon of salt and the *garganelli*. Cook, uncovered over high heat until the pasta is tender but still a bit firm to the bite.

Drain the pasta and add it to the skillet. Season lightly with salt. Mix quickly over medium heat until the pasta is well coated with the sauce. Stir the pasta and its sauce into the egg-cream mixture, add about half of the cheese, and mix thoroughly until the pasta is well coated with the eggs. Taste, adjust the seasoning, and serve with the remaining cheese on the side.

Potato Gnocchi with Shrimp, Squid, and Clams

Gnocchetti di Patate con Scampi, Calamari, e Vongole

A fifteen-minute taxi ride took us from our centrally located hotel to Da Giacomo, an old-fashioned restaurant that is well known for seafood dishes and desserts. The place was already bustling with what seemed to be very happy diners. The dining room's high ceiling, the thick ornate columns, the round windows, and the mosaic-like floor created a vibrant, warm feeling. But what captivated me most was an aroma that made me incredibly hungry. Of the several dishes I had, my favorite was the potato gnocchi with shellfish. The fluffy, light gnocchi, were topped with a delicious sauce of shrimp, baby squid, and very tiny clams in a flavorful tomato-wine sauce. This sauce also pairs perfectly well with spaghettini or spaghetti. ◆ *serves 4 to 6*

1 recipe Basic Potato Gnocchi (page 304)

3 pounds littleneck clams or cockles (the smallest you can get), cleaned (see note)

1 cup dry white wine

1/3 cup plus 2 tablespoons extra-virgin olive oil

1 pound shrimp, peeled, deveined, rinsed, and cut into I-inch pieces

1/2 small onion, minced (about 1/2 cup)

1 garlic clove, minced

1 (28-ounce) can Italian plum tomatoes, preferably San Marzano (see note, page 35), with their juices, put through a food mill to remove the seeds

Salt and crushed red pepper flakes to taste

1 pound whole squid, with bodies about 6 inches long, cleaned (see note), or 1/2 pound cleaned squid with tentacles, cut into I-inch-wide rings

1 tablespoon coarse salt

1 tablespoon unsalted butter

1 tablespoon finely chopped fresh flat-leaf parsley

Prepare the potato gnocchi and refrigerate, uncovered, until ready to use.

Put the clams and wine in a large skillet over medium heat. Cover the skillet and cook just until the clams open. Transfer the clams to a bowl as they open, and discard the ones that remain tightly shut. Line a strainer with paper towels, strain the liquid into a bowl, and set aside. Remove the clams from their shells and add to their liquid. Cover and set aside.

Wipe the skillet clean. Add ⅓ cup of the oil and return the pan to medium-high heat. As soon as the oil is hot, add the shrimp and stir until they just begin to color, 1 to 2 minutes. With a slotted spoon, transfer the shrimp to a bowl.

Return the skillet to medium heat. Add the remaining oil and the onion and cook, stirring, until the onion is pale yellow and soft, 4 to 5 minutes. Add the garlic and stir until it is lightly colored, about 1 minute. Add the tomatoes, season with salt and red pepper flakes, and simmer until the sauce has a medium-thick consistency, 7 to 8 minutes. Reduce the heat to low, then add the shrimp, clams with their juice, and squid. Simmer for 1 to 2 minutes, then turn off the heat. Taste and adjust the seasoning. (Do not cook the shellfish too long or it will become tough.)

Meanwhile, bring a large pot of water to a boil over high heat. Add the coarse salt and the gnocchi. Cook until the gnocchi rise to the surface, about 2 minutes. Remove with a slotted spoon, draining off the excess water against the side of the pot.

Place the gnocchi in the skillet with the sauce. Add the butter and the parsley, and mix quickly over low heat until the gnocchi and sauce are well combined. Taste, adjust the seasoning, and serve at once.

HOW TO CLEAN CLAMS AND SQUID

For clams: Soak in a large bowl of salted water for 20 to 30 minutes. Drain and scrub them well under cold running water. Discard any open clams that do not shut when handled. Place the clams in a bowl, cover with a wet towel, and refrigerate. Use the same day, if possible.

For squid: Put in a bowl of cold water and soak for a couple of hours. Drain, then pull away the tentacles. Cut the tentacles straight across, just above the eyes. Discard the head. Squeeze out the small beak at the base of the tentacles, and remove the long cartilage from the squid body. Rinse the inside of the body under cold running water. Peel away the skin under running water, then drain and pat dry. The squid body can now be stuffed or cut into rings.

Minestrone with Beans and Rice Milan-Style

Minestrone alla Milanese

What defines a Milanese minestrone, besides a large array of seasonal vegetables, is rice, which thickens the soup and turns a simple dish into a nurturing, wholesome meal. The Milanese minestrone can be prepared with chicken broth, meat broth, vegetable broth, or water. Pancetta, lard, or pork rinds are added to the savory base, and in summer beans are sometimes omitted in favor of larger amounts of fresh vegetables. Trattoria Mauselli San Marco, one of the oldest, most traditional trattorie of Milan, serves this summer soup at room temperature, with a generous topping of Parmigiano. Because this type of soup is even better a day or two after being made, I encourage you to double the amount and freeze what you don't use right away (see note). ◆ *serves 10 to 12*

2 tablespoons unsalted butter

$1/4$ cup extra-virgin olive oil

1 large onion, minced (about $1^{1}/2$ cups)

1 garlic clove, minced

$1/4$ pound thickly sliced pancetta, minced

2 tablespoons chopped fresh flat-leaf parsley

4 large tomatoes, diced (about $2^{1}/2$ cups), or $2^{1}/2$ cups diced canned plum tomatoes

2 medium russet or Idaho potatoes, diced (about $2^{1}/2$ cups)

3 large carrots, diced (about 3 cups)

3 large zucchini, diced (about 3 cups)

$1/2$ pound string beans, washed and cut into 1-inch pieces

$1/2$ medium head of Savoy cabbage, coarsely chopped (about 6 cups)

2 medium leeks, white parts only, cut into rounds and washed (about 2 cups)

Salt and freshly ground black pepper to taste

2 quarts Vegetable Broth (page 299), Chicken Broth (page 298), or water

1 cup Arborio rice

1 cup freshly grated Parmigiano-Reggiano

In a large pot over medium heat, heat the butter and the oil. When the butter begins to foam, add the onion, garlic, pancetta, and parsley. Cook, stirring, until the onion and pancetta are lightly golden, 5 to 6 minutes. Add the tomatoes, potatoes, carrots, zucchini, string beans, cabbage, and leeks. Stir for a few minutes until the vegetables are coated with the savory base. Season with salt and pepper. Add the broth and bring to a boil. Reduce the heat to low and simmer, uncovered, for 40 to 45 minutes, stirring from time to time.

About 25 minutes before serving, raise the heat to medium high and add the rice. Cook, stirring occasionally, until the rice is tender but still a bit firm to the bite, 10 to 12 minutes. Taste and adjust the seasoning. Let the soup rest for 10 to 15 minutes, then sprinkle with the freshly grated Parmigiano.

ABOUT PROPER FREEZING

Freezing gives you the advantage of having a wonderful soup on hand to use on the spur of the moment. However, freezing needs to be done correctly. As soon as the soup is done, but before adding the rice, transfer the amount you want to freeze to a bowl and refrigerate immediately, uncovered, until the soup is completely cold. Then cover the bowl tightly (or transfer to a freezer container) and freeze until ready to use. Soup will keep well for a couple of months. The rice should be added to the soup after it has been defrosted and reheated.

Old-Fashioned Milanese Veal Shanks

Ossobuco alla Milanese di Una Volta

During one of our regular trips to Milan, my husband and I went to La Piola, a seriously traditional establishment that prides itself on keeping alive old favorites. This simple trattoria with its wooden, not-too-comfortable chairs and its minimal décor, was crowded with locals who greeted one another as they were arriving and leaving. Good, I thought, we are in Milanese country! The forty-something son of Camilla Bertolini, the owner and cook, scurried to our table to take the order. When we asked him to select a few of their best traditional dishes, he nodded appreciatively and disappeared. Our dinner that night consisted of succulent, fork-tender ossobuco in a rich sauce that was barely tinged with a bit of sweet local tomato paste and topped by a small mound of bright green gremolata. Next to it was a glorious mound of moist Milanese Saffron Risotto (page 184). I later learned that this virtually tomato-less version, which also excluded the typical carrot-celery combination found in today's more modern preparations, was pretty standard decades ago in Milan. Today, only a handful of eating establishments strive to keep alive these culinary gems. Serve with the Milanese Saffron Risotto, creamy soft polenta (see page 306), or mashed potatoes. • *serves 4*

FOR THE VEAL SHANKS

- 4 large (2-inch-thick), meaty veal shanks, about 2 to 3 pounds
- 1 teaspoon salt plus more to taste
- 1/4 teaspoon freshly ground black pepper plus more to taste
- 1 cup all-purpose flour
- 1/2 cup extra-virgin olive oil
- 3 tablespoons unsalted butter
- 2 large yellow onions, minced (about 3 cups)
- 3 to 4 ounces thickly sliced pancetta, diced
- 1 cup dry white wine
- 1 tablespoon double-concentrated Italian tomato paste
- 2 cups Meat Broth (page 298) or low-sodium canned beef broth

FOR THE GREMOLATA

- 1 garlic clove, finely minced
  Grated zest of 1 lemon
- 1 tablespoon chopped fresh flat-leaf parsley
- 1/2 tablespoon finely chopped fresh sage
- 1/2 tablespoon finely chopped fresh rosemary

PREPARE THE VEAL

Preheat the oven to 350°F.

Pat the veal shanks with paper towels, season them with the salt and pepper, and dredge them lightly in flour.

Heat the oil in a large, heavy, ovenproof pan over medium-high heat. When the oil is nice and hot, add the shanks and cook until golden brown on both sides, about 5 minutes per side. Transfer to a platter.

Discard most of the oil in the pan and return to medium heat. Add the butter. As soon as the butter begins to foam, reduce the heat to medium and add the onions. Cook, stirring, until the onions are pale yellow and soft, about 5 minutes. Stir in the pancetta and cook until lightly golden, 3 to 4 minutes.

Return the shanks to the skillet and move them around, turning once, for a minute or two, until well coated with the savory onion. Raise the heat to high and add the wine. Cook, stirring, until the wine is reduced approximately by half. In a small bowl, whisk together the tomato paste and broth. Add to the skillet and bring to a simmer.

Cover the pan with a lid or aluminum foil and place on the middle rack of the oven. Cook until the meat just begins to fall away from the bone, 1½ to 2 hours. Check from time to time and make sure the liquid stays at a gentle simmer. Reduce the heat to 325°F if the liquid evaporates too quickly. When done, the sauce should have reduced approximately by half and should have a rich brown color and dense consistency.

FINISH THE DISH

While the shanks are cooking, combine all the ingredients for the gremolata in a small bowl.

When the shanks are done, place them on warm serving plates. If the sauce is too thin, reduce it quickly over high heat. Taste and adjust the seasoning. Spoon some sauce over each shank and sprinkle with a bit of gremolata. (The gremolata can also be stirred into the sauce off the heat, just before serving.)

FOR A PERFECT OSSOBUCO

"Bone with a hole" is the literal translation of *ossobuco*. These milk-fed shanks, with their delectable bone marrow, are slowly braised in a wine-broth combination until the meat is so tender that it falls off the bone. For a perfect ossobuco:

• Ask for the hind shank, which is meatier.

• Brown the shanks in enough oil, over medium-high heat, so they won't stick to the pan. When seared, the meat should be golden and crusty, not brown and burned.

• The braising of the shanks should be done over very gentle heat. Fast cooking will toughen the meat.

• The whole dish can be prepared several hours ahead. Warm gently and, if necessary, reduce the sauce just before serving.

Sautéed Breaded Milanese Veal Chops

Costolette di Vitello alla Milanese

The breaded Milanese veal chop is one of my very favorite dishes, one that I never tire of. Every time I am in Milan, I head to Bice or Don Lisander, two well-known traditional restaurants, because I know their Milanese is out of this world. This simple yet refined dish is cooked entirely in the sweet, wonderful butter of the region. Try to secure the best veal possible, and then with about ten minutes of cooking time, you will have one of the most succulent dishes of Italy. Serve with a mixed lettuce salad in summer, or mashed potatoes in winter. ♦ *serves 4*

4 (¾-inch-thick) veal loin chops

2 large eggs, lightly beaten in a bowl with a nice pinch of salt

2 cups fine, dry, unflavored bread crumbs

3 tablespoons unsalted butter

2 tablespoons extra-virgin olive oil

Cut (or have the butcher cut) all meat and fat away from the thin strip at the end of the bone, leaving the bone attached to the medallion of meat. Put the meat part of the chops between two sheets of plastic wrap or wax paper. Pound until the meat is about half its original thickness.

Dip the meat part of each chop into the beaten eggs, letting the excess egg fall back into the bowl. Dredge each chop in bread crumbs, and press the crumbs into the meat with the palms of your hands. Place on a baking sheet and set aside.

Heat the butter and oil in a large, nonstick skillet over medium heat. As soon as the butter begins to foam, slide the cutlets into the skillet without crowding (you will have to cook the cutlets in two batches). Cook, turning once, until each side of the chops has a golden brown crust, about 4 minutes per side. If the butter should turn too dark during cooking, reduce the heat. When done, the chops should be slightly pink and juicy inside, and golden and crisp outside. Serve hot.

THE WINES OF MILAN

Milan is the capital of Lombardy, which produces excellent wines, many of which are now becoming readily available in the United States. With Milanese cooking and its fondness for butter, pork products, rich cheeses, game, and long-braised dishes, the taste in wine is for full-flavored, medium-bodied wines that refresh rather than fatigue the palate. Here are my favorites.

VALTELLINA

Valtellina, the Alpine valley located about 100 kilometers northwest of Milan, near the Swiss border, is home to several wines based on the nebbiolo grape (locally called chiavennasca): Grumello, Sasella, Valgella, and Inferno. A special type of red Valtellina is Sfursat or Sforzato, made from 100 percent nebbiolo that are semi-dried off the vine, becoming more concentrated, fermenting to a higher alcohol level, and giving a richer flavor. These fragrant red wines can accompany risotto alla Milanese, cotoletta alla Milanese, game, or even cheese.

The Sforzato is a favorite accompaniment to the Valtellina cheese called Bitto. Nino Negri is a well-respected producer, and his 5 Stelle Sforzato is my favorite. Other excellent producers are Rainoldi and Conti Sertoli Salis.

FRANCIACORTA

Between Milan and Brescia to the east, a rich and varied wine-growing area exists that produces mainly sparkling wines but also still whites such as chardonnay and pinot bianco, as well as classic Bordeaux varieties such as cabernet sauvignon, cabernet franc, and merlot. In the hills of Brescia to the south of Lago d'Iseo, some of Italy's finest sparkling wines are produced. The appellation "Franciacorta" is reserved for the sparkling wine made by the classic bottle-fermented method, utilizing chardonnay and pinot noir (pinot nero) grapes. A very special sparkling wine called Franciacorta Satèn, generally 100 percent chardonnay under slightly less pressure than Franciacorta itself, makes a wonderful food wine, especially with risotto. With delicate scents of white flowers and pineapple, Satèn has a soft, almost silky texture. The non-sparkling wines are sold under the appellation "Terre di Franciacorta," either red (rosso) or white (bianco), and are generally medium-bodied, varietally fragrant, and easy drinking. My favorite producers of Franciacorta, both sparkling and still red and white wines, are Bellavista, Ca' del Bosco, Guido Berlucchi, Contadi Castaldi, and Monte Rossa.

OLTREPÒ PAVESE

To the south of Milan and just south of Pavia is the Oltrepò Pavese area. *Oltrepò* means beyond (that is, to the south of) the Po River, and *Pavese* refers to the province of Pavia. Here, sparkling wines are made from international varietals such as cabernet sauvignon, chardonnay, pinot noir, Riesling, and sauvignon blanc. However, two red wines made from blends of local varieties—barbera, croatina, uva rara, and some pinot nero—are worth trying and have wonderful names: Oltrepò Pavese Buttafuoco ("fire thrower") and Oltrepò Pavese Sangue di Giuda ("blood of Judas"). Bonarda, an indigenous grape of Lombardy technically known as croatina, is a fruity, medium- to full-bodied red with a smooth finish. It is the wine the locals drink, and is not to be missed. Here, most red wines are either still or slightly fizzy (*frizzante* or *vivace*), which to most American wine drinkers is unusual. But with rich, meat-based dishes, the frizzante wines, both red and white, are quite appealing. The small amount of carbon dioxide refreshes the palate and combines well with the light tannins of the reds. Many Oltrepò Pavese wines are difficult to find in the United States, but are well worth the effort. Try the wines of Dino Torti, whose 100 percent pino nero (pinot noir) will surprise you, and the Bonarda is outstanding. Additionally, the Cantina Sociale La Versa makes excellent sparkling wines and a range of still wines.

Stuffed Roasted Veal

Vitello Arrosto Imbottito

Several years ago, my daughter Paola and I had a luscious dinner at the hip Osteria del Binari in Milan. The place was packed with local business people, Milanese couples, an Italian-American woman (me), and a beautiful young American girl (Paola). We were seated at a nice table and were promptly given the menu, which was quite large, with a small section featuring traditional Milanese dishes and a larger section devoted to regional Italian dishes. In my steadfast determination that "when in Rome eat Roman, when in Milan eat Milanese," I ordered the risotto of the day, which was deliciously full of fresh vegetables and saffron, and a stuffed veal roast, which could have been prepared by my own mother. It was good, uncomplicated food, the type of food I like to cook for my family. Here is the recipe. • *serves 6*

1 ounce dried porcini mushrooms, soaked in 2 cups lukewarm water for 20 minutes

$^1/_3$ cup plus 2 tablespoons extra-virgin olive oil

1 garlic clove, finely minced

1 tablespoon chopped fresh flat-leaf parsley

2 anchovy fillets packed in salt or in oil, rinsed and chopped

$^1/_2$ teaspoon salt plus more to taste

$^1/_4$ teaspoon freshly ground black pepper plus more to taste

3 to $3^1/_2$ pounds top round veal, butterflied and pounded thin

6 slices prosciutto, about $^1/_4$ pound

1 cup dry white wine

Juice of $^1/_2$ lemon

5 fresh sage leaves, shredded

2 tablespoons unsalted butter

Drain the porcini and reserve their soaking water for another preparation. Rinse the mushrooms well under cold running water and coarsely dice them.

Heat 2 tablespoons of the oil in a small nonstick skillet over medium-high heat. Add the mushrooms and stir until they begin to color, about 2 minutes. Add the garlic, parsley, and anchovies, and season with the salt and pepper. Stir until the mixture is fragrant, 1 to 2 minutes. Transfer to a bowl and cool.

Place the veal on a work surface and season with the salt and pepper. Cover the meat with 3 slices of prosciutto, leaving a 1 1/2-inch border all around. Spread the mushroom mixture over the prosciutto and top with the remaining prosciutto. Roll up the veal tightly and tie securely with string. Season the outside with salt and pepper.

Preheat the oven to 375°F.

Heat the remaining ⅓ cup of oil in a large ovenproof skillet or heavy casserole over medium heat. When the oil is nice and hot, add the veal and cook, turning occasionally, until it is lightly golden on all sides, about 10 minutes.

Place the pan on the middle rack of the oven and roast until the veal's juices run barely pink when pierced with a thin knife (150°F. on an instant-read thermometer), 50 minutes to 1 hour, basting the roast several times with the pan juices. Transfer the veal to a cutting board, cover loosely with foil, and let rest for 10 to 15 minutes.

Meanwhile, carefully tilt the pan and spoon off some of the fat. Place the pan over high heat and add the wine, lemon juice, and sage. As soon as the wine begins to bubble, stir with a wooden spoon to pick up the bits and pieces attached to the bottom of the pan. When the sauce begins to thicken, swirl in the butter. Cook and stir until the sauce has a glassy, thick consistency.

Remove the string from the veal and slice the meat. Arrange the slices on serving dishes, drizzle lightly with some of the sauce, and serve at once.

ROASTING MEAT

The cooking time of a roast depends on its thickness, not on its weight. If your 3-pound roast is long and thin, it will cook faster than a 3-pound roast that is short and thick. After 35 to 40 minutes, check the internal temperature with an instant-read thermometer. Remove the roast from the oven when it is still a bit pink, because it will continue cooking as it rests.

Roasted Capon with Pancetta, Sage, and Rosemary

Cappone Arrosto alla Pancetta, Salvia, e Rosmarino

In Northern Italy, capons—young, neutered roosters—are much appreciated for their tender white meat. They are succulent when roasted, and when simmered at length they produce an absolutely delicious broth. In this preparation, which in Milan is typically served at Christmas, the capon is seasoned with a flavorful mixture of pancetta, herbs, and garlic and roasted in a very hot oven that turns the capon skin crisp and absolutely delicious. As the bird rests and its juices settle, the potatoes are cooked in the capon's roasting pan, absorbing the juices. ◆ *serves 6 to 8*

3 pounds russet potatoes, peeled and cut into 1- to 1 1/2-inch pieces

1 (7- to 8-pound) capon, wing tips removed

1/2 cup plus 2 tablespoons extra-virgin olive oil

1/4 pound thickly sliced pancetta, minced

2 tablespoons chopped fresh rosemary

2 tablespoons chopped fresh sage

2 garlic cloves, finely minced

1 teaspoon salt plus more to taste

1/2 teaspoon freshly ground black pepper plus more to taste

Bring a large pot of water to a boil over high heat and prepare an ice-water bath in a large bowl. Add the potatoes to the pot and cook for 3 to 4 minutes, or until the potatoes just begin to soften. Drain and plunge them into the ice water. When cool, drain again and pat dry with paper towels. Place in a large bowl and set aside until ready to use.

Remove the neck, liver, and gizzards from the capon's cavity, and wash the bird thoroughly inside and out. Pat dry with paper towels.

Preheat the oven to 425°F. Pour 1/2 cup of the oil into a roasting pan large enough to fit the capon comfortably.

In a small bowl, combine the pancetta, rosemary, sage, and garlic, and season with the salt and pepper. Season the capon's cavity with half of this mixture; set aside the other half for the potatoes. Place the capon breast side up in the roasting pan. Rub the remaining 2 tablespoons of oil over the skin, and season generously with salt and pepper.

Place the pan on the middle rack of the oven and roast for 1 hour and 20 minutes, basting every 20 minutes or so with the pan juices, or until the capon has a nice golden brown color and the juices run clear when pricked in the thickest part of the thigh (170°F. on an instant-read thermometer). Cover the breast loosely with foil if the skin turns too dark.

When the capon is done, pick it up with 2 pot holders or with 2 large, flat metal spatulas and place on a cutting board. Put kitchen towels or paper towels around the capon to absorb the juices that will flow out of the bird. Cover the capon loosely with foil and let rest for 15 minutes. Leave the oven on.

Meanwhile, spoon off some of the excess pan juices from the roasting pan, leaving in the pan just enough liquid to barely coat the bottom of the pan. Mix the remaining pancetta-herb mixture with the potatoes, season with salt and pepper, and add to the roasting pan. Roast until the potatoes have a nice golden color, 10 to 15 minutes.

Carve the capon, place on warm serving plates, and serve with the roasted potatoes.

Pheasant Hunter-Style

Fagiano alla Cacciatora

In the trattorie of Milan, chicken, rabbit, lamb, or pheasant are often cooked *alla cacciatore*, a preparation that implies a method of cooking that gives the dish a rustic, robust character. The key ingredient is dried, wild porcini mushrooms, whose woodsy flavor enriches a flavorful, slowly cooked preparation. When I make a cacciatore dish, I generally increase the amount of sauce so I can use it over pasta or gnocchi later. I also let the dish rest for an hour or so before serving, so its flavor will be more pronounced. Serve with soft, grilled, or roasted polenta. ◆ *serves 6*

1 ounce dried porcini mushrooms, soaked in 2 cups lukewarm water for 20 minutes

1/2 cup extra-virgin olive oil

2 cups all-purpose flour

2 pheasants (about 3 pounds each), quartered, washed, and dried on paper towels

1 teaspoon salt plus more to taste

1/4 teaspoon freshly ground black pepper plus more to taste

3 tablespoons unsalted butter

1 large yellow onion, minced (about 1 1/2 cups)

2 garlic cloves, minced

2 tablespoons minced fresh rosemary

2 tablespoons chopped fresh flat-leaf parsley

1 cup dry white wine

1 (28-ounce) can Italian plum tomatoes, preferably San Marzano (see note, page 35), with their juices, put through a food mill to remove the seeds

Drain the mushrooms and reserve the soaking water. Rinse the mushrooms well under cold running water, then chop them coarsely. Line a strainer with a few layers of paper towels and strain the soaking liquid into a bowl to get rid of the sandy deposits. Set aside.

In a large, deep skillet or casserole, heat the oil over medium-high heat. Flour the pheasant lightly and add to the skillet skin side down. (You will probably need to brown in batches.) Season with the salt and pepper and cook, turning once, until golden brown on all sides, about 10 minutes. Transfer to a large platter.

Discard the oil in the skillet. Add the butter and return the skillet to medium heat. When the butter begins to foam, add the onion, garlic, rosemary, and parsley. Cook, stirring, until the onion is lightly golden and soft, 6 to 7 minutes. Add the reserved porcini and the wine, and stir with a wooden spoon, scraping up the bits and pieces on the bottom of the skillet, until the wine is almost all evaporated. Add the tomatoes and 1 cup of the reserved porcini liquid. Season lightly with salt and pepper.

As soon as the sauce begins to bubble, return the pheasant to the skillet, reduce the heat to low, and partially cover. Cook, stirring from time to time, until the meat is tender and flakes easily when pierced with a fork, and the sauce has a medium-thick consistency, 40 to 50 minutes. Add a bit more broth or reserved mushroom liquid if the sauce thickens too much. Taste and adjust the seasoning. Serve hot.

Milanese Meatballs Wrapped in Cabbage

Mondeghili nella Verza

Mondeghili are Milanese meatballs that were traditionally prepared with leftover cooked meats; in Italian kitchens, nothing was ever thrown away. So these meatballs were made with pieces of roasted or braised chicken, boiled meats, fried sausage, slices of ham, and whatever other meat was left in the refrigerator. Thus their flavor varied from batch to batch. The meats were chopped very fine and mixed with a few eggs, a bit of cheese, and some old bread that had been soaking in milk, to add moisture to the meats. There are two versions of mondeghili: one fries the meatballs; the other wraps them in cabbage and cooks them in a sauce, as below. Serve next to buttery, fluffy mashed potatoes. ◆ *serves 4 to 6*

FOR THE MEATBALLS

- 2 cups loosely packed Italian bread without the crust, 2 days old, broken into rough pieces
- 1 1/2 cups whole milk
- 1 1/2 pounds roasted, grilled, or boiled meats, very finely chopped by hand or with a food processor
- 1/4 pound sliced mortadella, finely chopped
- 1 garlic clove, minced
- 2 tablespoons chopped fresh flat-leaf parsley
- 3 large eggs, lightly beaten in a bowl
- 3/4 cup freshly grated Parmigiano-Reggiano
- 1/2 teaspoon salt plus more to taste
- 1/4 teaspoon freshly ground black pepper

TO COMPLETE THE DISH

- Salt
- 12 large Savoy cabbage leaves (see note, page 216), washed
- 3 tablespoons unsalted butter
- 1 to 2 tablespoons extra-virgin olive oil
- 1/2 very small yellow onion, finely minced (1/3 cup)
- 2 ounces thickly sliced pancetta, diced
- 1/2 cup dry white wine
- 1/2 cup Chicken Broth (page 298) or low-sodium canned chicken broth

PREPARE THE MEATBALLS

Put the bread in a small bowl, add the milk, and soak for 5 minutes. Drain the bread, place in a clean cloth napkin, and squeeze out all the milk.

In a large bowl, combine the soaked bread, chopped meat, mortadella, garlic, parsley, eggs, and Parmigiano, and season with the salt and pepper. Mix well with your hands or a large spoon until well combined. Set aside.

COMPLETE THE DISH

Bring a large pot of water to a boil and prepare an ice-water bath in a large bowl. Add a large pinch of salt and the cabbage leaves to the boiling water. Cook, uncovered, until the leaves are tender but just a bit firm to the touch, about 2 minutes. Remove with a large slotted spoon or tongs and place in the ice water to stop the cooking. When cool, transfer to paper towels, and pat dry thoroughly. With a mallet, flatten the thick center vein at the base of the leaves.

Place an egg-size amount of meat filling in the center of each cabbage leaf. Fold the sides of the cabbage over the filling, then roll up the leaves loosely around the filling to make a bundle. Secure each bundle with a toothpick.

Heat the butter and the oil in a large nonstick skillet over medium heat. When the butter begins to foam, add the bundles, without crowding. Cook until the bundles are lightly golden on all sides, 2 to 3 minutes. Transfer to a large platter.

Add the onion to the skillet and cook, stirring and scraping the bottom of the skillet, until the onion begins to soften, about 5 minutes. Add the pancetta and stir until it begins to color, 2 to 3 minutes. Add the wine and broth and bring to a fast simmer. Return the bundles to the skillet, reduce the heat to medium low, and partially cover. Cook until the sauce has a medium-thick consistency, 4 to 5 minutes.

Place the bundles on serving dishes, top with a bit of the sauce, and serve hot.

VARIATION

Deep-Fried Meatballs ◆ Take an egg-size amount of meat mixture between the palms of your hands and shape into a ball. When all the meatballs have been shaped, dip them in beaten eggs, then roll them into fine unseasoned bread crumbs. Heat olive oil or vegetable oil, and fry a few meatballs at a time until they are golden brown on all sides. Serve hot or at room temperature.

ABOUT SAVOY CABBAGE

Mild, sweet Savoy cabbage, with its crinkled leaves, is used in many Italian preparations. Choose a head that has dark green, unblemished leaves and a compact, heavy body. Keep your cabbage in a plastic bag in the coldest part of your refrigerator, and try to use it at its freshest state, within a few days. For this dish, choose the nicest, larger leaves of approximately the same size.

WHEN IN MILAN
Specialty Food Stores and Cooking Schools

Gastronomia Peck
Via Spadari 9
Tel. 802 3161

While there are many small and large food shops spread throughout Milan, here I will mention only Gastronomia Peck, because this enormous store is truly a temple of Italian gastronomy. Just a few blocks from Piazza del Duomo, Peck is famous throughout Europe. Massive display cases showcase all kinds of delicacies: large platters of colorful cold salads; marinated vegetables and mozzarella; deep-fried artichokes; aspics and pâtés; rosy prosciutto, large mortadella, sausages, salami, and cheeses from all over Italy; white truffles and marinated porcini mushrooms; stuffed handmade pasta; spit-roasted *porchetta,* quails, and rabbit; large wheels of perfectly aged Parmigiano-Reggiano; balsamic vinegars; fresh breads, pastries, and panettone; and so much more.

The four Stoppani brothers who own Peck have added five other stores that used to be independently run in nearby locations: Bottega del Maiale, Gastronomia Peck, Rosticceria Peck, Casa del Formaggio, and La Bottega del Vino are now all under one large, expanded roof. If you are a wine lover, make sure to check out the Bottega del Vino, on the lower level of the store, which carries more than 3,000 labels from many parts of the world and offers tastings.

Q.B. (Quanto Basta)
Via Farini 70
Tel. 6900 6546

Claudio Sadler is the creative director and star chef of Q.B., Italy's premier cooking school. The classes are taught in Italian and English by well-known, highly esteemed celebrity Italian chefs, covering a very large gamut: from regional Italian cooking to seafood and game; from homemade pasta to polenta, risotto, and soups; from breads and savory pies, to sweet pastries and gelatos; even on wine. For information, e-mail qb@enogastronomica.com.

Cuttlefish and Warm Potato Salad

Insalata di Seppie e Patate

Santa Lucia is a quaint Neapolitan restaurant a few blocks from Piazza del Duomo that also serves dishes from Milan and other regions. The day my husband and I had lunch at Santa Lucia, while the rain was coming down in buckets, we feasted. One of my favorite dishes was this salad of warm potatoes with cuttlefish that was tossed simply with garlic, parsley, and olive oil. The cuttlefish was so tender that I asked my waiter how they cooked it. "We boil it gently with the addition of a wine cork," he said. As I was looking at him with an obvious puzzled expression, he added wearily, "I know, I know, you don't believe me, but it works!" Later, I found out that the enzymes in the cork tenderize the fish. ◆ *serves 4*

I medium yellow onion, cut into wedges

I celery stalk, cut into large pieces, plus 2 small celery stalks, diced (about I cup)

I carrot, cut into large pieces

I cup dry white wine

I bay leaf

I^1/$_2$ pounds cleaned, frozen cuttlefish bodies

I wine cork—yes, I wine cork

I pound medium Idaho potatoes, scrubbed

I medium red onion, diced (about I^1/$_2$ cups)

I garlic clove, minced

I tablespoon finely chopped fresh flat-leaf parsley

Salt and freshly ground black pepper to taste

I tablespoon freshly squeezed lemon juice

Extra-virgin olive oil to taste

In a large pot, combine the wedges of onion, large pieces of celery and carrot, wine, bay leaf, and enough water to come halfway up the side of the pot. Bring to a boil, then reduce the heat to medium and simmer for about I hour. Strain the broth through a large sieve directly into a large bowl.

Return the broth to the pot and bring it back to a boil. Add the cuttlefish and the wine cork. As soon as the water begins to bubble, reduce the heat to low and simmer, uncovered, until the cuttlefish is tender, about I hour. (The cuttlefish can be cooked several hours or a day ahead. Place it in a bowl with its broth and cool in the refrigerator until ready to use.)

Drain the cuttlefish, pat dry with paper towels, and cut into $1/2$-inch-wide strips. Place in a salad bowl and set aside.

Meanwhile, put the potatoes in a medium pot with enough cold water to cover over high heat. As soon as the water begins to bubble, reduce the heat to medium and cook until the potatoes are tender, 30 to 40 minutes. Drain. As soon as you are able to handle them, peel and cut into 1-inch pieces. Add to the salad bowl with the cuttlefish. Add the diced celery, diced red onion, garlic, and parsley. Season with salt and pepper, add the lemon juice, and drizzle generously with the olive oil. Toss well, taste, and adjust the seasoning. Serve while the potatoes are warm.

ABOUT CEPHALOPODS

Cuttlefish, squid, and octopus belong to the cephalopod family and are abundant on the Italian seacoasts. They taste great when hot off the grill, are delicious when slowly braised with tomatoes and fresh herbs (see Cuttlefish with Wine, Tomatoes, and Paprika, page 276), and are wonderful when simmered in a flavorful broth and turned into salads. Their sac of black ink is added to flour and eggs to make black pasta, and to flavor and color risottos and sauces. Most of the cuttlefish and octopus available in the United States come from the Philippines and Vietnam, and can be found frozen and already cleaned in specialty seafood stores and Asian markets. Octopus or squid can be used in this recipe instead of cuttlefish.

Asparagus with Parmigiano and Fried Eggs

Asparagi con Parmigiano e Uova Fritte alla Milanese

It was a rainy, soggy day in Milan that looked more like November than the end of September. My husband and I were hungry, so we left the hotel and walked the two blocks to Don Lisander, a well-known, always busy trattoria. We ate outdoors under a large, heavy canvas with the raindrops tapping overhead. Little birds were chirping wildly while diving from the surrounding trees straight to the crumbs scattered under the tables. The chill in the air made us enjoy our food and our wine even more. In spite of the rain, we lingered long after most people had left, savoring the moment. This is one of Don Lisander's simple but very delicious dishes, which can be served for brunch, for lunch, or as a light supper. In Milan, this dish is often preceded by a simple risotto, or by steamed or boiled rice dressed only with sweet butter and Parmigiano. ◆ *serves 4*

1 1/2 pounds asparagus
Salt
5 tablespoons unsalted butter

1/2 cup freshly grated Parmigiano-Reggiano
4 large eggs
8 small slices grilled, crusty bread

Wash the asparagus under cold running water and cut off the tough ends. If the stalks are thick, peel off the outer skin with a vegetable peeler. Tie them in a couple of bunches with string or rubber bands.

Bring 2 to 3 inches of water to a boil in an asparagus cooker or in a narrow pot over medium heat, and add salt. Place the asparagus upright in the water and cover the tips loosely with foil. Simmer until the asparagus are tender but still a bit firm to the bite, 3 to 5 minutes, depending on thickness. Transfer to paper towels and pat dry. Discard the string or rubber bands.

Heat 3 tablespoons of the butter in a large skillet over medium heat. When the butter begins to foam, add the asparagus. Sprinkle with about half of the Parmigiano, and cover the pan. Cook just long enough to allow the cheese to melt, 1 to 2 minutes. Place on 4 warm serving dishes.

Return the skillet to medium heat and add the remaining 2 tablespoons of butter. As soon as the butter turns lightly brown, break the eggs into the skillet, leaving space between them, and season lightly with salt. As the egg whites begin to solidify but the yolks are still uncooked, scoop up each egg with a large, flat spatula, and place over the asparagus. Dribble each egg with the browned butter and sprinkle lightly with Parmigiano. Serve with the slices of grilled bread.

WHEN IN MILAN
Caffès and Pastry Shops

Biffi
Corso Magenta 87
Tel. 4800 6702
Another great historic bar-pasticceria that opened in the last part of the nineteenth century. Biffi's house-made panettone is one of the best in the city.

Caffè Pasticceria Sant Ambroeus
Corso Matteotti 7
Tel. 7600 0540
Located in the historic center of Milan, this elegant landmark serves some of the best pastries in the city. A great place to indulge in a leisurely breakfast or an aperitivo while relaxing and people watching.

Zucca in Galleria
Piazza del Duomo 21
Tel. 8646 4435
The magnificent Galleria facing Piazza del Duomo is the home of several historic caffès, bars, and restaurants. Sit at this charming caffè and order a Campari, the slightly bitter, very popular Italian aperitivo that was invented here at the end of the nineteenth century.

Celery Root and Green Apple Salad

Insalata di Sedano di Verona e Mele

Casa Fontana in Milan is the home of great risottos and great salads. As my husband and I were waiting for our risotto to arrive, we ordered a somewhat unusual salad of celery root and green apples with mustard seeds and mustard-lemon dressing. When the large salad came to the table, I remember thinking, "there is no way I can finish this." But as I began eating, the crispness and freshness won me over. By the time the risotto was served, nothing was left on my salad plate. • *serves 4 to 6*

FOR THE DRESSING

- 3 teaspoons Dijon mustard
- 3 teaspoons lemon juice
- 1/3 cup extra-virgin olive oil
- Salt to taste
- 3 teaspoons mustard seeds

FOR THE SALAD

- 2 medium celery roots (see note), about 2 pounds
- 2 green apples, unpeeled
- Freshly ground black pepper to taste

MAKE THE DRESSING

In a small bowl, combine the mustard and lemon juice. Add the oil slowly and whisk until the mixture is thick and smooth. Season with salt and stir in the mustard seeds. Set aside until ready to use.

MAKE THE SALAD

Bring a large pot of salted water to a boil and prepare an ice-water bath in a large bowl. Peel the celery roots and slice into 1/8-inch-thick rounds. Drop the rounds into the boiling water and cook for about 1 minute. Drain and cool in the ice water. Drain again and dry with paper towels. Cut the rounds into 1/4-inch-thick strips, and place in a large salad bowl.

Cut the apples in half, then into thin slices. Cut the slices into 1/4-inch strips and add to the bowl. Season with salt and pepper. Add the mustard-lemon dressing, and toss well to combine. Serve slightly chilled.

ABOUT CELERY ROOT

Sedano rapa or *sedano di Verona* are the Italian names of celery root, a heavy, bulbous vegetable that is harvested when its weight is about 2 pounds. It has a clean, aromatic taste not unlike that of celery. Celery root can be used in soups, vegetable dishes, and salads. In buying celery root, look for a bulb that is heavy and firm to the touch. Wrap it in a plastic bag and store it in the refrigerator until ready to use. It keeps well for a couple of weeks.

Marinated Artichoke Hearts

Carciofini Marinati

I had just finished a hefty lunch at Trattoria Milanese, a charming old-fashioned place in the heart of Milan. The waiter had won me over with his descriptions of the day's specials. So I ordered *Mondeghili nella Verza,* Milanese meatballs wrapped in blanched cabbage leaves (page 214), which came to the table with a pile of mashed potatoes. After I cleaned my plate, the waiter came over with a large platter of marinated baby artichokes and said, "Signora, and now to cleanse your palate . . ." This simple dish can be served as an appetizer, alone or in conjunction with a few slices of prosciutto, mortadella, or smoked ham; or as a light refreshing vegetable served alone or next to grilled seafood. If the artichokes are completely covered with oil, they can be kept for several days at room temperature. Or refrigerate them and leave them at room temperature for a few hours before serving. ◆ *serves 4*

3 pounds baby artichokes (see note)
Juice and zest of 1 lemon
Salt
1 garlic clove, finely minced

2 tablespoons chopped fresh flat-leaf parsley
1 cup extra-virgin olive oil
Salt and freshly ground black pepper to taste

Remove the green leaves from the artichokes by snapping them off at the base until you reach the pale yellow, tender leaves of the heart. Slice off the green top, cut off the stem at the base, and use a small knife to trim off the green part at the base. Drop the artichokes in a large bowl of cold water with about half of the lemon juice.

Bring a large pot of water to a boil over medium-high heat and prepare an ice-water bath in a large bowl. Drain the artichokes and add them to the boiling water with the remaining lemon juice and a generous pinch of salt. Cook uncovered over medium heat until the artichokes are tender and the bottom can easily be pierced with a thin knife, 4 to 8 minutes, depending on size. Drain and place in the ice water to cool. Drain again, pat dry with paper towels, and place in a salad bowl.

In a small bowl, combine the garlic, parsley, lemon zest, and olive oil. Stir well to blend. Season the artichokes with salt and several grindings of pepper, and add the olive oil mixture. Mix well and leave the artichokes at room temperature for a few hours, tossing them every 30 minutes or so. Taste, adjust the seasoning, and serve.

ABOUT BABY ARTICHOKES

"Baby" artichokes are the same artichokes as their bigger counterparts, for they come from the same plant. Their size is determined not by their age but by their placement on the plant, which is way down among the shady fronds. In selecting baby artichokes, choose those that are firm and compact. To store, sprinkle with some water and put them in plastic bags in the coldest part of the refrigerator; they will keep for one week. Baby artichokes are available all year round, but they are especially plentiful in the spring.

Peppers, Onions, and Tomatoes in a Skillet, Milan-Style

La Peperonata Milanese

Peperonata is a medley of peppers, onions, and tomatoes that are cooked at length in a skillet, and is typical of many Italian cities. In Milan, celery and carrot are added, along with a splash of good red-wine vinegar at the end of cooking. This is one of those straightforward, comforting dishes that belongs in the homes and trattorie of Italy. Trattoria Masuelli San Marco in Milao serves peperonata hot, next to a *bollito misto* (mixed boiled meats), but it is equally delicious at room temperature next to grilled fish, steaks, or chops. ♦ *serves 6 to 8*

1/3 cup extra-virgin olive oil

1 large celery stalk, thinly sliced

2 small carrots, cut into 1/4-inch rounds

1 small yellow onion, thinly sliced

4 large red and yellow bell peppers, washed, seeded, and cut into 2-inch pieces

1 pound ripe tomatoes, seeded and diced

Salt and freshly ground black pepper to taste

1/4 cup red-wine vinegar

Heat the oil in a large skillet over medium heat. Add the celery, carrots, and onion and cook, stirring, until the vegetables begin to color, 6 to 8 minutes. Add the peppers and stir until they are lightly charred, 10 to 12 minutes.

Add the tomatoes and season with salt and pepper. Reduce the heat to medium low and cook, uncovered, stirring occasionally, until the vegetables are soft and tender and the juices in the skillet have thickened, 15 to 20 minutes.

Raise the heat to high and add the vinegar. Stir until the vinegar is completely evaporated, 2 to 3 minutes. Taste, adjust the seasoning, and serve hot or at room temperature.

Milan's Crumbly Cake

Torta Sbrisolona

This is a homey, unassuming, easy-to-prepare crumbly cake that does not need refrigeration and keeps well for several days. When cutting into the cake, you will probably see the slices crumble into large chunks; after all, the characteristic of a crumbly cake is . . . to crumble. I love it in the morning with a cappuccino, or at night with a glass of dessert wine. ◆ *serves 8*

6 ounces (1½ sticks) unsalted butter, melted, plus more for greasing the pan

1 cup all-purpose flour

¾ cup fine cornmeal

1 cup granulated sugar

6 ounces almonds, finely chopped

Grated zest of 1 lemon

Grated zest of 1 orange

3 large eggs, lightly beaten

Confectioners' sugar, for dusting

Preheat the oven to 350°F. Butter the bottom and sides of a 9-inch cake pan.

In a large bowl, place the flour, cornmeal, granulated sugar, chopped almonds, and lemon and orange zests. Mix until the ingredients are thoroughly combined. Sprinkle the melted butter all over the dried ingredients. Add the eggs and stir with a spatula or your hands until the ingredients are well combined into a soft, moist, slightly sticky dough. Pour the mixture into the greased pan. With your hands, press it gently and evenly into the pan, smoothing the top with a spatula.

Place the cake on the middle rack of the oven and bake until the top has a nice golden brown color and a thin knife inserted in the center comes out clean, 30 to 35 minutes. Let the cake cool on a rack.

When unmolding, gently detach the sides of the cake with a knife, then invert onto a plate. Cool to room temperature.

Sprinkle the cake with confectioners' sugar and serve with whipped cream or a glass of dessert wine.

Rice, Almond, and Raisin Cake

Torta di Riso, Mandorle, e Uvetta Sultanina

Rice, a fairly modest staple of Northern Italy, is transformed into mouthwatering risottos, refreshing salads, wholesome soups, and even delicious cakes. Milanese cooks boil rice in milk and combine it with a variety of savory ingredients. Rice cake in Milan often has the addition of raisins, Amaretti di Saronno cookies, candied citron, and almonds or hazelnuts; often a little liqueur is added. This is not a glamorous dessert, but its straightforward, down-home goodness and simple execution make it a staple of Milanese trattorie. ◆ *serves 8 to 10*

4 cups whole milk

$^1/_2$ cup plus 2 tablespoons granulated sugar

Grated zest of $^1/_2$ lemon

1 cup Arborio rice

4 Amaretti di Saronno (see note)

$^1/_2$ cup blanched almonds

Butter for greasing the pan

3 large eggs

$^1/_2$ cup golden raisins, soaked in lukewarm water for 20 minutes, drained, and dried

$^1/_4$ cup finely minced candied citron

$^1/_4$ cup Amaretto di Saronno liqueur

3 large egg whites

Confectioners' sugar, for dusting

In a medium saucepan, combine the milk, the $^1/_2$ cup sugar, and lemon zest. Bring to a gentle boil over medium heat. Add the rice, reduce the heat to low, and simmer, uncovered, stirring from time to time, until the rice is tender and the milk has been completely absorbed, 25 to 30 minutes. During the last 5 to 6 minutes of cooking, as the milk evaporates, make sure to stir constantly or the rice will stick to the bottom of the pot. When done, the rice should have a moist, thick consistency. Transfer to a medium bowl and cool to room temperature.

Break the amaretti cookies and place in the bowl of a food processor fitted with the metal blade. Pulse until the amaretti are chopped into very small granular pieces, about the consistency of fine dried bread crumbs. Place in a bowl and set aside.

Put the almonds in the food processor and chop very fine, just like you did with the amaretti.

Preheat the oven to 375°F. Butter an 8- or 9-inch cake pan. Sprinkle about half of the chopped amaretti on the bottom and sides of the pan and shake off any excess.

In a large bowl, beat the eggs and stir in the remaining chopped amaretti cookies, all the chopped almonds, the plumped raisins, the candied citron, and about half of the Amaretto. Gradually add the rice and stir well to incorporate. Beat the egg whites with the remaining 2 tablespoons sugar, and fold into the rice mixture. Pour into the prepared pan, and shake the pan to settle the mixture.

Place the pan on the middle rack of the oven and bake until the cake has a nice golden brown color and a thin knife inserted in the center comes out clean, 40 to 45 minutes.

Cool the cake to room temperature, then remove from the pan and place on a large, round serving dish. Prick the top of the cake in several places with a fork, and sprinkle the remaining Amaretto over the top. Let the cake rest for several hours or refrigerate overnight. Just before serving, dust with confectioners' sugar.

ABOUT AMARETTI DI SARONNO

Amaretti di Saronno are imported Italian macaroons that taste like no other. Amaretti, which are used as a component in many Italian desserts, can be found in Italian and specialty food markets and are sold in small or large red tins. The cookies are wrapped by the pair, and can be kept for months.

Cherries Poached in Red Wine and Spices

Ciliege Cotte nel Vino Rosso

Italians often end their meal not with a dessert but with fresh fruit. Often a trattoria will have a special fruit preparation, such as these cherries poached in wine; or stuffed, baked peaches or apricots; or mixed berries served with whipped cream. At Da Giacomo, a trattoria on the outskirts of Milan that is famous for seafood dishes, I ordered the cherries cooked in wine. The wine was thick and glazy; the cherries were large, black, and sweet; and the combination was the perfect ending to a very enjoyable meal. ✦ *serves 4*

4 cups dry, medium-bodied red wine	I whole clove
$^3/_4$ cup sugar	Zest of I lemon, in large pieces
$^1/_2$ cinnamon stick	I $^1/_2$ pounds large, ripe dark cherries, pitted

In a medium saucepan, combine the wine, sugar, cinnamon, clove, and lemon zest. Bring to a simmer and cook, uncovered, over medium heat, until the wine is reduced approximately by half.

Add the cherries, reduce the heat to medium low, and simmer until the cherries are tender, 7 to 8 minutes. Strain the cherries and wine in a large, fine sieve over a bowl. Put the wine back in the saucepan and bring it back to a simmer. Cook over medium-high heat until reduced again by half, to a medium-thick consistency.

Meanwhile, pick out and discard the lemon zest, clove, and cinnamon stick. Put the cherries in a nice serving bowl and add the reduced wine. Serve hot or at room temperature.

THE MILANESE TABLE

APPETIZERS

Asparagi alla Milanese: Boiled asparagus tossed in butter and Parmigiano-Reggiano. When the asparagus are topped with a fried egg, this dish becomes an entrée.

Bresaola: Air-dried, salted beef filet that is aged a minimum of one month. Served thinly sliced with slivers of Parmigiano-Reggiano, oil, and lemon.

Nervetti in Insalata: A salad of calf's foot with onions, and potatoes or cabbage.

FIRST COURSES

Malfatti: "Badly made" ricotta and spinach dumplings tossed with melted butter, sage, and Parmigiano-Reggiano.

Minestrone alla Milanese: A thick vegetable soup made with seasonal fresh vegetables, dried beans, and rice.

Risotto: Short-grained rice that is slowly cooked in butter, onions, and broth, with the addition of mushrooms, seafood, cheese, vegetables, or other ingredients. Risotto alla Milanese, the signature risotto of Milan, is flavored with saffron, which gives the dish a bright yellow-orange color.

Risotto al Salto: Leftover risotto pan-fried in butter and turned into golden, flat, crisp cakes.

Tortelli: Fresh stuffed pasta.

Tortelli di Zucca: Fresh pasta stuffed with squash, a favorite dish of many Milanese trattorie.

ENTRÉES

Animelle: Sweetbreads coated with bread crumbs and Parmigiano, then deep-fried.

Bollito Misto: Assorted boiled meats such as beef, veal, pork, tongue, and capon, served with assorted condiments.

Büsecca: Tripe, slowly braised with beans, onions, and tomatoes.

Cassoeula: An old-fashioned robust pork-cabbage stew that includes sausage, spareribs, and other parts of the pig.

Costoletta alla Milanese: A breaded veal rib chop, sautéed in clarified butter.

Mondeghili: Breaded meatballs made with boiled or roasted meat leftovers, sausage, and other savory ingredients, then fried in butter.

Ossobuco: Veal shanks slowly braised with butter, onions, and white wine. A small amount of *gremolada* (or *gremolata*), a cold condiment of chopped parsley, garlic, sage, rosemary, and grated lemon zest, is stirred into the sauce before serving.

Rostin Negaa: Veal chop slowly braised with pancetta, rosemary, sage, and white wine.

Vitel Tonè (Vitello Tonnato): A boneless veal roast that is slowly braised in a flavorful light broth, then chilled, sliced, and topped with a creamy tuna-mayonnaise sauce.

VEGETABLES AND SALADS

Bietole in Padella: Boiled Swiss chard, generally tossed in oil and garlic.

Funghi Trifolati: Mushrooms sautéed with parsley and garlic.

Insalata Russa: Boiled, diced mixed vegetables tossed with mayonnaise.

Verdure Fritte: Deep-fried vegetables coated in bread crumbs or in flour, or dipped into a thick batter.

Verzata: Cabbage stew, often paired with sausages.

DESSERTS

Chiacchiere: Deep-fried pastry fritters.

Panettone: A tall, rich Milanese cake made with butter, eggs, and candied fruit, traditionally eaten at Christmas.

Torta di Riso: Rice cake.

Torta Sbrisolona: A crumbly cake made with cornmeal, almonds, and butter.

SOME BASIC INGREDIENTS

Amaretti di Saronno: Small, crisp almond cookies that are used as a component of many desserts. They are also an indispensable ingredient in the stuffing of squash tortelli.

Bresaola: Air-dried, salted, cured beef, a specialty of the Valtellina area in Lombardy, served thinly sliced with olive oil and slivers of Parmigiano-Reggiano.

Burro: Butter, sweet and unsalted, is essential to the cooking of Milan and its region.

Erbe: In the cooking of Milan, just as in Bologna, fresh herbs are used sparingly. Thyme, sage, and parsley are the favorites.

Gorgonzola: A creamy, scented, blue-veined cow's-milk cheese that is used extensively in Milanese dishes.

Grana Padana: A granular cheese similar to the Parmigiano-Reggiano of Parma made with cow's milk, generally grated over pasta.

Mascarpone: A very soft, sweet, creamy cheese made with cow's milk, used in a large variety of desserts. It is the indispensable ingredient in tiramisù.

Mostarda: A sweet-and-sour condiment of large pieces of assorted fruit, preserved in a thick sugar-mustard syrup. Mostarda is usually served with mixed boiled meats. (The city of Cremona in Lombardy makes the best and best-known mostarda.)

Polenta: Yellow or white cornmeal cooked in salted water until thick and creamy.

Prosciutto cotto: Cooked ham, boneless and mildly cured with a salt brine and flavored with spices, then steamed or baked.

Riso: Rice. Of the fifty or so varieties grown in Italy, Vialone Nano, Carnaroli, and Arboria, with their chubby kernels and large amount of starch, are the favorites of Milanese cooks.

Salame Milano: A typical Milanese *salame* made with lean pork, beef, wine, garlic, and spices.

Stracchino: A straw-yellow, soft, creamy cow's-milk cheese.

Strutto: The soft lard that used to be the fat of choice for old-style Milanese dishes.

Verza: Savoy cabbage, one of the favorite vegetables of Milan, used in stews, soups, and salads.

Zafferano: Saffron, made with the stigma of *Crocus sativus,* a flower that grows wild in Sicily, Abruzzo, and Sardinia. It is the essential ingredient in Risotto alla Milanese.

VENICE

APPETIZERS

Whipped Creamy Salt Cod with Soft Polenta {*Baccalà Mantecato con la Polenta*}

Fried Sardines in Savory Sauce {*Sarde Fritte all'Agro*}

Shrimp and Mushrooms with Soft Polenta {*Gamberetti e Funghi con Polenta*}

Fried Green Olives {*Olive Fritte*}

Carpaccio with Baby Artichokes and Parmigiano {*Carpaccio con Carciofini e Parmigiano*}

Venetian Salame with Honey and Wilted Radicchio
{*La Soppressa Veneziana con Miele e Radicchio Scottato*}

FIRST COURSES

Risotto with Radicchio and Sea Scallops {*Risotto con Radicchio e Cape Sante*}

Risotto with Shrimp and Summer Vegetables {*Risotto con Gamberi e Verdurine Estive*}

Risotto with Squash and White Truffle {*Risotto con Zucca e Tartufo Bianco*}

Whole-Wheat Pasta with Onion, Capers, and Anchovies
{*Bigoli con Cipolle, Capperi, e Acciughe*}

Risotto with Wild Mushrooms and Smoked Ham {*Risotto con Funghi e Speck*}

Rice with Peas and Pea Pods {*Risi e Bisi*}

Spaghetti with Tuna, Olives, and Tomatoes {*Spaghetti con Tonno, Olive, e Pomodori*}

Pasta and Bean Soup, Venetian-Style {*Pasta e Fagioli alla Veneziana*}

ENTRÉES

Shellfish Stew {*Brodetto di Pesce*}

Scallops with Capers, Anchovies, Lemon, and Wine {*Cape Sante in Padella*}

Sweet-and-Sour Shrimp {*Scampi in Saor alla Veneziana*}

Cuttlefish with Wine, Tomatoes, and Paprika {*Seppie alla Busara*}

Venetian Calf's Liver with Onions {*Fegato alla Veneziana*}

Roasted Guinea Hen with Peppery Sauce {*Faraona in Peverada*}

Venetian Lamb Stew with Cabbage {*Castradina*}

VEGETABLES

Stuffed Roasted Vegetables {*Verdure Ripiene al Forno*}

Radicchio Salad with Anchovy Dressing {*Insalata di Radicchio con Acciughe*}

DESSERTS

Venetian Cornmeal Cake with Raisins and Grappa {*Pinza di Polenta alla Veneziana*}

Hazelnut Cookies {*Cornetti alle Nocciole*}

San Marco Basilica

Imagine a city built on water. A city that has no cars, buses,

motor scooters, and bicycles. A city that is made up of 118 islands that are linked by 400 bridges, under which the waters of 150 canals converge, mix, and languorously follow a prescribed path. Venice is such a city, a city that since its birth has attracted masses of visitors from every corner of the world.

To a first-time visitor, Venice—which has been called by many the most beautiful city in the world because of its stunning architecture based on Byzantine, Gothic, and Renaissance styles—seems like a mirage rising out of the water. Its amazing gold-decorated buildings, churches, and bridges sparkle under the sun and reflect in the water, creating a surreal, dreamy landscape. Gondolas float lazily on the shining water while motorboats, water taxis, and yachts zigzag through the city's main thoroughfare, the Grand Canal.

The history of Venice, like the history of most other Italian cities, is complex. Ruled in turn by the Etruscans, Greeks, Gauls, and Celts, the original colony of settlers not only survived but through the centuries grew in number and importance. By the ninth century they had formed the city of Venice, which eventually grew into the Venetian Republic. Through sheer will, perseverance, and genius, Venice became one of the most loved, feared, and admired cities in the world.

The palaces of Venice are evidence today of the tremendous riches that the city had in its medieval and Renaissance days. It was the only city in Italy that for centuries remained independent of popes, emperors, and ruling families, and it grew into one of the greatest maritime powers, connecting the Far East to Europe. Venice was also the center of the spice trade in what were then rare and unusual ingredients: sugar, salt, pepper, coffee, saffron, nutmeg, cinnamon, and cloves were eagerly adopted and made lavish use of, developing a subtle and flavorful cuisine.

I am sitting on the rooftop *terrazzo* of the Hotel Danieli at sunset, looking out at a magnificent view of Baroque churches, bell towers, the Grand Canal, and the waterways. I am sipping a Bellini, the most famous of all Venetians cocktails, invented by Arrigo Cipriani, of the famed Harry's Bar. My mood is mellow, the sunset is breathtakingly beautiful, and I feel blessed to be here. Tomorrow morning I will be ready to explore Venice by foot.

For me the best time to visit Venice is in late fall, when the air is crisp, the crowds of visitors have thinned out, and I don't have to wait for a table at any caffès in Piazza San Marco or at my favorite restaurants. Even though I have been to Venice many times, and visited most of the spectacular sights and masterpieces of the city, I generally stick to the same pattern and head straight for Piazza San Marco. I sit at Florian, one of the most beautiful, historical (and expensive) caffès of Venice, established in 1720. I order a cappuccino and a brioche, then decide on a plan of action. What *sestiere*, neighborhood, will I visit? What historical site will I check out? And where will I eat?

Begin as I do, in Piazza San Marco, which has been the center of Venetian life for centuries and was described by Napoleon as "the most beautiful living room in Europe." Some of the best shops in Venice are located under the arcades that line three sides of the piazza. Check out the San Marco Basilica, one of Europe's most opulent churches, sparkling with mosaics. Then stop at the Campanile just outside the basilica. The spectacular view of the city and lagoon from the top of the Campanile will take your breath away. Take a vaporetto and explore the island of Murano, famous for its glassblowers' craft. Make sure to stop at the Palazzo Ducale, the seat of the Venetian government, with its amazing Gothic architecture. Then go on to the Accademia, the premier art gallery of Venice, packed with amazing paintings. Make a stop at Santa Maria della Salute, a splendid Baroque church on the Grand Canal, then go on to the Ponte dei Sospiri, the Bridge of Sighs. Climb the steps of the famed Rialto Bridge and observe the traffic of motorboats below. When you are desperately hungry, get completely lost in the narrow Venetian streets. Walk over humble bridges, not following signs, while moving away from the crowds, through a labyrinth of narrow passageways called *calli.* Before you know it, you will discover a whole world of real Venetian life with places to eat that serve delicious, unpretentious food.

The cooking of Venice has been dependent on and inspired by the agriculturally rich region that encompasses the Dolomites, a mountain area in the north; the fertile planes of the Po Valley in the south, with its miles of rice paddies and cornfields; and a coastal area with an abundance of seafood. The cooking of Venice is based on fish, vegetables, rice, and polenta. In the Veneto, polenta is more important than bread (thus the Venetian nickname *polentoni,* which means "big polenta eaters") and is a vital staple of restaurants, trattorie, and wine bars. Made with yellow or white cornmeal, this luscious, creamy, dense mush can be served as an appetizer, side dish, or entrée, either soft, fried, baked, grilled, or roasted.

For me, the best way to appreciate the gastronomy of Venice at its source is to wander through the famed Rialto food market, near the sixteenth-century Rialto Bridge. Crustaceans and fish of all kinds are on display: baby cuttlefish, crabs, small sea bass, spider crabs, large scallops in their shells, clams, razor clams, baby shrimp. The market is humming, and the clean scent of fresh fish is everywhere, mingling with the aroma of the colorful vegetables and fruit from the mainland and the gardens of the lagoons. I am mesmerized by the speed with which the produce man cleans the large, purple artichokes all the way down to their bottoms, then drops them into a bucket of water speckled with slices of lemon. That night they will be sautéed or boiled and turned into a delicious appetizer or side dish. It is early morning, the weather is cold and damp, and the market is in full swing.

The best places to taste real, old-fashioned Venetian dishes is at the humble *bacari,* the wine bars, especially those located in the back alleys. Bacari are unpretentious, friendly, stand-up bars and *osterie* that sell *ombre,* the traditional small glasses of local wine, and *cicheti,* bite-size snacks much like the tapas of Spain. One of the oldest

Venetian traditions, and unique in Italy, is to eat progressively from one bacaro to another, savoring along the way gulpfuls of local wines and morsels such as tuna croquettes, fried olives, hard-cooked eggs topped with anchovies, grilled sardines, fried polenta with creamy cod, and marinated artichoke hearts.

Every time my husband and I are in Venice, we eat at bacari several days in a row. At about seven in the evening we walk to our pre-selected bacaro and order an ombra and a cicheto, then eat standing up, often shoulder to shoulder with other customers. If one of the few, small tables becomes available, we sit down and order one of the specials. Otherwise we move on to the next bacaro and start over again. This informal, unusual way of eating allows one not only to taste several dishes, but also to reconnect with rituals and traditions that have been at the center of the city's social life for centuries.

And then there is the food of the stylish, well-known restaurants. After several days of the straightforward traditional food of the area, we dress in our best garb and dine in calmer, subdued atmospheres. We begin our dinner with a flute of local *prosecco.* The lights are low, the mood is romantic, and the waiter is impeccably dressed. The food is fantastic and our mood is, too. I simply cannot forget a risotto of butternut squash topped with freshly sliced white truffle we had at Da Fiore. And the sea bass baked in salt of Al Covo. The light-as-air fried seasonal vegetables of Fiaschetteria Toscana. The sole with sweet-and-sour onions, pine nuts, and raisins of La Corte Sconta . . . Enough, I have to stop dreaming!

To be sure, Venice has to cope with many problems. The sinking of the city. The congested, narrow streets jammed with the fourteen million people who visit each year. The uninspired, expensive restaurants that take advantage of the tourists. The slow exodus of Venetians to the mainland. There is no doubt that Venice is not as serene as she once was. And yet when I think about Venice, I see a shining star in the landscape of a country that has given the world so many jewels. I see her as a formidable 1,600-year-old grand dame that has survived invasions, domination, floods, and diseases. She just needs to rest for a while, then she will solve her problems and will reappear embellished and proud, ready to show the world her intoxicating, beautiful face.

Whipped Creamy Salt Cod with Soft Polenta

Baccalà Mantecato con la Polenta

Baccalà Mantecato is the creamy salt-cod dish similar to France's *brandade*; it has been a staple in the Venetian home kitchen for centuries. It is also a signature dish of the local *bacari*, wine bars, where it is generally paired with soft, grilled, or fried polenta. The combination is a match made in heaven. ◆ *serves 4*

1 pound dried, unsalted cod, preferably imported *stoccafisso ragno*, or salt cod, skinned and boned (see note)

5 cups whole milk

1 cup extra-virgin olive oil

2 garlic cloves, very finely minced

1/4 cup chopped fresh flat-leaf parsley

Salt and freshly ground white pepper to taste

1/2 recipe Basic Polenta (page 306)

Place the cod in a large bowl and cover with cold water. Cover the bowl and refrigerate for 2 to 3 days, changing the water 3 to 4 times per day.

Drain the cod and place it in a saucepan. Add 4 cups of the milk and just enough water to cover. Bring to a simmer and cook gently until the cod is tender and begins to flake when pierced with a fork, about 20 minutes.

Drain the cod and pat dry with paper towels. Pick out and discard any pieces of bone and skin. With your fingers, shred the cod, then place it in the bowl of a stand mixer fitted with the paddle. While the cod is still warm, beat it on low speed for a couple of minutes into smaller pieces.

Increase the speed and add the oil in a slow, steady stream while beating constantly for about 10 minutes. Pour in the remaining cup of milk a little at a time, beating steadily, until the cod is creamy and well emulsified, 2 to 3 minutes.

Add the garlic and parsley, season with pepper and, if needed, a little salt. Mix gently with the paddle or with a spatula to combine. You can make the cod 2 to 3 hours ahead and keep it covered at room temperature. Before serving, reheat lightly in a skillet with a little olive oil. Serve next to a mound of soft, buttery polenta.

ABOUT SALT COD

Baccalà and *stoccafisso* identify a single fish, cod (*merluzzo*), which reached Italy from the icy waters of Norway. For centuries, cod has been preserved throughout Europe either by salting it (baccalà) or drying it, unsalted, in the sun (stoccafisso). While in most parts of Northern Italy baccalà and stoccafisso are often used interchangeably, in Venice the preferred type is the saltless stockfish. Both can be found in Italian markets and specialty food stores. In selecting baccalà look for a piece that is meaty, has a minimal amount of bones, and has a nice creamy color with no dark spots.

Rialto market

Fried Sardines in Savory Sauce

Sarde Fritte all'Agro

Venetians love sardines, which are plentiful in local waters. This small, rich, oily fish is served many ways, but perhaps the most delicious and best-known is fresh sardines topped with a sweet-and-sour onion mixture and marinated for a couple of days. Below is another delicious version that fries the sardines until crisp, then tops them with a dressing of garlic, parsley, olive oil, and lemon—a delicious way to start a meal.

◆ *serves 4*

8 large fresh sardines, about I pound, scaled, gutted, boned, heads and fins removed, and butterflied (see note)

I cup olive oil or vegetable oil, for frying

I cup all-purpose flour

$^1/_2$ cup extra-virgin olive oil

I garlic clove, finely minced

I tablespoon finely chopped fresh flat-leaf parsley

Juice of I medium lemon (about $^1/_4$ cup)

Salt to taste

Rinse the sardines under cold running water and pat dry with paper towels.

Heat the olive oil or vegetable oil in a medium skillet over medium-high heat. Dredge the sardines in the flour, shaking off the excess. When the oil just begins to smoke, carefully lower the sardines into the hot oil without crowding (fry in 2 batches if necessary). Cook until golden and crisp on both sides, about 2 minutes per side. Transfer to paper towels and blot.

Meanwhile, in a small bowl, combine the extra-virgin olive oil with the garlic, parsley, and lemon juice. Season lightly with salt and stir with a small whisk to combine.

Transfer the sardines to individual serving plates, top with some of the dressing, and serve while still warm, perhaps next to a slice of grilled or fried polenta.

HOW TO CLEAN FRESH SARDINES

I am not going to kid you here: Cleaning fresh sardines is a thankless job. But someone has to do it. If your fishmonger refuses, here's how: Pull off the heads, fins, and tails. Butterfly by cutting the belly horizontally and opening up the sardines like a book. With your fingers, pull out all the innards. Remove the central bone by pulling it from the tail upward toward the head, and remove any bones that are still attached to the meat. Trim the sardines evenly of any hanging skin. Rinse thoroughly but gently under cold running water, and pat dry with paper towels. Set aside until ready to use. (If you have a pair of thin plastic kitchen gloves, this is the time to use them.)

Shrimp and Mushrooms with Soft Polenta

Gamberetti e Funghi con Polenta

When in Venice, one must eat seafood. And when the delectable seafood of the lagoons is paired with creamy Venetian polenta, it becomes a marriage made in heaven. At Vini da Gigio, one of my favorite trattoria-wine bars, I was served a delicious appetizer of *gamberetti*, small local shrimp, that were quickly sautéed with sliced porcini mushrooms and served over hot, creamy polenta.

Even though I make this dish with medium shrimp and use shiitake mushrooms instead of the almost-impossible-to-obtain porcini, this appetizer is a winner. ◆

serves 4

$^1/_2$ recipe Basic Polenta (page 306)

$^1/_3$ cup extra-virgin olive oil

$^1/_2$ pound medium shrimp, peeled and deveined

$^1/_2$ pound shiitake or chanterelle mushrooms, wiped clean and thinly sliced

1 garlic clove, finely minced

1 tablespoon chopped fresh flat-leaf parsley

$^1/_2$ cup dry white wine

2 tablespoons unsalted butter

Salt and freshly ground black pepper to taste

Prepare the polenta and keep it warm and soft (as instructed on page 306).

Heat about half of the oil in a large skillet over medium-high heat. When the oil is nice and hot, add the shrimp and stir until they are lightly golden, about 2 minutes. With a slotted spoon, transfer to a plate.

Return the skillet to high heat and add the remaining oil. Let the oil get hot again, then add the mushrooms. Cook, stirring, until the mushrooms begin to color, about 2 minutes. Add the garlic and parsley, stir a few times, then add the wine and butter. Stir until the wine is reduced approximately by half, about 2 minutes.

Return the shrimp to the pan, season with salt and pepper, and stir just long enough to reheat the shrimp, about 1 minute. Taste, adjust the seasoning, and turn off the heat.

Stir the polenta energetically. If it is too firm, add a little milk. Spoon the soft polenta onto serving plates, top with the mushroom-shrimp mixture, and serve hot.

Fried Green Olives

Olive Fritte

In Venice, almost every other *bacaro* serves fried green olives that come from Lake Garda. At a bacaro one evening, the man standing next to me, a glass in one hand, a crisp fried olive in the other, said, "Boy, this is good!" Fried olives are a perfect, casual *cicheto,* or bar snack, because the olives can be fried a few hours ahead and reheated in a 300°F. oven. Place them in a nice bowl and let your guests pick them up with their fingers. ◆ *serves 6 to 8*

30 pitted green olives (see note)
1/3 cup all-purpose flour
2 large eggs, lightly beaten

1/2 cup fine, dry bread crumbs
Vegetable oil for frying

To remove some salt, place the olives in a bowl of cold water and soak for about 1 hour. Drain, rinse, and pat dry with paper towels.

Place the olives in a strainer. Add the flour and toss lightly to coat. Dip each olive in the eggs and roll them in the bread crumbs. With your hands, press the bread crumbs lightly onto the olives. Line the olives on a sheet pan or plate, and refrigerate for about 1 hour.

Heat 1 inch of oil in a medium skillet over medium-high heat. When the oil is hot, fry a handful of olives at a time until they are golden on all sides, 1 to 2 minutes. Remove with a slotted spoon and spread on paper towels to dry. Serve while warm.

BUYING OLIVES FOR FRYING

Do not buy olives packed in oil, because the coating of flour and bread crumbs will not adhere to their slippery skin. Pitted green olives stuffed with anchovies or other savory ingredients can also be used.

THE WINES OF VENETO

The Veneto region, of which Venice is the capital, is the largest producer of wine in Italy, with a major share of it classified as DOC or DOCG. The wines range from simple and light wines to powerful cabernet- and merlot-based reds, with practically everything in between. Some of my favorites originate from the western province of Verona, in the hills between Lake Garda and the town of Soave:

SOAVE

A white wine, perhaps the most famous white in Italy, made from a minimum of 70 percent garganega grapes with an optional addition of trebbiano di Soave; some producers choose to make the wine entirely from garganega. Much of Soave is mass-produced as a simple quaffing wine. But Soave Classicos, especially single-vineyard offerings, have more character, structure, and even aging potential, and can be remarkably refreshing and crisp, perfect as an aperitivo or as an accompaniment to fish.

VALPOLICELLA

Made from a blend of corvina, rondinella, and molinara grapes, Valpolicella is known worldwide. Much of Valpolicella is simple and straightforward—a light- to medium-bodied, all-purpose red, best consumed within one to three years. In recent years, though, quality-conscious producers have made more complex wines, with greater concentrations of fruit, structure, and appealing mouthfeel. These wines can accompany most pasta and meat dishes. Masi, Dal Forno, Allegrini, Zenato, and Quintarelli are among the best producers.

BARDOLINO

A light, refreshing, and dry red, made from the same grape varieties as Valpolicella, grown on the southeast shore of Lake Garda, around the town of Bardolino; also made in a *rosato* fashion. Both can accompany fish dishes and lighter fare quite well. Corte Gardoni and Le Fontane, while not always easy to find, produce classic examples.

AMARONE DELLA VALPOLICELLA

More commonly known simply as Amarone, this dry red was, until recently, one of Italy's best-kept red-wine secrets—and its most often misunderstood. *Amarone* means "bitter," or, more precisely, "bitter in a big way." Yet the wine is not bitter. The term *Amarone* was applied, according to legend, when grapes that were intended for sweet Recioto fermented out their sugars during the drying process, and the result was a dry wine. The same grapes as Valpolicella are dried for up to several months before fermentation.

Amarone has been described as a "supercharged Valpolicella" or a "Valpolicella on steroids," although both characterizations are misleading. Amarone is a distinctive wine, full-bodied, rich in taste, deep garnet in color, with a dried, ripened cherry taste and an almost sweet finish, although technically it is a dry wine. It is an excellent accompaniment to richly flavored meat dishes, beef, venison, or ossobuco. Masi, Allegrini, Quintarelli, and Brigaldara are fine producers of Amarone. From the central, hilly area in the provinces of Vicenza, Padova, and Treviso, some of my favorite wines are:

BREGANZE ROSSO

Predominantly merlot (85 to 100 percent), these wines are ruby red, well structured, with firm tannins, and they age well. Often blended with cabernet, the wines complement most meat or fowl dishes. Maculan is the foremost producer.

COLLI EUGANEI ROSSO

Cabernet- and merlot-based reds, with full bouquet, rich complex flavors, and aging potential, from the hills southwest of Padova. Serve with most red-meat dishes. Vignalta and Marlunghe are fine producers.

PROSECCO DI CONEGLIANO-VALDOBBIADENE

Perhaps the most famous wine of the Veneto is *prosecco*, especially the sparkling version. Made by the tank-fermentation method, introduced at the end of the eighteenth century by the Enology School at Conegliano to exalt its varietal aromas and freshness, prosecco is served in every establishment in Venice and is the aperitivo of choice for many. Prosecco, together with white peach juice, is the base for the famous Venetian cocktail, the Bellini. Many prefer prosecco with their food, especially delicately flavored *risotti* or pasta dishes. Ruggeri, Bele Casel, Zardetto, Nino Franco, and Carpenè Malvolti are excellent prosecco producers.

TORCOLATO DI BREGANZE

Made from semi-dried vespaiolo (85 percent), tocai, and garganega, this dessert wine is golden in color with a fruity and flowery aroma; it develops a warm mellowness with age. It is perfect for after-dinner sipping or with cheeses. Maculan is the producer of choice.

Carpaccio with Baby Artichokes and Parmigiano

Carpaccio con Carciofini e Parmigiano

In early spring, when the first baby artichokes of the year appear on the Venetian markets, they are used in countless preparations. Carpaccio with baby artichokes is one of my favorites. Very thin slices of impeccably fresh raw beef are layered on a plate and topped with thin wedges of raw baby artichokes that are tossed in olive oil and lemon juice, and topped with shavings of Parmigiano-Reggiano. This simple, clean-tasting dish is typical of the trattorie and wine bars of the city. ♦ *serves 6*

1 pound beef eye of round, trimmed of fat

1 pound baby artichokes

Juice of 2 lemons

¹/₄ to ¹/₃ cup extra-virgin olive oil

Salt and freshly ground black pepper to taste

3 ounces Parmigiano-Reggiano, thinly shaved with a vegetable peeler

Put the meat in the freezer for 1 to 2 hours to "firm" it a little. Using a very sharp knife, slice the meat paper-thin. If the slices are not very thin, place them between 2 sheets of wax paper and pound until they are almost transparent. (You might also ask your butcher to do the job for you.)

Brush 6 salad plates with just a bit of oil (so the meat will not stick to the plate) and arrange the slices on each plate to cover the entire surface. The meat can be prepared up to this point 1 hour or so ahead. Cover with plastic wrap and refrigerate.

Meanwhile, remove the green leaves of the artichokes by snapping them off at the base. Stop when the leaves at the base are pale yellow and the tips are pale green. Slice off the green top. Cut the stems off at the base and trim off the remaining green parts around the base. Place the artichokes in a bowl of cold water with the juice of one of the lemons to prevent discoloring.

Just before you are ready to serve, drain and pat dry the artichokes, and cut them in half. (Generally, baby artichokes don't have fuzzy chokes; if they do, remove them with a small knife.) Slice the artichoke halves very thin, place them in a bowl, and dress them with the olive oil and the remaining lemon juice. Season with salt and pepper and mix to combine.

Brush the meat lightly with oil and season with a bit of salt and pepper. Scatter the artichokes and dressing over the meat, and top with shavings of Parmigiano.

CARPACCIO

The most famous carpaccio in the world—and certainly the granddaddy of them all—is the one invented in 1950 at Harry's Bar in Venice. The dish was created for a regular customer whose doctor forbade her to eat cooked meat, and was inspired by Vittorio Carpaccio, a great Renaissance Venetian painter known for his use of sparkling red and white colors.

Venetian Salame with Honey and Wilted Radicchio

La Soppressa Veneziana con Miele e Radicchio Scottato

Soppressa with sweet-and-sour sauce is a typical dish of the Venetian countryside, and it has many variations. In this simple, straightforward version, the soppressa is quickly browned in butter then placed over a mound of wilted radicchio that has been tossed with a mixture of honey and vinegar. ◆ *serves 4*

2 heads radicchio di Treviso (about 1 1/2 pounds)

1/3 cup extra-virgin olive oil

Salt to taste

1/3 cup plus 2 tablespoons good-quality honey

1/3 cup white-wine vinegar

1 tablespoon unsalted butter

2 tablespoons good-quality balsamic vinegar

1/2 pound *soppressa* or good-quality *salame,* (see note) cut into 4 equal slices

Santa Maria della Salute

Remove any bruised outer leaves from the radicchio and cut off the hard white stems. Starting at the tips, cut the radicchio crosswise into $^1/_2$-inch slices. Wash thoroughly, drain, and pat dry with paper towels. Set aside until ready to use.

Heat the oil in a large skillet over medium-high heat. When the oil is hot, add the radicchio and season with salt. Cook, stirring, until the radicchio begins to wilt, about 5 minutes. Reduce the heat to medium, add $^1/_3$ cup of the honey and all the white-wine vinegar, and stir quickly for about 1 minute, or just long enough to coat the radicchio. Place the radicchio in the center of each of 4 plates and set aside.

Meanwhile, wipe the skillet clean with paper towels and return it to medium heat. Add the butter. As soon as the butter begins to foam, add the remaining 2 tablespoons honey and the balsamic vinegar, and stir to combine. Add the *soppressa* and drag it in the honey-butter sauce, turning once, for less than 1 minute. Arrange each slice of soppressa over the radicchio and serve.

SOPPRESSA

Soppressa is a large *salame* made from 70 percent lean pork and 30 percent pork fat. This delicious, cured Venetian salame can be eaten thinly sliced in a sandwich, as an antipasto next to other cured meats, next to a boiled chicory salad, or simply next to fried or grilled polenta. Italian-American soppressa can occasionally be found in Italian specialty food stores. If unavailable, substitute with any high-quality pork salame.

Risotto with Radicchio and Sea Scallops

Risotto con Radicchio e Cape Sante

Even though risotto is a staple of many Northern Italian regions, the most memorable risottos I have ever had were those of Venice. This one, which I enjoyed at the well-known Corte Sconta, combines the mild bitterness of richly colored radicchio with the creaminess of scallops—a marriage made in heaven. I use the intensely red radicchio of Treviso. Its brilliant color changes during cooking to a darker burgundy, and its leaves turn meltingly soft while loosing a bit of their pungency, forming a perfect union with the sweetness of scallops and the creamy risotto. ◆ *serves 4 to 6*

FOR THE SCALLOPS

1/4 cup extra-virgin olive oil

1/2 pound sea scallops, muscles removed and diced into 1/2-inch pieces

1 garlic clove, minced

1/2 teaspoon salt plus more to taste

FOR THE RISOTTO

6 cups Vegetable Broth (page 299) or canned low-sodium chicken broth

4 tablespoons (1/2 stick) unsalted butter

1/2 small onion, minced (about 1/2 cup)

2 cups Arborio, Carnaroli, or Vialone Nano rice

1 cup dry white wine

Leaves from 3 medium heads of Treviso radicchio, about 1 1/2 pounds, finely chopped

Freshly ground black pepper to taste

PREPARE THE SCALLOPS

Heat the oil in a medium skillet over high heat. When the oil is nice and hot, add the scallops. Stir until they are barely golden, about 2 minutes. Add the garlic and stir until it is pale yellow, 30 to 40 seconds. Season with the salt, and set the skillet aside.

Bring the broth to a boil in a medium saucepan and keep warm over low heat.

Melt 3 tablespoons of the butter in a large, heavy skillet over medium heat. When the butter begins to foam, add the onion. Cook, stirring with a wooden spoon, until the onion is pale yellow and soft, 4 to 5 minutes. Add the rice and stir until it is well coated with the butter and onion, and begins to whiten, about 2 minutes.

Stir in the wine. When the wine is almost all evaporated, add the radicchio and 1 cup of the hot broth. Cook and stir until most of the broth has been absorbed. Continue cooking and stirring the rice in this manner, adding 1 cup or so of broth at a time, for about 16 minutes.

Add the scallops and their juices and stir constantly until most of the liquid has been absorbed, about 2 minutes. At this point the rice should be soft but still a bit al dente.

Swirl in the remaining tablespoon of butter and stir for about 1 minute, until the rice has a moist, creamy consistency. Taste, adjust the seasoning, and serve at once.

RADICCHIO

Radicchio is a purplish-reddish, slightly bitter type of chicory that is typical of the Veneto region, where there are many varieties. Although the shapes of radicchio differ, they all retain that tempting bitter edge, which softens and sweetens as it cooks. Until fifteen or twenty years ago, radicchio was basically unknown in this country, but today most specialty food markets carry it. There are several types available in the United States: radicchio di Treviso, a prized variety with large red leaves; radicchio di Chioggia, which looks like a round, dark-red cabbage; radicchio di Castelfranco, my favorite, with soft, speckled leaves (easily available); and radicchio di Treviso Tardivo, with red and white long, pointy leaves, a wonderful newcomer on the American scene.

Risotto with Shrimp and Summer Vegetables

Risotto con Gamberi e Verdurine Estive

When risotto is made with very fresh seafood and fresh, ripe vegetables, and when it is served *all'onda* (soft, moist, and creamy) as it is in Venice, it becomes a small masterpiece. Add to that a pleasant waiter and a view of Piazza San Marco, one of the most breathtaking settings in the world, and the experience is complete. The restaurant is Quadri, one of the oldest in the city. Have an aperitivo in the ground-floor bar, then experience the food and the view on the second floor. • *serves 4 to 6*

FOR THE SHRIMP-VEGETABLE SAUCE

- 1 medium zucchini, diced (about 1 cup)
- 1/4 cup extra-virgin olive oil
- 1 garlic clove, peeled and crushed
- 1/2 pound medium shrimp, peeled, deveined, and cut into 1/2-inch pieces
- 4 medium tomatoes, peeled, seeded, and diced (see note, page 27), about 2 cups

  Salt and freshly ground black pepper to taste

FOR THE RISOTTO

- 6 cups Vegetable Broth (page 299) or canned low-sodium chicken broth
- 4 tablespoons (1/2 stick) unsalted butter
- 1/2 small onion, minced (about 1/2 cup)
- 2 cups Arborio, Carnaroli, or Vialone Nano rice
- 1 cup dry white wine

PREPARE THE SHRIMP-VEGETABLE SAUCE

Bring a small saucepan of water to a boil. Blanch the zucchini for about 1 minute. Drain and set aside.

Heat the oil in a large nonstick skillet over medium-high heat. Add the garlic and cook just long enough to flavor the oil, about 1 minute. Discard the garlic and add the shrimp. Cook, stirring, until the shrimp begins to color, 1 to 2 minutes. With a slotted spoon, transfer to a bowl.

Return the skillet to medium-high heat and add the tomatoes. Cook, stirring a few times, until the tomatoes are soft and the juices have thickened, 2 to 3 minutes. Add the reserved zucchini and shrimp. Stir once or twice, season lightly with salt and pepper, and turn off the heat.

PREPARE THE RISOTTO

Heat the broth in a medium saucepan and keep warm over low heat.

Melt 3 tablespoons of the butter in a large, heavy skillet over medium heat. When the butter foams, add the onion and cook, stirring, until pale yellow and soft, 4 to 5 minutes. Add the rice and stir until it is well coated with the butter and onion, and begins to whiten, about 2 minutes. Stir in the wine. When the wine is almost all evaporated, add 1 cup of the hot broth, and stir until most of the broth has been absorbed. Continue cooking and stirring the rice in this manner, adding 1 cup of broth at a time, for about 16 minutes.

Add the shrimp-vegetable mixture and stir until most of the liquid has been absorbed, 2 to 3 minutes. At this point the rice should be tender but still firm to the bite.

Add the remaining tablespoon of butter and stir for about 1 minute, until the rice has a moist, creamy consistency. Taste, adjust the seasoning, and serve.

Risotto with Squash and White Truffle

Risotto con Zucca e Tartufo Bianco

The arrival of fall in Italy signifies different things to different people. For food lovers, it means they finally can luxuriate in the arrival of magic ingredients such as white truffle, porcini mushrooms, and squash. These ingredients are used in a multitude of dishes, but especially in conjunction with pastas and risottos. At the well-known Da Fiore restaurant, I was served a squash risotto that was richly golden and creamy, topped with paper-thin slices of intensely aromatic white truffle from the Piedmont region. Heavenly! ◆ *serves 4 to 6*

Half of a 2-pound butternut squash

6 cups Vegetable Broth (page 299) or canned low-sodium chicken broth

4 tablespoons ($^{1}/_{2}$ stick) unsalted butter

$^{1}/_{2}$ small onion, minced (about $^{1}/_{2}$ cup)

2 cups Arborio, Carnaroli, or Vialone Nano rice

1 cup dry white wine

$^{1}/_{2}$ cup freshly grated Parmigiano-Reggiano

Salt to taste

4 ounces white truffle (optional), cleaned with a small brush

Preheat the oven to 350°F.

Cut the squash lengthwise, discard the seeds, and wrap loosely in foil. Place on a baking sheet and bake on the middle rack of the oven until the squash is tender when pierced with a thin knife, 1 hour and 15 minutes. Cool the squash, then unwrap it. With a tablespoon, scoop up the pulp from the shell and place in a bowl. Mash the squash against the sides of the bowl with the spoon, then cover the bowl and set aside until ready to use.

Heat the broth in a medium saucepan and keep warm over low heat.

Melt 3 tablespoons of the butter in a large skillet over medium heat. When the butter foams, add the onion and cook, stirring, until pale yellow and soft, 4 to 5 minutes. Add the rice and stir until it is well coated with the butter and the onion, and begins to whiten, about 2 minutes. Stir in the wine. When the wine is almost all evaporated, add 1 cup of the hot broth. Cook and stir until most of the broth has been absorbed. Continue cooking and stirring the rice in this manner, adding a cup or so of broth at a time, for about 15 minutes.

Add ½ cup of squash pulp to the rice and stir to incorporate. Stir in a little more broth, then add another ½ cup of squash; this may be all the squash you need (see note). Cook and stir, adding small additions of broth until the rice is tender but still firm to the bite, 3 to 4 minutes.

Swirl in the remaining tablespoon of butter and about half of the Parmigiano. Stir quickly until the cheese and butter are melted and the rice has a moist, creamy consistency. Taste and adjust the seasoning.

Divide the risotto among serving plates. Shave thin pieces of truffle over each plate, and serve with the remaining Parmigiano on the side.

NOTE

Because the squash is quite starchy, make sure to leave your risotto a little "wetter" than usual. After you have stirred 1 cup of squash into the risotto, wait a few minutes before adding what is left, because you might not need it. Keep in mind that you can always add it, but once you've added more you can't take it out.

WHITE TRUFFLE

Late fall and early winter is truffle season. This amazing aromatic fungi grows in several Italian regions, underground, near the roots of hazel and poplar trees. Sniffed out by dogs at night, the truffle is then dug up by the *trifolaro*, the truffle hunter, who wisely tries to keep his whereabouts a secret. Perhaps the most precious truffle in the world is the white truffle of Alba, a small town in Piedmont. Thinly sliced white truffle piled over steaming risotto, tagliolini, or gnocchi is simply an unforgettable culinary experience. Today fresh Italian truffles can be found more often than in the past. Here are some truffle tips:

- Good white truffle should be firm and compact, with no softness whatsoever. Each truffle should be approximately the size of an egg. It should have a strong fragrance and a pale beige color.

- Use truffle as soon as possible. If you need to hold it for a while, wrap in newspaper, then wrap tightly in aluminum foil. Bury the truffle in a jar filled with sea salt or rice and place in the coldest part of your refrigerator.

- When you are ready to use it, clean the truffle with a small, stiff brush. Remove stubborn dirt with a small knife and rub the surface with a barely moist—not wet—paper towel. Never wash truffles.

- Buy a truffle slicer, the only tool that can slice the truffle paper-thin.

Whole-Wheat Pasta with Onions, Capers, and Anchovies

Bigoli con Cipolle, Capperi, e Acciughe

One of the oldest, most traditional pastas of the Veneto is *bigoli,* thick whole-wheat spaghetti, which used to be made religiously at home and enjoyed particularly on Christmas Eve. There are several variations of the classic bigoli sauce, but the ever-present ingredient in each is onions that are cooked at length over low heat until they have a meltingly soft consistency and a sweet taste. In my version, the onions are given an assertive kick by the addition of chopped capers and anchovies. ◆ *serves 4 to 6*

3/4 cup extra-virgin olive oil

2 large onions, thinly sliced (about 3 1/2 to 4 cups)

2 tablespoons capers preserved in salt, rinsed and finely chopped

8 anchovy fillets, packed in oil, chopped

I tablespoon coarse salt

I pound whole-wheat spaghetti

2 tablespoons chopped fresh flat-leaf parsley

Freshly ground black pepper to taste

Heat 1/2 cup of the oil in a large skillet over medium heat. Add the onions and stir until well coated. Reduce the heat to low and cook, stirring from time to time, until the onions are very soft and pale yellow, 15 to 20 minutes. (Stir in a few tablespoons of water if the onions start to brown.)

Add the capers and anchovies, raise the heat to medium, and cook, stirring with a wooden spoon, for 2 to 3 minutes, until the ingredients are thoroughly mixed and the anchovies are melted. Turn off the heat.

Meanwhile, bring a large pot of water to a boil. Add the coarse salt and the pasta. Cook uncovered, over high heat, until the pasta is tender but still firm to the bite. Scoop out and reserve about 1/2 cup of the cooking water.

Drain the pasta and place in the skillet with the sauce. Add the parsley, a few grindings of black pepper, and the remaining 1/4 cup of oil. If needed, stir in a few tablespoons of the cooking water. Toss well over medium heat until the pasta and sauce are well combined. Taste, adjust the seasoning, and serve.

Risotto with Wild Mushrooms and Smoked Ham

Risotto con Funghi e Speck

One of the joys of fall in Italy is the abundance of wild mushrooms, especially the prized porcini. While porcini are not always available in American markets, other equally delicious *funghi* are: in this dish, shiitake are quickly tossed in fragrant olive oil with garlic, smoked ham, and herbs and added to risotto a few minutes before it is completed. ◆ *serves 4 to 6*

FOR THE MUSHROOMS

- $1/2$ pound shiitake mushrooms
- $1/3$ cup extra-virgin olive oil
- 1 large garlic clove, minced
- 2 ounces sliced speck or other smoked ham (see note), diced
- $1/2$ tablespoon finely chopped fresh flat-leaf parsley
- 1 teaspoon fresh thyme leaves
  Salt and freshly ground black pepper to taste

FOR THE RISOTTO

- 6 cups Vegetable Broth (page 299) or canned low-sodium chicken broth
- 4 tablespoons ($1/2$ stick) unsalted butter
- $1/2$ small onion, minced (about $1/2$ cup)
- 2 cups Arborio, Carnaroli, or Vialone Nano rice
- 1 cup dry white wine
- $1/2$ cup freshly grated Parmigiano-Reggiano

PREPARE THE MUSHROOMS

Remove and discard the stems. Wipe the mushrooms clean with a damp towel, then thinly slice them.

Heat the oil in a large skillet over medium-high heat. As soon as the oil begins to smoke, add the mushrooms. Cook, stirring, until lightly golden, about 2 minutes. Add the garlic and smoked ham, and stir until the garlic begins to color, about 1 minute. Stir in the parsley and thyme, season lightly with salt and pepper, and remove from the heat.

Heat the broth in a medium saucepan and keep warm over low heat.

Melt 3 tablespoons of the butter in a large skillet over medium heat. When the butter foams, add the onion and cook, stirring, until pale yellow and soft, 4 to 5 minutes. Add the rice and stir until it is well coated with the butter and onion, and begins to whiten, about 2 minutes. Stir in the wine. When the wine is almost all evaporated, add 1 cup of hot broth and cook, stirring, until most of the broth has been absorbed. Continue cooking and stirring the rice in this manner, adding a cup or so of the broth at a time, for about 15 minutes.

Add the mushrooms and their juices and stir to incorporate. Continue cooking and stirring, adding broth a little at a time, until the rice is tender but still firm to the bite, about 3 minutes.

Add the remaining tablespoon of butter and half of the Parmigiano. Stir quickly until the butter and cheese are melted and the rice has a moist, creamy consistency. Taste, adjust the seasoning, and serve with the remaining Parmigiano on the side.

SPECK

Speck is smoked ham from the Alto Adige and is available in Italian and specialty food stores. Substitute with a mild smoked American or French ham.

Rice with Peas and Pea Pods

Risi e Bisi

Risi e bisi (rice and peas) is a cross between a very thick soup and a soupy risotto. My favorite version is a traditional one that begins by cooking the rice as a regular risotto, and keeps cooking it with a large amount of broth and the addition of puréed pea pods. The sweetness of the fresh pea pods infuses the already flavorful broth. Risi e bisi is traditionally prepared in spring, when the tiny, sweet green peas of the lagoons appear in the Rialto food market. Risi e bisi should be served with a spoon.

• serves 4 to 6

1 pound fresh peas in their pods (about 2 cups shelled), the smallest you can get

Salt to taste

8 cups Vegetable Broth (page 299)

4 tablespoons (1/2 stick) unsalted butter

1/2 small onion, minced (about 1/2 cup)

3 ounces thickly sliced pancetta, finely minced

2 cups Arborio, Carnaroli, or Vialone Nano rice

1 cup dry white wine

1 tablespoon minced fresh flat-leaf parsley

1/2 cup freshly grated Parmigiano-Reggiano

Shell the peas and set them aside. Wash the pea pods, place them in a large pot, and add enough cold water to cover by a couple of inches. Season with salt and bring to a boil over medium heat. Cook, uncovered, until the pods are tender, 45 to 50 minutes.

Scoop up the pods and purée them in the bowl of a food processor with 1 cup of their cooking water. Put the puréed pods through a food mill or a sieve to remove the tough fibers.

Heat the vegetable broth in a medium saucepan, add the puréed pods, and keep warm over low heat.

Melt 3 tablespoons of the butter in a large skillet over medium heat. When the butter foams, add the onion and the pancetta and cook, stirring with a wooden spoon, until the onion is soft and the pancetta is lightly golden, 4 to 5 minutes. Add the rice and stir until it is well coated with butter and onion, and begins to whiten, about 2 minutes. Stir in the wine. When the wine is almost all evaporated, add I cup of the hot vegetable-pea broth and the reserved peas. Stir until most of the broth has been absorbed. Continue cooking and stirring the rice in this manner, adding I cup of broth at a time, until the rice and peas are tender but still firm to the bite, I5 to I6 minutes.

Turn off the heat, then add the remaining tablespoon of butter, the parsley, $1/3$ cup of the Parmigiano, and just enough broth to give the rice a soupier consistency. Cover the pot and let rest for a couple of minutes before serving with an additional sprinkling of Parmigiano.

VARIATION

When fresh tiny peas in their pods are not available, make this dish with small frozen peas and flavorful homemade Vegetable Broth.

WHEN IN VENICE
Restaurants, Trattorie, and Wine Bars

From the U.S., dial 011, followed by the country code of 39. The area code for all numbers below is 041.

Al Bacareto
Calle de le Boteghe
San Marco 3447
Tel. 528 9336
A quaint, casual place that has a large selection of wines by the glass and delicious *cicheti*. Try the batter-fried *baccalà*, the rice and potato *polpette*, or the stuffed fried olives. Or sit at one of their small tables and indulge in a dish of cuttlefish and polenta.

Al Covo
Campiello della Pescaria
Castello 3968
Tel. 522 3812
A magnet for Venetians and gourmands from all over the world, this rustic, unpretentious seafood restaurant will win you over with the freshness of their simply prepared fish. Al Covo is consistently busy, so make a reservation. (This restaurant is also one of the few in Venice that does not accept credit cards.)

Al Mascaron
Calle Lunga Santa Maria Formosa
Castello 5225
Tel. 522 5995
A former *bacaro*, or wine bar, that evolved into a much-loved upscale trattoria, with food that is traditional to the core. Try liver with sweet caramelized onions, creamy *baccalà* on roasted polenta, or one of their great seafood risottos.

Ca' d'Oro, alla Vedova
Ramo Ca' d'Oro
Cannaregio 3912
Tel. 528 5324
A very well known, historic *bacaro* that serves many wines by the glass and a large number of traditional Venetian *cicheti:* meatballs, seafood salads, sausages, stuffed vegetables, marinated sardines, stuffed olives, fried cod, and more. This is a fun place to spend an hour or so, to eat and listen to the Venetians who, after several cicheti, will probably begin to sing.

Cantina Do Mori
Calle dei Do Mori
San Polo 429
Tel. 522 5401
A picturesque old-fashioned wine bar near the Rialto Bridge that offers a regularly revised wine list and delicious *cicheti*, the succulent Venetian snacks.

Osteria Da Fiore
Calle del Scaleter
San Polo 2202a
Tel. 721 308
Perhaps the best Venetian restaurant, serving exceptionally delicious food in an elegant, refined setting. The menu changes with the seasons, taking advantage of the freshest ingredients.

Dalla Marisa
Cannaregio 652b
Fondamenta San Giobbe 652b
Tel. 720 211
This is perhaps the only trattoria in Venice that offers an authentic meat-based menu. So if after all the fish dishes of Venice you yearn for duck, beef, veal, chicken, and wild boar, Dalla Marisa is the place for you.

Fiaschetteria Toscana
San Giovanni Grisostomo
Cannaregio 5719
Tel. 528 5281
An understated, elegant, and memorable restaurant that serves great traditional Venetian dishes prepared with the highest-quality seasonal ingredients, with attentive service and a relaxed atmosphere.

Harry's Bar
Calle Vallaresso
San Marco 1323
Tel. 528 5777
The best-known and most popular restaurant of the city, which makes it almost impossible to get a reservation. One goes to Harry's not only for the food, but also to see and be seen, for its clientele seems to belong in the pages of *Vanity Fair*. If you do get a table, be sure to start with a Bellini, a lovely drink that was invented here, made with *prosecco* and peach juice or peach purée.

Il Refolo
Campo San Giacomo dall'Orio
Santa Croce 1459
Tel. 524 0016
A pizzeria that serves delicious pizza and other dishes, and a good spot to drop in for a quick, reasonably priced lunch. Try the salad of tiny shrimp and avocado.

La Cantina
Campo San Felice
Cannaregio 3689
Tel. 522 8258
A very popular wine bar. Sit at one of the outdoor tables and sip a glass of *prosecco* while enjoying one of La Cantina's many wonderful *cicheti*.

La Corte Sconta
Calle del Pestrin
Castello 3886
Tel. 522 7024
For many, La Corte Sconta is a cult trattoria, with terrific food, casual feeling, and colorful way of dressing the tables (butcher paper instead of tablecloths, and colorful napkins). Here you are going to find traditional Venetian cuisine with an amazing number of seafood appetizers; don't miss the sweet-and-sour sardines.

Vini da Gigio
Fondamenta San Felice
Cannaregio 3628a
Tel. 528 5140
One of my favorite trattorie. Small and always packed, but the service is attentive and unrushed. The food is terrific, the wine list is impressive, and the prices are moderate. Don't miss it.

Spaghetti with Tuna, Olives, and Tomatoes

Spaghetti con Tonno, Olive, e Pomodori

This dish belongs to Fiaschetteria Toscana, one of the best-known Venetian restaurants. When I first opened the enticing menu, the choices were so appealing that I decided to give up my daily risotto. As I took the first bite of this spaghetti, I liked it so much that I asked our waiter what went into the sauce. "Signora," he said, "we go to the market every morning and we buy what is fresh. If we can't get tuna, we buy swordfish, or calamari, or shrimp, or cuttlefish. Then we go into the kitchen and decide what to do. And frankly, the simpler the dish is, the happier we are."

♦ *serves 4 to 6*

1/3 cup extra-virgin olive oil

3/4 pound tuna or swordfish steak, cut into 1/2-inch cubes

1 garlic clove, finely minced

1 tablespoon finely minced sun-dried tomatoes packed in oil

8 large green olives, pitted and finely chopped

1/2 cup dry white wine

6 large, ripe tomatoes, peeled, seeded, and diced (see note, page 27), 2 1/2 to 3 cups; or 3 cups canned Italian plum tomatoes, diced

Salt and freshly ground black pepper to taste

6 to 8 fresh basil leaves, shredded, or 1/2 tablespoon chopped fresh flat-leaf parsley

1 pound spaghetti

1 tablespoon coarse salt

Heat the oil in a large skillet over medium-high heat. When the oil is nice and hot, add the tuna and stir until it begins to color, about 2 minutes. With a slotted spoon, transfer to a plate.

Add the garlic, sun-dried tomatoes, and olives to the skillet and stir over medium heat for a minute or two. Stir in the wine and let it bubble until it is all evaporated, 2 to 3 minutes. Add the tomatoes, season with salt and pepper, and simmer until the juices have thickened, 4 to 5 minutes. Add the tuna, simmer for 2 to 3 minutes, then stir in the basil or parsley.

Meanwhile, bring a large pot of water to a boil over high heat. Add the coarse salt and the pasta and cook, uncovered, until the pasta is tender but still a bit firm to the bite. Scoop up and reserve about ½ cup of the pasta cooking water.

Drain the pasta and add it to the sauce. Toss over medium heat until the pasta and sauce are well combined; add some of the pasta water if the sauce seems too dry. Taste, adjust the seasoning, and serve.

Pasta and Bean Soup, Venetian-Style

Pasta e Fagioli alla Veneziana

Every region of Italy has its own *pasta e fagioli.* In Venice, this old standby can be found in basically every wine bar, trattoria, and restaurant. In fall or winter, when dense fog envelopes the city, head straight to Al Bacareto or Vini da Gigio, two of Venice's most colorful establishments, and order a nice bottle of local red wine and a steaming bowl of comforting, filling pasta e fagioli, a dish that has fed Venetians for centuries.

◆ *serves 8 to 10*

1 pound (about 2 cups) dried cranberry beans, picked over and soaked overnight in cold water to cover generously (see note)

1/3 cup plus 2 tablespoons extra-virgin olive oil

1/2 small onion, minced (about 1/2 cup)

1 small celery stalk, minced (about 1/2 cup)

1 small carrot, minced (about 1/2 cup)

3 ounces thickly sliced pancetta, diced

2 garlic cloves, finely minced

2 tablespoons chopped fresh flat-leaf parsley

3 to 4 fresh sage leaves, finely chopped

1 small sprig of rosemary, leaves only, finely chopped

Salt and freshly ground black pepper to taste

6 ounces spaghetti, broken into 2- to 3-inch pieces

Drain the beans of their soaking water and rinse well. Put the beans in a large saucepan and add enough cold water to cover by 3 inches (about 3 quarts). Partially cover the pot and bring to a boil over medium heat. As soon as the water begins to bubble, reduce the heat to low and simmer, uncovered, until the beans are tender, 40 to 45 minutes.

In a blender or food processor fitted with the metal blade, purée about half of the beans with 1 cup of their liquid. Stir the purée back into the pot.

Meanwhile, prepare the savory base. Heat 1/3 cup of the oil in a medium skillet over medium heat. Add the onion, celery, carrot, and pancetta and cook, stirring from time to time, until the mixture is lightly golden and soft, 8 to 10 minutes. Add the garlic, parsley, sage, and rosemary and stir for a couple of minutes. Add the base to the beans, season generously with salt and pepper, and simmer over low heat for about 10 minutes.

Add the spaghetti to the simmering soup and cook over medium heat, stirring from time to time, until the pasta is tender but still a bit firm to the bite. Taste and adjust the seasoning. Ladle the soup into serving bowls, dribble the reserved oil over, and serve.

QUICK-SOAKING BEANS

If you forget to soak dried beans overnight, this quick-soak method will tenderize them in a few hours: Pick over the beans, place them in a large saucepan, and add enough cold water to cover by 3 inches. Bring the water to a gentle simmer and cook, partially covered, for about 3 minutes. Turn off the heat and leave the beans in the warm water for a couple of hours. Drain the beans, rinse them under cold running water, and add enough water to cover by 3 inches. Cook as instructed in the recipe.

Shellfish Stew

Brodetto di Pesce

Italy boasts hundreds of miles of white, sandy seacoasts and an enormous wealth of seafood dishes. One of the most loved and famous is a stew that changes from region to region, with variations according to local traditions and the imagination of the cook. This *brodetto*, or *broeto* as the Venetians call it, relies heavily on the variety of seafood native to the northern Adriatic, and on the lightness of the broth. Although Venetian seafood is not available here in the United States, we can still try to duplicate the essence of this beautiful dish by selecting the best, freshest seafood available.

◆ *serves* *4*

6 cups Fish Broth (page 300)

1 pound littleneck clams or cockles, scrubbed and thoroughly rinsed under cold running water

1 1/2 pounds mussels, beards removed, scrubbed and thoroughly rinsed under cold running water

1/2 cup dry white wine

1/3 cup extra-virgin olive oil

2 garlic cloves, peeled and lightly crushed

1 small yellow onion, finely chopped

1 celery stalk, finely chopped

1 small carrot, peeled and finely chopped

5 large tomatoes, peeled, seeded, and chopped, with their juices (see note, page 27), about 3 cups

Salt and freshly ground black pepper to taste

1/2 pound medium shrimp, peeled and deveined

1/2 pound sea scallops, halved

8 fresh basil leaves

Heat the fish broth in a medium saucepan and keep warm over low heat until ready to use.

Put the clams and mussels in a large skillet with 1/2 cup of water and the wine. Cook over medium heat, covered, until the shellfish open. Transfer them to a bowl as they open. (If some clams and mussels do not open, cook them a little longer. If after a few minutes they fail to open, discard them.)

Reduce the liquid in the pan to about half its original amount. Line a small strainer with paper towels and strain the juice. Set aside.

Heat the oil in a large saucepan over medium heat. Add the garlic and cook until lightly golden on both sides, 1 to 2 minutes; discard the garlic. Stir in the onion, celery, and carrot. Reduce the heat to medium and cook, stirring with a wooden spoon, until the vegetables are soft and pale yellow, 10 to 12 minutes. (Do not let the vegetables brown.) Add the tomatoes and their juices, and simmer until they begin to soften, 4 to 5 minutes.

Add the warmed fish broth and the reserved mussel and clam liquid. Season with salt and pepper and simmer for about 5 minutes. Add the shrimp and the scallops, and cook for 2 minutes. Add the reserved clams and mussels, stir once or twice, then turn off the heat. Taste and adjust the seasoning. Let the *brodetto* sit for at least 1 hour. Just before serving, tear the basil into small pieces with your hands and add to the brodetto. Reheat it gently and serve hot.

PREPARING THE BRODETTO AHEAD

When I make this dish, I prepare it 1 or 2 hours ahead so its flavor increases and concentrates as it sits. If I want to prepare it several hours ahead or overnight, I transfer the stew to a large bowl, place that bowl over another bowl of ice water, and stir until the stew is cool. Then I refrigerate it, uncovered, until completely cold. At that point it can be covered with plastic wrap and left in the refrigerator overnight. The next day, reheat it gently and serve.

Scallops with Capers, Anchovies, Lemon, and Wine

Cape Sante in Padella

A simple dish that becomes terrific when very fresh, sweet scallops are used. At the Ca' d'Oro, alla Vedova, one of Venice's historic wine bars, the scallops are quickly sautéed and combined with a savory lemon-anchovy-garlic-wine sauce, then placed over slices of crisp, fried polenta. Here's my version: see page 306 for the polenta.

♦ *serves 4*

1/3 to 1/2 cup extra-virgin olive oil

2 garlic cloves, peeled and lightly crushed

16 sea scallops (1 1/2 pounds), washed and patted dry

1 cup all-purpose flour

1/2 teaspoons salt plus more to taste

1 tablespoon capers, drained and rinsed

3 anchovy fillets packed in salt, rinsed and chopped

1 1/2 cups dry white wine

1 lemon, half zested, whole juiced

2 tablespoons unsalted butter

1 tablespoon chopped fresh flat-leaf parsley

Heat the oil in a large skillet over high heat. Add the garlic and stir until golden brown on all sides. Discard the garlic.

Place the scallops in a sieve and toss them with the flour, shaking the sieve to remove excess. Add the scallops to the skillet without crowding (if necessary, cook them in batches). Season with the salt and cook over high heat, stirring, until they are lightly golden on both sides, about 4 minutes.

With a slotted spoon, transfer the scallops to a bowl. Add the capers and anchovies to the skillet, stir once or twice, then add the wine and the lemon juice. Cook over high heat, stirring and scraping the bottom of the pan with a wooden spoon, until the liquid has a medium-thick consistency, 3 to 4 minutes. Add the lemon zest, butter, and parsley and stir for about 1 minute.

Return the scallops to the skillet and cook just long enough to coat with the sauce. Taste, adjust the seasoning, and serve at once.

GARLIC IN VENICE

In the Veneto, garlic is used with considerable restraint. In fact, most of the time a peeled garlic clove is added to the sizzling oil, browned gently, and then discarded, leaving behind only a whiff of its aroma to enrich the food in the pan without shouting.

Sweet-and-Sour Shrimp

Scampi in Saor alla Veneziana

Saor is a centuries-old sweet-and-sour marinade that before refrigeration was used to preserve meat and fish for several days. The technique for saor, which has changed little through the years, cooks onions at length, then combines them with sugar, vinegar, pine nuts, and raisins into a thick, glazy marinade. This savory mixture is then paired with fried fish that is left to marinate overnight, as in this dish. Today this sweet-and-sour tradition can be found in Venice's most traditional eating establishments and in many *bacari*, or wine bars. ◆ *serves 4*

$^1/_2$ cup olive oil

1 cup all-purpose flour

$1^1/_2$ pounds medium shrimp, peeled and deveined

Salt to taste

2 large onions, thinly sliced ($3^1/_2$ to 4 cups)

$^1/_2$ cup pine nuts

$^1/_2$ cup golden raisins, soaked in warm water for 15 minutes

1 tablespoon sugar

$^1/_3$ cup white-wine vinegar

$^1/_2$ cup dry white wine

Freshly ground white pepper to taste

Heat the oil in a large, heavy skillet over high heat. When the oil is nice and hot, lightly flour the shrimp and add to the oil without crowding (cook in batches if needed). Cook until the shrimp are golden on both sides, about 2 minutes. Transfer to paper towels and season lightly with salt.

Discard a little of the oil and return the skillet to medium-low heat. Add the onions and cook, stirring, until golden and soft but not limp, about 15 minutes.

Meanwhile, toast the pine nuts in a dry frying pan over medium heat.

Drain the raisins and add to the onions together with the toasted pine nuts, sugar, vinegar, and wine. Season with salt and white pepper. Cook over medium heat, stirring, until the vinegar and wine are almost all evaporated. Taste and adjust the seasoning. Transfer the onions to a bowl and cool to room temperature.

Place half the onions in a serving dish, top with the shrimp, and cover with the remaining onions. Cover and refrigerate for a day or two. Leave at room temperature for a couple of hours before serving.

WHEN IN VENICE
Caffès, Pastry Shops, and Gelaterie

The Historic Caffès of Piazza San Marco
Three of the most famous caffès in the world are located in Venice's breathtakingly beautiful Piazza San Marco, also known as the drawing room of Europe: Caffè Florian, Caffè Quadri, and Caffè Lavena. These historic caffès all opened their doors in the eighteenth century and have since been a magnet for Venetians and visitors from all over the world. During the warm months, Piazza San Marco is a magic place. Sit at an outdoor table, sip an aperitivo, or indulge on a decadent gelato while listening to the sound of the orchestras, and watch the whole world go by.

Caffè Florian
Piazza San Marco 56
Tel. 528 5338

Caffè Quadri
Piazza San Marco 121
Tel. 522 2105

Caffè Lavena
Piazza San Marco 133
Tel. 522 4070

Gelateria Paolin
San Marco 2962/a, Campo Santo Stefano
Tel. 522 5576
While it is almost impossible in Italy to eat a so-so gelato, some *gelaterie* outdistance everyone. Gelateria Paolin does not have a large variety, but Venetians seem to agree that Paolin makes some of the best.

Harry's Dolci
Fondamenta San Biagio
773 Giudecca
Tel. 522 4844
You can go to Harry's Dolci for the great view or for a light meal. Or you can go there simply because of Harry's legendary sweets. It is also a romantic spot in which to linger over a superb cocktail.

La Boutique del Dolce
San Polo 890, Fondamenta Rio Marin
Tel. 718 523
A small, unassuming caffè that serves very good cappuccino and espresso and delicious pastries, cookies, and croissants. A great breakfast spot.

Pasticceria Marchini
San Marco Spadaria 676
Tel. 522 9109
If you ask a true Venetian how to go to Marchini, he will smile broadly and probably escort you to this wonderful pastry shop.

Cuttlefish with Wine, Tomatoes, and Paprika

Seppie alla Busara

Vini da Gigio is a small, quaint trattoria that I discovered many years ago while researching one of my very first books. I remember entering the small, cramped dining room, which was already filled to capacity with locals and tourists, and thinking that because I was alone, I had absolutely no chance to get a table. Instead, a waiter escorted me to a little table in a corner. I began my meal with a selection of *cicheti*, typical Venetian bar snacks, then proceeded to order a stew of small cuttlefish that had simmered gently in wine and tomatoes, served next to slices of grilled, golden polenta. The leftover stew is turned into a sauce for *bigoli*, Venice's traditional buckwheat pasta, or bucatini, a thick spaghetti-like pasta. ◆ *serves 4*

1/3 cup extra-virgin olive oil

3 garlic cloves, peeled and lightly crushed

1/2 medium yellow onion, finely minced (about 3/4 cup)

2 to 3 anchovy fillets packed in salt, rinsed and chopped

1 1/2 pounds cleaned, fresh or frozen cuttlefish bodies (see note), cut into 1-inch strips

Salt and freshly ground black pepper to taste

Hot paprika to taste

2 cups dry white wine

2 cups imported Italian plum tomatoes, preferably San Marzano (see note, page 35) with their juices, put through a food mill to remove the seeds

2 tablespoons fine, unflavored, dried bread crumbs

1 tablespoon chopped fresh flat-leaf parsley

Heat the oil in a large skillet over medium-high heat. Add the garlic and stir until golden brown on all sides; discard the garlic. Lower the heat to medium and add the onion and anchovies. Cook, stirring, until the onion is soft and pale yellow, 4 to 5 minutes. Add the cuttlefish and season with salt, pepper, and paprika. Cook, stirring and shaking the pan, until the cuttlefish is coated with the savory base, about 2 minutes.

Raise the heat to high and add the wine and the tomatoes. As soon as the liquid begins to bubble, reduce the heat to low and cover the skillet. Cook at the gentlest simmer, stirring from time to time, until the cuttlefish is tender, 50 to 55 minutes.

Stir the bread crumbs and parsley into the sauce, cover the pan, and simmer 10 minutes longer. Taste, adjust the seasoning, and turn off the heat. Let the stew sit for a few minutes before serving.

CUTTLEFISH *(SEPPIE)*

A member of the cephalopod family that includes calamari and octopus, cuttlefish is plentiful in the waters of the Venetian lagoon, and is used in many preparations. The large cuttlefish, available in the fall, are often stuffed and cooked in savory sauces or grilled and dressed simply with olive oil and lemon. In summer, when the cuttlefish are small and tender and called *seppiolina* they are generally fried. The ink of the cuttlefish is used to add taste and drama to the much-admired, sleek black risotto of Venice.

When cuttlefish or octopus slowly simmers in a sauce, its natural, watery juices tend to thin out the sauce. The addition of a little bread crumbs stirred into the sauce during the last few minutes of cooking will absorb and thicken the sauce while giving it texture.

Venetian Calf's Liver with Onions

Fegato alla Veneziana

Calf's liver and onions is a much-loved traditional Venetian dish. While I am not an avid fan of liver, I must admit that once in Venice I can't bypass this succulent dish. Serve with grilled, fried, or roasted polenta (page 306). ◆ *serves 4*

1/3 cup extra-virgin olive oil

2 large onions, thinly sliced (3 1/2 to 4 cups)

3 tablespoons unsalted butter

1 1/2 pounds calf's liver, cleaned, thin membrane peeled off, and cut into 1/2-inch-wide and 3- to 4-inch-long strips

1/2 teaspoon salt

1/4 teaspoon freshly ground black pepper

1 tablespoon chopped fresh flat-leaf parsley

Heat the oil in a large skillet over medium heat. When the oil is nice and hot, add the onions and cook, stirring with a wooden spoon, until soft and golden brown, about 25 minutes. With a slotted spoon, transfer the onions to a bowl, letting the juices and oil fall back into the skillet.

Return the skillet to medium-high heat and add 1 tablespoon of the butter. As soon as the butter begins to foam, add the liver without crowding (cook in 2 batches if necessary) and cook, stirring, until golden brown, about 3 minutes. Season with the salt and pepper.

Return the onions to the pan and stir until the onions and liver are thoroughly combined, 1 to 2 minutes. Transfer the contents of the skillet to a warm serving platter.

Add the remaining 2 tablespoons of butter to the skillet and stir, scraping up the brown bits attached to the bottom of the pan. Add the parsley, stir once or twice, and pour the butter sauce over the liver and onions. Serve hot.

WHAT YOU NEED FOR *FEGATO ALLA VENEZIANA*

- The fresh, shining liver of a young calf, sliced into $1/4$-inch pieces. (The younger the calf and the thinner the liver, the faster it will cook and the better it will taste.)
- The sweetest onion available. The traditional recipe calls for equal amounts of onion and liver.
- A 12- or 14-inch skillet, so that the onion and the liver will have a large space to cook evenly and quickly.
- Before adding the liver to the skillet, make sure the fat is very hot so the liver will brown immediately.
- Even though not traditional, adding a bit of cubed pancetta to the skillet, at the same time you add the liver, will give an extra kick to this delicious preparation.

Roasted Guinea Hen with Peppery Sauce

Faraona in Peverada

Peverada is a traditional peppery sauce that dates back to medieval times and used to be paired with spit-roasted game. Today, the hens are cooked in a hot oven, while the savory sauce of *salame*, pancetta, onion, anchovies, lemon zest, and peppercorns is prepared on top of the stove. Polenta—soft, grilled, roasted, or fried (see page 306)—is the perfect accompaniment to this hearty dish. ◆ *serves 4*

2 guinea hens (about 2 pounds each)

1/2 cup extra-virgin olive oil

Salt and freshly ground black pepper

2 garlic cloves, peeled and lightly crushed

1/2 small yellow onion, finely minced (1/2 cup)

I ounce *soppressa* or any good-quality *salame*, minced

I ounce thinly sliced pancetta, minced

2 salt-preserved anchovies, rinsed and chopped

1/2 tablespoon chopped fresh sage

Grated zest of 1/2 lemon

I teaspoon crushed black peppercorns

1/4 cup white-wine vinegar

I cup dry white wine

I tablespoon unsalted butter

I tablespoon chopped fresh flat-leaf parsley

Preheat the oven to 400°F.

Cut the hens in half on each side of the backbone, and discard the backbone. Wash under cold running water and pat dry with paper towels.

Put half the oil in a large heat-proof pot or casserole, add the hen pieces, and turn to coat with the oil. Season with salt and generously with pepper on both sides. Transfer the pan to the center rack of the oven and roast until the hens are golden brown and cooked all the way through, 40 to 45 minutes (170°F on a meat thermometer inserted in the thickest part of the leg).

Meanwhile, prepare the sauce. Heat the remaining oil in a medium skillet over medium heat. Add the garlic and cook until golden on both sides; discard the garlic. Add the onion to the skillet and stir with a wooden spoon until pale yellow and soft, about 5 minutes. Add the *salame*, pancetta, anchovies, sage, lemon zest, and crushed peppercorns. Stir for 2 to 3 minutes. Stir in the vinegar, season lightly with salt and pepper, and turn off the heat.

When the guinea hens are done, carefully remove the casserole from the oven (pay attention, because at this point the casserole is very hot) and place the hens on 4 heated serving plates. Cover loosely with foil and set aside while you finish the sauce.

Scoop up and discard most of the fat from the casserole and place it on high heat. Add the wine and stir, scraping the bottom of the pan with a wooden spoon, until the wine and the pan juices have thickened. Stir the reserved peppery sauce into the casserole, then add the butter and the parsley. Cook, stirring constantly, until the sauce has a medium-thick consistency, 3 to 4 minutes. Taste and adjust the seasoning.

Remove the foil from the plates, spoon the sauce over the hens, and serve immediately.

Venetian Lamb Stew with Cabbage

Castradina

This lamb stew is a cross between a stew and a soup, and in the traditional trattorie of Venice it is often served in a bowl with a large amount of brothy sauce. As always, there are several variations of *castradina*. Some omit the tomatoes. Others add radicchio instead of cabbage. And others again add cinnamon and cloves. However, most Venetian cooks seem to agree that this stew needs to cook at length on moderate heat to produce a melt-in-the-mouth tender meat. Serve next to soft, grilled, or roasted polenta (see page 306), or grilled slices of bread. ◆ *serves 4*

$1/3$ cup extra-virgin olive oil

$1/2$ medium onion, minced

$1/2$ medium head of Savoy cabbage, thinly sliced (about 7 cups)

1 garlic clove, minced

2 ounces thickly sliced pancetta, minced

3 pounds boneless lamb shoulder, trimmed of fat and cut into 2-inch pieces

Salt and freshly ground black pepper

1 cup dry white wine

4 medium-size, ripe tomatoes, peeled, seeded (see note, page 27), and minced (about 2 cups), or 2 cups minced, canned plum tomatoes

4 cups Meat Broth (page 298) or low-sodium canned beef broth

Preheat the oven to 325°F.

Heat the oil in a large, heavy ovenproof pot or casserole over medium heat. Add the onion, cabbage, garlic, and pancetta. Cook, stirring, until the vegetables begin to soften, 10 to 12 minutes. Raise the heat to medium high and add the lamb. Season with salt and pepper. Stir for 2 to 3 minutes, or until the lamb is coated with the savory base.

Add the wine, bring to a fast simmer, then add the tomatoes. Stir just long enough to combine, 1 to 2 minutes. Add the broth. As soon as the broth begins to bubble, turn off the heat. Cover the pot and place on the middle rack of the oven. Bake for 2 to 2½ hours, stirring occasionally, until the meat is tender enough to be cut with a fork.

Serve the stew hot.

WHEN IN VENICE
Food Markets, Specialty Food Stores,
and Cooking Schools

Casa del Parmigiano
214/215 Erberia Rialto
Tel. 520 6525
Great cheeses from many parts of Italy, especially
the perfectly aged Parmigiano-Reggiano.

Fulvia Sesani
Palazzo Morosini della Trezza
Castello 6140
Tel. 522 8923
Fulvia Sesani is the aristocratic, much-respected
owner and teacher of her namesake cooking school
at her Palazzo Morosini, near Piazza San Marco.
Fulvia, a former chemist and the author of several
cookbooks, is a formidable teacher of Venetian
cuisine.

Il Pastaio
219 Calle dei Varoteri
San Polo-Rialto
If pasta made by hand is what you are looking for,
this is the place.

L'Arte del Pane
Fondamenta San'Eufemia
655 Giudecca
Tel. 520 6737
Claudio Crosara, baker and owner of this well-
known shop, makes superior bread, bread sticks,
and traditional Venetian cookies. For a perfect
morning snack, buy some cookies and enjoy them
while touring the city.

Mascari
Ruga dei Speziali
381 San Polo
Tel. 522 9762
A well-known gourmet food shop located near the
Rialto Bridge.

Panificio Giovanni Volpe
Cannaregio 1143
This bakery, located in the old Jewish ghetto, has
a nice assortment of Venetian and Jewish breads,
cookies, and pastries.

Rialto Market
The famous fish and vegetable market, just around
the corner of the Rialto Bridge, is not to be missed.
I can spend hours walking around, inhaling the
salty breeze of the sea and the sweet aroma of the
fresh fish. This market is the gastronomic heart of
Venice.

Stuffed Roasted Vegetables

Verdure Ripiene al Forno

One of the joys of being in Venice is to eat like the locals do, in the friendly wine bars and *osterie*. Because Venice is a uniquely pedestrian city, you quickly learn the paths to the many eating establishments that serve delicious, simple, local food. One dish that can often be found is the mix of seasonal stuffed vegetables. In summer, tomatoes, peppers, and zucchini are filled with a mixture of chopped bread, *salame*, parsley, Parmigiano, and flavorful olive oil, then baked until soft and topped with a nice golden color. You can prepare it ahead and serve at room temperature as an antipasto or next to grilled or roasted meats. ◆ *serves 4 to 6*

3 medium-size, ripe tomatoes

2 large red bell peppers

4 small zucchini

1 large egg, lightly beaten

1 cup freshly grated Parmigiano-Reggiano

1 1/2 cups coarsely chopped fresh Italian or French bread, without the crust

3 ounces sliced *salame* or baked ham, minced

2 garlic cloves, minced

1 cup finely chopped fresh flat-leaf parsley

1/2 teaspoon salt plus more to taste

1/4 teaspoon freshly ground black pepper plus more to taste

1 cup extra-virgin olive oil

Slice the tomatoes in half horizontally. With your fingers, remove the seeds. Place the tomatoes cut side down on paper towels, and let them drain for about 1 hour.

Wash and dry the bell peppers, trim both ends, and discard the stems. Cut the peppers into quarters lengthwise. Core and seed them, and remove the white membranes.

Trim both ends of the zucchini and halve them lengthwise. With a teaspoon, scoop out about half of the flesh, leaving 1/2-inch-thick shells. Chop the flesh and place in a medium bowl. Add the beaten egg, 3/4 cup of the Parmigiano, the bread, *salame*, garlic, and parsley. Season with the salt and pepper and drizzle with about half of the olive oil. Mix well, taste, and adjust the seasoning. The stuffing should have a soft, moist texture. Add a little more oil if needed.

Preheat the oven to 350°F. Coat a baking dish lightly with oil.

Place some of the stuffing in the cavities of the tomatoes, zucchini, and bell peppers. Arrange the vegetables in the baking dish. Sprinkle the tops with the remaining Parmigiano and drizzle with a little more oil.

Place the pan on the center rack of the oven and bake until the vegetables are soft and the stuffing is golden brown, 30 to 40 minutes. Serve hot or at room temperature.

Radicchio Salad with Anchovy Dressing

Insalata di Radicchio con Acciughe

Radicchio di Treviso is perhaps the most loved Venetian vegetable. With its rich purplish-red leaves; mildly bitter taste; and crisp, crunchy texture, it can be turned into a lovely, refreshing salad in no time at all. In Venice there are many versions of radicchio salad. This one uses a dressing of chopped anchovies, olive oil, and lemon juice, and a garnish of crisp Parmesan-coated bread cubes. ◆ *serves 4 to 6*

2 to 3 tablespoons unsalted butter

1½ cups crust-free, ½-inch-cubed, day-old bread

2 tablespoons freshly grated Parmigiano-Reggiano

4 heads of Treviso radicchio or 2 heads of round radicchio, bruised leaves removed

4 to 6 anchovy fillets packed in salt, rinsed and chopped

¼ to ⅓ cup extra-virgin olive oil

Juice of 1 lemon

Salt and freshly ground black pepper to taste

Preheat the oven to 375°F.

Heat the butter in a medium skillet over medium heat. As soon as the butter begins to foam, add the bread cubes and stir until they are coated with the butter. Remove from the heat, sprinkle the Parmigiano over the bread, and stir quickly to coat. Transfer the bread to a baking sheet and bake until the cubes are lightly golden and crisp, 8 to 10 minutes. Set aside to cool. (The bread can be prepared several hours or a day ahead. Store in an airtight container.)

Separate the radicchio leaves, wash them under cold running water, and pat dry with paper towels. Cut or shred the leaves into 1- to 2-inch pieces, and place in a salad bowl.

Put the anchovies in a small bowl, add the oil and the lemon juice, and stir with a small whisk until well emulsified.

Season the radicchio with salt and pepper, add the dressing, and toss well. Taste and adjust the seasoning. Mound the salad on serving plates, top with the toasted cubed bread, and serve.

THE RADICCHIO SALAD OF VENICE'S WINE BARS

Venice's wine bars offer a variety of radicchio salads:

- With hard-boiled eggs, tuna, and anchovy dressing
- With cubed cheese (Pecorino, Toma, Fontina, or Gorgonzola) in a balsamic–olive oil dressing
- With blood orange or pink grapefruit segments, and olive-oil-and-lemon dressing
- With crisp pancetta, crisp cubed bread, olive oil, and balsamic vinegar

Venetian Cornmeal Cake with Raisins and Grappa

Pinza di Polenta alla Veneziana

In spite of its name, Fiaschetteria Toscana is not a Tuscan eatery at all; it serves some of the best Venetian food in the city. The ever-changing tempting menu and the impeccable, friendly service, not to mention the homemade desserts prepared daily by Mariuccia, the owner of the restaurant, will lure you back time after time. I loved this classic cornmeal cake studded with raisins, dried figs, and pine nuts and infused with grappa, a strong brandy-like distilled spirit made from grape must. This is not a dessert for all seasons, for it is quite rich. But in the fall and winter, when our bodies need more caloric input, it will put a blissful smile on anyone's face. ♦ *serves 8 to 10*

Butter for greasing the pan

Amaretti di Saronno (see note, page 229), finely crushed, or $^1/_3$ cup all-purpose flour

$^3/_4$ cup golden raisins soaked for 20 minutes in lukewarm water

$^1/_3$ cup pine nuts

$1^1/_2$ cups dried figs, minced (7 ounces)

$^1/_2$ cup grappa or rum

5 cups whole milk

1 cup granulated sugar

4 tablespoons ($^1/_2$ stick) unsalted butter

Pinch of salt

2 cups coarsely ground cornmeal (11 ounces)

1 cup all-purpose flour

4 large eggs

$^1/_2$ pound (1 cup) whole-milk ricotta

1 teaspoon pure vanilla extract

$1^1/_2$ tablespoons baking powder

Confectioners' sugar, for dusting

Preheat the oven to 350°F. Butter a 10- or 12-inch springform pan generously and coat with the finely crumbled cookies. Set aside.

Drain the raisins and place in a bowl. Add the pine nuts, dried figs, and grappa. Mix well and set aside.

In a large saucepan, combine the milk with the granulated sugar, butter, and salt. Bring to a fast simmer over medium heat. In a mixing bowl, combine the cornmeal and flour. As soon as the milk begins to simmer, add the cornmeal-flour mixture by the handful in a slow, thin stream, stirring constantly with a wooden spoon or a wire whisk. Reduce the heat to low and cook, stirring, until the cornmeal begins to detach itself from the sides of the pan, 10 to 15 minutes.

Add the raisin mixture and stir over low heat until combined, 2 to 3 minutes. Turn off the heat and transfer to a large bowl.

With a wire whisk, beat the eggs in a large bowl with the ricotta, vanilla, and baking powder until the mixture has a nice, creamy consistency. Fold into the cornmeal mixture.

Pour the batter into the prepared pan and level the top with a wet spatula. Place the pan on the middle rack of the oven and bake until the top is golden brown and a thin knife inserted in the center comes out clean, 40 to 45 minutes. Cool on a rack to room temperature.

Remove the cake from the pan and place on a round serving plate. Sprinkle with confectioners' sugar and serve.

Hazelnut Cookies

Cornetti alle Nocciole

Venetians love cookies probably more than anybody else in Italy, and the large displays in the pastry shops prove it. When I am in Venice, my breakfast often consists only of a cappuccino and a couple of freshly baked cookies, a wonderfuly civilized way to start the day. ◆ *makes about 30 cookies*

5 ounces whole hazelnuts (1 cup)

2 cups all-purpose flour

³/₄ cup granulated sugar

Grated zest of 1 lemon

2 large eggs, lightly beaten, plus 2 large egg yolks, beaten

8 tablespoons (1 stick) unsalted butter, melted, plus more for greasing the pan

Confectioners' sugar, for dusting

Preheat the oven to 350°F.

Put the hazelnuts in a single layer on an ungreased baking sheet. Bake until lightly golden, 5 to 6 minutes, then turn off the oven. Wrap the hazelnuts in a large kitchen towel, and rub off as much skin as possible. Put the nuts in a food processor and chop into very fine pieces, but not into powder. (The hazelnuts can be prepared a couple of days ahead.)

In a large bowl, combine the hazelnuts, flour, granulated sugar, and lemon zest. Mound the mixture on a large wooden board or other work surface. With your fingers, make a round well in the center. Place the beaten eggs and the melted butter in the well and mix thoroughly with a fork. Draw the flour mixture into the eggs a little at a time and mix with your fingers or the fork, working it into a dough. Knead until the dough is compact and has a nice, smooth texture, 3 to 4 minutes. Wrap in plastic and refrigerate for 1 hour or overnight.

Preheat the oven to 350°F. Lightly butter a large baking sheet and line it with parchment paper. (The butter will keep the paper in place.)

Pull off a small piece of dough about the size of a walnut. With the palms of your hands, roll it into a 4-inch-long, chubby rope. Bend both ends of the rope slightly toward each other, shaping it into a half-moon. When all the dough has been rolled out and shaped, place the cookies on the prepared baking sheet about 1 inch apart. Brush them lightly with the beaten egg yolks. Bake on the middle rack of the oven until the cookies have a rich golden color, 13 to 15 minutes. Cool for a few minutes, then transfer to a rack or a large serving dish and cool completely. Sprinkle with confectioners' sugar just before serving.

THE VENETIAN TABLE

APPETIZERS

Antipasto Misto di Pesce Crudo: Mixed raw-seafood platter, often dressed simply with extra-virgin olive oil and lemon.

Baccalà Fritto: Chunks of salt cod that are dipped in an egg-flour batter and deep-fried.

Baccalà Mantecato: A whipped, soft, creamy salt cod that is generally spooned over grilled or fried polenta.

Fondi di Carciofi: Large globe artichoke bottoms are sold already cleaned in the Rialto market and are a staple of wine bars. They are fried or boiled, and when still hot are covered and marinated with oil, garlic, and parsley.

Olive Fritte: Crisp, deep-fried green olives to snack on while enjoying a glass of cool, crisp white wine.

Polpette: Deep-fried small balls made of seafood, potatoes, or meat. Polpette are staples in local wine bars, where they are piled on large platters and served as finger food.

Sarde in Saor: Fresh-fried sardines layered with a mixture of sweet-and-sour onions, raisins, and pine nuts, served at room temperature.

Verdure Ripiene: Roasted, mixed, stuffed vegetables.

FIRST COURSES

Bigoli in Salsa: Whole-wheat pasta with sardine or anchovy sauce.

Gnocchi di Zucca: Squash gnocchi generally served simply with butter, sage, and Parmigiano, or topped with fresh truffle.

Pasta e Fagioli: Pasta-and-bean soup is the quintessential Venetian soup.

Risi e Bisi: A delicious soup of peas, pea pods, and rice that is a cross between a very thick soup and a soupy risotto.

Risotto di Peoci e Capparosoli: Risotto with local mussels and small clams.

Spaghetti Neri: Black spaghetti or black risotto made with cuttlefish ink, often topped with a sauce of white scallops or squid for a striking contrast.

ENTRÉES

Bisato in Umido: Eel braised in tomato, wine, and vinegar, a traditional Christmas Eve dish.

Brodetto di Pesce: Venetian seafood stew.

Castradina: A delicious, brothy lamb-and-cabbage stew.

Faraona in Peverada: Guinea hen with a peppery sauce, a dish that seems to date as far back as the sixteenth century.

Fegato alla Veneziana: Calf's liver smothered with soft, golden onions and placed over soft or grilled polenta. A true Venetian classic.

Frittura Mista di Pesce e Verdure: A mixture of local fish and local vegetables coated in a flour-egg batter and fried.

Moleche con il Pien: Stuffed soft-shell crab, generally deep-fried and served with grilled or fried polenta.

Seppie alla Griglia con Polenta: Grilled cuttlefish with polenta.

Sogliola ai Ferri: The fresh, local sole, often simply grilled, generally sprinkled with a light olive oil and lemon juice.

VEGETABLES AND SALADS

Carciofini in Insalata: Salad of small, tender choke-less baby artichoke, with Parmigiano shavings, lemon juice, and extra-virgin olive oil. Often spelled as *castrature* in Venice.

Cipolline in Agro-Dolce: Small onions in a sweet-and-sour preparation served as a side dish or appetizer or even as an unusual salad.

Fondi di Carciofi: Artichoke hearts cooked with oil, garlic, parsley, and broth, served as an appetizer or a side dish.

Frittura Mista di Verdure: Mixed, seasonal vegetables fried in a batter, served as an appetizer or next to grilled fish.

Radicchio di Treviso alla Griglia: Grilled marinated radicchio, generally served at the beginning or the end of a meal.

DESSERTS

Cornetti alle Nocciole: Hazelnut cookies shaped as a half-moon, generally served at the end of a meal, next to espresso.

Crema Fritta: Deep-fried cream flavored with liqueur.

Crostata di Frutta di Stagione: Seasonal fruit tart.

Galani: Fried Carnival pastries.

Torta Dolce di Polenta e Uvetta: Sweet cornmeal cake with raisins. A wholesome fall or winter treat.

Zabaglione all'Amaretto: Zabaglione with Amaretto liqueur.

SOME BASIC INGREDIENTS

Aceto: Vinegar. Red or white vinegars are staples of the Venetian pantry.

Aglio: Garlic, used by Venetians with restraint, often browned in oil or butter and then discarded, so what is left in the pan is only a whiff of its aroma.

Asparagi: Besides the usual green and slightly purple asparagus, the region also cultivates a prized white variety.

Baccalà: Cod, either sun-dried or salt-dried, is turned into a creamy mush or slowly stewed with savory ingredients.

Pangrattate: Homemade bread crumbs are indispensable in the Venetian kitchen, since they are often used to coat delicate fish and young, spring vegetables.

Burro: Butter is the predominant fat in Venice and the Veneto. The sweet, unsalted butter of the area is traditionally used in risotto, sauces, sautéed dishes, and the majority of desserts.

Cannocchie or Canoce: Long, grayish-white local shrimp that are generally grilled or boiled and dressed simply with oil, lemon juice, parsley, and garlic.

Carciofi: The two types of artichokes eaten in Venice are the *carciofino*, baby artichoke, and the regular, large size. They can be boiled, stuffed, or fried. The hearts of large artichokes can be bought already cleaned at the vegetable market.

Fagioli: Beans, which along with polenta and rice are an important local staple. *Borlotti* beans, similar to cranberry beans and a favorite of the Venetians, are usually available dried, and are turned into thick, hearty soups.

Formaggi: Some of the region's best cheeses are Asiago, Montasio, and Morlacco, all made from cow's milk.

Grappa: A strong distilled spirit made from grape skins and vines left behind during wine making. It is used to flavor desserts and is served at the end of a meal.

Moleche: Soft-shell crabs, often stuffed and deep-fried.

Olio Vergine d'Oliva: Extra-virgin olive oil is almost as indispensable in the Venetian kitchen as butter, for it replaces heavier fats such as lard. The Veneto region, especially the area around Lake Garda, produces outstanding olive oils that are soft and delicate.

Polenta: Ground cornmeal cooked in water or milk into a thick mass and often served instead of bread, soft, fried, baked, or grilled. Yellow or white polenta is a staple of the Venetian table.

Radicchio: A chicory that comes in many sizes and shapes. Its prevalent red color and slightly bitter taste make it a Venetian favorite.

Riso: Rice. Of the many varieties grown in Italy, Arborio, Carnaroli, and Vialone Nano are the ones available in the United States. All have short, stubby grains that cook to a firm yet moist and creamy consistency. Their high starch content make them the perfect rice for risotto.

Scampi: Known in other parts of the world as Dublin Bay prawns or langoustine. With their delicate, tasty flesh, scampi are terrific grilled, fried, or broiled, or tossed with pasta.

Seppia: Cuttlefish, a cephalopod of the same family as octopus and squid. Their sac of black ink turns dishes such as risottos and pastas into dramatic, glossy presentations.

Soppressa: A delicious pork *salame* that is typical of the Veneto, made from 65 percent lean pork and 35 percent pork fat. It is used as an appetizer or as a savory base for soups and stews.

Spezie: Spices such as cinnamon, nutmeg, cloves, saffron, and pepper are often used, usually in moderation, in Venetian cooking.

Uvetta Sultanina: Raisins. Large, plump golden raisins are an essential ingredient to the many sweet-and-sour Venetian dishes.

Zucca: Squash, which originally came to Italy from the New World, is very popular in the cooking of Venice. Its golden yellow color and porous flesh adds taste, color, and consistency to dishes such as risotto and gnocchi.

BASIC RECIPES

MEAT BROTHS Capon Broth, Chicken Broth, Meat Broth ◆

VEGETABLE BROTH ◆ FISH BROTH ◆ BASIC PASTA DOUGH ◆

BASIC POTATO GNOCCHI ◆ BASIC POLENTA ◆

BASIC PIE DOUGH

Meat Broths

Homemade meat broth, absolutely vital to the cooking of many Italian regions, is the basis for wonderful soups, risottos, sauces, braised dishes, and stews. (My father's favorite winter dish was a soup of homemade tagliolini in a light, clear meat broth.) The Italian *brodo* is made by assembling vegetables, meats, bones, and scraps from chicken, capon, beef, and veal (lamb and pork are not used because of their assertive flavors), covering generously with cold water, and cooking at the lowest simmer for about 3 hours. The long, slow cooking and the careful skimming of the foamy impurities are the keys. Do not confuse the Italian brodo with the French stock, for they are two completely different preparations.

CAPON BROTH ◆ *makes about 5 quarts*

Half of an 8- to 9-pound capon
1 pound beef brisket or rump roast
1 pound veal brisket or veal rump
2 pounds veal and beef bones
1 large yellow onion, peeled and quartered

2 carrots, cut into large pieces
2 celery stalks, cut into large pieces
2 canned Italian plum tomatoes
Salt to taste

Wash the meats and the vegetables, except the tomatoes, well under cold running water. Put everything except the salt in a large stockpot and cover by 2 to 3 inches with cold water. Set the cover askew and bring to a gentle boil over medium heat. As soon as the water begins to bubble, reduce the heat to low. With a slotted spoon or a skimmer, skim off the foam that has risen to the surface. Cover the pot partially and cook at the gentlest of simmers for 2½ to 3 hours, skimming off the foam every 20 to 30 minutes. Season with salt during the last few minutes of cooking.

Remove the meats and set aside. If using the broth right away, strain it through a fine-mesh strainer directly into another pot. If using within a few days, strain it into a metal bowl and set it over a larger bowl filled with ice water until cool. Refrigerate the broth for a day or two, or freeze it. Before using, remove the fat that has solidified on the surface.

CHICKEN BROTH • *makes about 4 quarts*

1 (4-pound) stewing chicken
  or boiling hen

3 pounds bones and meat scraps from
  veal and chicken

1 large yellow onion, peeled and
  quartered

2 carrots, cut into large pieces

2 celery stalks, cut into large pieces

1 canned Italian plum tomato

Salt to taste

Wash all the meats and vegetables, except the tomato. Place everything except the salt in a large stockpot and cover by 2 to 3 inches with cold water. Cook as instructed for Capon Broth on previous page.

MEAT BROTH • *makes about 2½ quarts*

5 pounds bones and meat scraps from
  beef, veal, and chicken

1 large yellow onion, peeled and
  quartered

2 carrots, cut into large pieces

2 celery stalks, cut into large pieces

1 canned Italian plum tomato

Salt to taste

Wash all the bones, meat scraps, and vegetables, except the tomato. Place everything except the salt in a large stockpot and cover by 2 to 3 inches with cold water. Cook as instructed for Capon Broth on previous page.

FREEZING BROTH

Since making broth is time-consuming, it makes sense to prepare a large batch and freeze it. When the broth has chilled, ladle it into small containers, plastic bags, or ice cube trays (when the broth is frozen, unmold the cubes and freeze in several plastic bags).

PUTTING THE MEAT IN THE BROTH TO GOOD USE

During the long, slow cooking, the meats will literally fall apart in the broth. That is fine, since the emphasis here is on the quality of the broth, not the perfect cooking of the meat. Scoop up the meat pieces, remove the bones, and cut into cubes or strips. Serve the hot meat with mashed potatoes, with a *salsa verde*, or simply with spicy mustard. Or chill the meat for a few hours, then toss with mixed greens, radicchio, or arugula and dress with extra-virgin olive oil and balsamic vinegar.

Vegetable Broth

Brodo Vegetale

It is so simple to make a vegetable broth: just look into your refrigerator and take that lonely carrot, half onion, wilted celery, and any other vegetables and turn them into a light broth to use for risotto and soups and to give body and flavor to sauces. ◆ *makes 2 to 2½ quarts*

2 pounds assorted fresh vegetables,
  such as onions, leeks, zucchini, carrots,
  celery, peas, asparagus, and spinach
Salt

Peel, shell, and wash all the vegetables. Cut them into large pieces and place in a medium pot. Add enough water to cover by 2 to 3 inches. Bring to a boil, then reduce the heat to medium low and simmer, skimming the foam that comes to the surface, for about 1 hour. Season with salt to taste.

Strain the broth into a large bowl and discard the vegetables or set aside (see note). Strain the broth again through a strainer lined with cheesecloth or paper towels, directly into another bowl. If you are not using the broth right away, chill it over a larger bowl filled with ice water, then refrigerate it for a few days, or freeze it.

NOTE

Not everybody in the world loves boiled vegetables, especially when they are seriously overcooked. But I do. So when I make vegetable broth, I cool the vegetables, then toss them with just some salt, pepper, and good extra-virgin olive oil.

Fish Broth

Brodo di Pesce

Cooking a seafood risotto with a light, flavorful fish broth will enrich the dish considerably. • *makes about 6 cups*

2 pounds fish bones from white-flesh fish

1 cup sliced onion

1 cup sliced carrots

1 cup sliced celery

3 to 4 sprigs of fresh flat-leaf parsley

1 sprig of thyme

$1/2$ tablespoon whole black peppercorns

1 cup dry white wine

Rinse the fish bones under cold running water and wash the vegetables. Place the bones in a large saucepan, add the vegetables and herbs and pepper, and cover by about 3 inches with cold water. Bring to a boil over medium-high heat. Reduce the heat to low and simmer, uncovered, for about 1 hour. With a slotted spoon or a skimmer, skim the surface to remove any foam and impurities that rise to the surface.

Line a strainer with cheesecloth or a few layers of paper towels, and strain the broth into a bowl. If you are not using the broth right away, chill it over a larger bowl filled with ice water, then refrigerate it for a few days, or freeze it.

Basic Pasta Dough

Making pasta from scratch can be very satisfying—all you need are a few eggs, a bunch of flour, your hands, a rolling pin or a pasta machine, and a little bit of patience. Here you will find two basic methods, Making dough by hand can be really pleasurable—you will feel the changes in the texture as you knead. The machine method is quicker. Either way, if you are a beginner, read the instructions carefully and follow them to the letter. And don't worry if your first batch is less than satisfactory.

♦ makes about 1 pound pasta dough, 4 to 6 servings

2¹/₃ cups unbleached all-purpose flour, plus more for kneading

4 extra-large eggs

HAND METHOD

Mound the flour on a large wooden board or other work surface. With your fingers, make a round well in the center of the flour. Crack the eggs into the well, and stir thoroughly with a fork. Using the fork, begin to incorporate the flour, starting from the inner rim of the well, into the eggs, until about half of the flour has been incorporated and a soft paste begins to form.

With a dough scraper, push all the remaining flour to one side of the board. Scrape off and discard the bits and pieces of dough attached to the board. Wash your hands, then begin adding some of the flour you have pushed aside into the dough. Knead gently with the heels of your hands. As you keep incorporating a little flour at a time, the dough will become firmer. Keep the board clean and dust it lightly with flour as you knead. After 8 to 10 minutes of good kneading, the dough should be smooth, elastic, and just a little sticky. (Press one finger into the center of the dough. If it comes out barely moist, the dough is ready to be rolled out. If the dough is quite sticky, add a bit more flour and knead it 2 to 3 minutes longer.)

Wrap the dough in plastic wrap and let it rest at room temperature for 20 to 30 minutes. Just before using, knead again for a minute or two.

MACHINE METHOD

Crack the eggs into a food processor fitted with the metal blade. Process quickly to mix. Add the flour in a couple of batches, and pulse until the dough gathers in several soft lumps around the blade. (Do not let the dough form a ball, or it will be tough.)

Put the soft, sticky dough on a lightly floured wooden board or other work surface. Dust your hands with flour and knead for a few minutes, adding a bit more flour if the dough is very sticky, until smooth and pliable.

Wrap the dough in plastic wrap and let it rest at room temperature for 20 to 30 minutes. Just before using, knead again for a minute or two.

ROLLING OUT PASTA DOUGH WITH A PASTA MACHINE

Set the rollers of a hand-cranked or electric pasta machine at their widest opening. Cut off a piece of dough about the size of a large egg, and flatten it with the palms of your hands. Keep the rest of the dough wrapped in plastic. Dust the small piece of dough lightly with flour, and run it once through the machine. Fold the dough in half, pressing it down with your fingertips, and run through the machine again. Repeat this step four or five times, dusting the dough lightly with flour if needed, until the dough is smooth and elastic.

Now change the rollers of the pasta machine to a decreasing setting, and roll out the dough once without folding. Keep rolling the sheet through the machine on decreasing settings until you reach the desired thinness.

FOR STUFFED PASTA

Run one sheet of dough at a time through the *last* (thinnest) setting of the machine. Cut, stuff, and shape the pasta sheet immediately (see individual recipes) before rolling out another sheet, so that the sheet will not dry out.

FOR STRING PASTA

Roll out one sheet of dough at a time, running it twice through the setting next to the last (thinnest). Place the pasta sheets on a lightly floured tablecloth and let them all dry for 10 to 12 minutes before putting them through the cutters of the machine. Then to cut into string:

* For Tagliatelle, Fettuccine, and Tagliolini: Run the dry sheets of pasta through the widest cutters of the pasta machine for tagliatelle and fettuccine; use the narrow cutters for tagliolini. Arrange the noodles in loose bundles on a tablecloth. They can be cooked immediately or allowed to dry, uncovered. Once dried, they can be kept at room temperature for a few days.
* For Tonnarelli: This pasta is thicker than tagliatelle or tagliolini. In rolling out the sheets, stop when you get halfway through the notches of the machine, approximately at number 3 of a hand-cranked pasta machine. Dry the sheets for about 15 minutes before putting them through the narrow cutters of the pasta machine. Arrange the noodles in loose bundles on a tablecloth. They can be cooked immediately or allowed to dry, uncovered. Once dried, they can be kept at room temperature for a few days.

VARIATION

Basic Spinach Dough ◆ Boil 2 cups spinach leaves for about 1 minute. Drain in a small colander, then plunge the colander into a large bowl of ice water. Drain, place in a large clean towel, and squeeze out as much water as possible. Purée the spinach in a food processor, then stir into the beaten eggs. Make the dough following one of the methods listed above.

Basic Potato Gnocchi

Gnocchi di Patate

Legions of people in Italy grew up eating gnocchi, especially potato gnocchi, which are by far the most popular version and pair so well with a variety of sauces. To make good potato gnocchi:

- Bake the potatoes instead of boiling them, so their water content will be reduced and less flour will be used.
- Knead your dough for only a few minutes; it should feel a bit sticky.
- Before rolling out a whole batch of gnocchi, drop a few in boiling water. They should rise to the surface within a minute or two. If they fall apart, knead a bit more flour into the dough.
- Use a large, wide pot to boil the gnocchi, so they will not stick together.

◆ *serves 4 to 6*

4 large russet potatoes (about 2 pounds)

2 teaspoons salt

1 1/2 to 2 cups all-purpose flour

Preheat the oven to 375°F.

Wash and dry the potatoes. With a large knife, make a deep incision in the potatoes. Put the potatoes on a baking sheet, place on the center rack of the oven, and bake until tender, about 1 hour.

Cool the potatoes briefly, but peel them while still quite warm. Put them through a potato ricer directly into a large bowl. Season with salt. Cool the potatoes a bit more, then add 1 1/2 cups of the flour, a little at a time, and mix well with your hands until the flour and the potatoes stick together into a rough dough.

Transfer the mixture to a work surface and knead lightly, gradually adding the remaining flour if the dough sticks heavily to the board and to your hands. Knead for 2 to 3 minutes, until it is smooth, pliable, and just a bit sticky.

Cut off a piece of dough about the size of an orange. Flour your hands lightly (do not flour the work area, or the dough will not slide smoothly). Using both hands, roll out the piece of dough with a light back-and-forth motion into a roll about the thickness of your index finger. Cut the roll into 1-inch pieces.

Hold a fork with its tines against the work surface, the curved part of the fork facing away from you. Starting from the curved outside bottom of the fork, press each piece of dough with your index finger firmly upward along the length of the tines. Let the gnocchi fall back onto the work surface. Repeat with the remaining dough until all the gnocchi have been formed.

Line a large tray with a clean kitchen towel, and flour the towel lightly. Line the gnocchi on the towel without crowding them. They can be cooked immediately or kept in the refrigerator, uncovered, for several hours.

Basic Polenta

For the past 250 years polenta, not pasta, has been the staple of life for several Northern Italian regions. This wonderfully wholesome dish is so versatile that it is hard to categorize: it can be used as an antipasto, first course, entrée, or side dish. It can be served soft, straight from the pot. It can be fried, grilled, baked, or sautéed. Polenta's mellow flavor makes it the perfect vehicle for a staggering number of sauce-based dishes. The addition of butter and Parmigiano is by choice, but that is how my mother and the people of Bologna have always made it. ◆ *serves 8 to 10*

1 tablespoon salt

1 cup coarse-ground cornmeal

1 cup fine-ground cornmeal

2 to 3 tablespoons unsalted butter

3/4 cup freshly grated Parmigiano-Reggiano

Bring 8 cups cold water to a boil in a heavy, medium pot. Add the salt and reduce the heat to low. When the water comes to a steady simmer, add the cornmeals slowly by the handful in a continuous fine stream, letting the cornmeal fall through your fingers. Stir constantly with a long wooden spoon or a wire whisk to prevent lumps.

When all the cornmeal has been incorporated, reduce the heat to low. Cook at a gentle simmer, stirring every couple of minutes with the wooden spoon reaching all the way to the bottom and sides of the pot. As the polenta cooks it will thicken considerably, and it will bubble and let off puffs of steam. Cook the polenta for 40 to 45 minutes, stirring occasionally. It is done when it pulls away from the sides of the pan.

Add the butter and the Parmigiano, and stir until the polenta is smooth and creamy. The polenta can be used immediately while soft, straight out of the pot.

VARIATIONS

Make-Ahead Soft Polenta ◆ As soon as the polenta is done, transfer to a large stainless-steel bowl and place the bowl *over* a large pot containing 3 to 4 inches of gently simmering water. Make sure that the bowl doesn't touch the simmering water. Cover the bowl tightly with aluminum foil and stir every 30 minutes or so. Polenta will stay soft for 2 to 3 hours. If the polenta has become too firm when you are ready to serve, add a little hot water or milk, and stir with a wire whisk until soft again.

Firm, Warm Polenta ◆ Turn the cooked soft polenta onto a large wooden board. Shape it with a wet spatula into a thick round. Let the polenta firm up for 20 to 25 minutes before slicing.

ROASTED, GRILLED, OR FRIED POLENTA

Spread the cooked polenta 1 inch thick on a baking sheet and cool to room temperature. Refrigerate, uncovered, for several hours or overnight. When needed, cut the polenta into squares or rectangles.

Roasting ◆ Heat the oven to 400°F. Brush the polenta pieces on both sides with a little oil, and roast until the polenta is golden brown on both sides.

Grilling ◆ Brush the polenta pieces on both sides with olive oil. Place on a hot grill until golden and crisp on both sides.

Frying ◆ Heat 1 inch of oil in a medium skillet. When the oil is very hot, fry a few pieces of polenta at a time. Remove when they are golden brown on both sides, and drain on paper towels.

Each of these methods will give the polenta a different appearance and texture.

Basic Pie Dough

Pasta Frolla

This is a basic pastry dough recipe. Once you have the right proportions of flour, butter, and liquid, it's a snap to make a dough with a soft, pliable consistency. Have all your ingredients well chilled; don't overwork the dough, or the butter will heat up, making it too soft and sitcky. Simply gather the dough lightly into 2 balls, one a little larger than the other, and refrigerate a few hours or overnight. Then leave the dough 5 to 10 minutes at room temperature before using. This pastry dough can be used for all kinds of pies and tarts. It can also be frozen. *• makes 1 double-crust 10-inch pie, or 2 single 10-inch tart shells*

2 cups unbleached all-purpose flour

2 tablespoons sugar

5 tablespoons unsalted butter, at room temperature for hand mixing, or cold, cut into small pieces for the food processor

1 large egg, lightly beaten

4 to 5 tablespoons chilled dry white wine or water

TO MAKE THE DOUGH BY HAND

Combine the flour and sugar in a large bowl. Add the butter. With your fingertips, rub the butter into the flour until the mixture has a fine, crumbly texture. Stir in the egg and the chilled wine with a fork, then mix gently with your hands until the dough begins to come together.

TO MAKE THE DOUGH IN A FOOD PROCESSOR

Place the flour and sugar in a food processor and pulse with the metal blade a few times to combine. Add the butter and pulse briefly until the mixture has a crumbly texture. Add the egg and the wine and pulse briefly, until the dough is loosely gathered into large clumps around the blade.

Transfer the dough to a work surface and shape into 1 or 2 disks, depending on the recipe. Wrap in plastic wrap and refrigerate for 1 hour, or until ready to use.

Fontana di Trevi, Rome

Sources for Italian Specialties

Even though Italian ingredients can be found in Italian markets, specialty food stores, and some supermarkets across the country, they are not available everywhere. Most of the sources below have a wide range of cured meats, cheeses, olive oils, vinegars, pastas, spices, mushrooms, rices, wines, and more, and will ship across the country.

Armandino's Salumi
309 Third Avenue South
Seattle WA 98104
(206) 621-8772

Convito Italiano
Plaza del Lago
1515 Sheridan Road
Wilmette IL 60091
(847) 251-3654
www.convitoitaliano.com

Corti Brothers
5810 Folsom Boulevard
Sacramento CA 95819
(800) 509-3663
www.cortibros.biz

Dean & Deluca
560 Broadway
New York NY 10012
(212) 226-6800
www.deandeluca.com

Dean & Deluca
607 South St. Helena Highway
St. Helena CA 94574
(707) 967-9980
www.deandeluca.com

Di Palo
200 Grand Street
New York NY 10013
(212) 226-1033

Todaro Brothers
555 Second Avenue
New York NY 10016
(212) 679-7766
www.todarobros.com

Vivande Porta Via
2125 Fillmore Street
San Francisco CA 94115
(415) 346-4430

Acknowledgments

I could not have written this book without the inspiration and support of many people.

Thank you to my family and friends in Bologna, my native city, who throughout the years have consistently shared with me their table, their knowledge, and their love.

Thank you to the talented "kids" in my restaurant kitchen: Don Brown, John Eichhorn, Tony Sanguinetti, and

to all the supporting crew who consistently helped me with sometimes overwhelming work and impending deadlines.

Thank you to my husband, Vincent, and to Darrell Corti for their much needed help about the sections on wine.

Thank you to my customers who kept asking me to write a book about the food and the best eating places of several grand Italian cities.

Thank you for my new agent, Jane Dystel. I am honored to be one of your authors.

Thank you to Stacey Glick, who showed me the way.

Thank you to Chris Pavone, a most talented and patient editor. And finally, a big thank-you to Ann Bramson, the publisher of this book, who opened a new door for me. I will not let you down.

A PERSONAL NOTE AND A SPECIAL THANK-YOU

Back in 2001, only four or five months after I began working on this book, the unexpected happened: I was diagnosed with breast cancer. The cancer was removed, the prognosis seemed good, and my husband, a cancer doctor, together with my physician, guided me through some difficult times. Throughout this ordeal—surgery, chemotherapy, and radiation—I doubted whether this book would ever happen. Then I regained my health, my energy, and the strong desire to finish this book. Here it is.

A big, heartfelt thank-you to the many cancer survivors who wrote, and encouraged me to fight this battle, and to the hundreds and hundreds who cheered me on.

And lastly, a special thank-you to Martha Stewart, for not only allowing me to be on her show when my hair was just beginning to sprout, but who encouraged me to remove my "silly hat" and to be proud of the way I looked.

Index

stew of fava beans, peas, and
artichokes, 52
guinea hen, roasted, with
peppery sauce, 280–81

ham, smoked, risotto with wild
mushrooms and, 260–61
hazelnut cookies, 290–91
honey, Venetian salame with
wilted radicchio and,
250–51

ice cream, Parmigiano-Reggiano,
with balsamic vinegar, 169
incapriata, 9–11
ingredients, sources for, 310
insalata:
di funghi, sedano, e Pecorino, 107
di radicchio con acciughe, 286–87
di sedano di Verona e mele,
222–23
di seppie e patate, 218–19

kale:
fettunta with, 68–69
twice-cooked Florentine
vegetable soup, 78–79

lamb:
abbacchio, 39
buying, 45
hunter-style, 38–39
rack, of Ristorante Troiani,
44–45
Venetian stew with cabbage,
282
legumes, about, 31
lentils, braised, zampone sausage
with, 154–55
lombatine di vitello del Battibecco,
144–45

maccheroni with stracotto sauce
(var.), 95
maritozzi Romani, 58–59
mascarpone-ricotta fritters,
170–71
meat, roasting, 209
meatballs:
deep-fried (var.), 216
wrapped in cabbage,
Milanese, 214–16
meat broth, 298
Milan, 174–233
caffès and pastry shops, 221
local dishes and ingredients,
231–33
restaurants, trattorie, and
wine bars, 189–91
specialty food store and
cooking school, 216
wines, local, 206–7
minestra di pasta e ceci, 30–31
minestrone alla Milanese, 200–201
minestrone with beans and rice
Milan-style, 200–201
mondeghili nella verza, 214–16
monkfish with white wine,
tomatoes, and basil,
160–61
mortadella:
creamy mousse, crostini with,
124
fava beans with, 166
Mostarda di Cremona, 193
mushroom(s):
chestnut-flour tagliatelle with,
194–95
crisp risotto cakes with, 180
garganelli with sausage,
porcini, and cream,
132–33
penne with porcini, 86
pheasant hunter-style, 212–13
risotto with chanterelles,
Fontina, and sparkling
wine, 188
roasted quail wrapped in
pancetta, 98–99

salad with celery and
Pecorino, 107
and shrimp with soft polenta,
244
stuffed roasted veal, 208–9
wild, risotto with smoked
ham and, 260–61
mussels, shellfish stew,
270–71

octopus, about, 219
olive(s):
buying, for frying, 245
green, fried, 245
panzanella with tuna and,
77
rabbit braised with wine, sage
and, 96
spaghetti with fresh tomatoes,
capers and, 19
spaghetti with tuna, tomatoes
and, 266–67
olive fritte, 245
onions:
peppers, and tomatoes in a
skillet, Milan-style, 226
Venetian calf's liver with,
278–79
whole-wheat pasta with
capers, anchovies and, 259
ossobuco, perfect, 204
ossobuco alla Milanese di una volta,
202–4
oxtail:
about, 36
oxtail stew, Roman, 34–36

pancetta:
bucatini with Pecorino, black
pepper and, 22–23
crisp, garganelli with spring
peas, Pecorino and,
196–97
potato gnocchi with classic
Bolognese ragù, 140–41